Establishing Validity

ESTABLISHING VALIDITY

The First Chapter of Karmapa Chödrak Gyatso's
Ocean of Literature on Logic and the
Corresponding Chapter from Dharmakīrti's
Commentary on Validity

WITH FOREWORDS BY
The 17th Gyalwang Karmapa Ogyen Trinley Dorje
& Khenchen Thrangu Rinpoche

KTD PUBLICATIONS
WOODSTOCK, NY

Establishing Validity: The First Chapter of Karmapa Chödrak Gyatso's
Ocean of Literature on Logic and the Corresponding Chapter from Dharmakīrti's
Commentary on Validity
Chos-grags-rgya-mtsho, Karma-pa VII, 1454–1506. *Tshad ma kun las btus pa sde bdun
dang rigs pa'i gzhung mtha' dag gi sgo nas bshad pa/ tshad ma rjod par byed pa thams cad kyi
chu bo yongs su 'du ba rigs pa'i gzhung lugs kyi rgya mtsho zhes
bya ba las le'u dang po/ tshad ma grub pa.*
Dharmakīrti, 7th c. *Pramāṇavārttikakārikā, Prathamaḥ paricchedaḥ, Pramāṇasiddhi.*

Published by:
KTD Publications
335 Meads Mountain Road
Woodstock NY 12498

International Standard Book Number (ISBN) 978-1-934608-54-8
Library of Congress Control Number: 2015951254

Designed and typeset by Gopa & Ted2, Inc.
Jacket design by Louise Light of Light Graphics

Printed on 100% PCR, acid-free paper.

Printed in the United States of America

Contents

FOREWORD

BY HIS HOLINESS THE GYALWANG KARMAPA
OGYEN TRINLEY DORJE

THE SEVENTH KARMAPA CHÖDRAK GYATSO was a respected scholar, an artist and a realized meditator. He spent much of his life travelling throughout Tibet, accompanied by the *Garchen* or Great Encampment, a huge nomadic community of monks, nuns and lay practitioners. During his time, the Garchen reached its peak, numbering 10,000 people. The community comprised scholars, meditators, a shedra for the study of Buddhist philosophy, and a school of thangka painters, as well as skilled metal workers. The Seventh Karmapa founded an annual Garchen prayer festival which was held during the Festival of Miracles in the First Month of the Tibetan year. Whenever he appeared at public events such as this, tens of thousands of people would gather from all over Tibet just for the chance to glimpse him. Wherever the Garchen went, Chödrak Gyatso and the members of the encampment would bring benefit to the people of that area by settling disputes, giving advice and help, and teaching the Dharma.

The Seventh Karmapa spent much of his time in private, meditating, teaching, and engaging in scholarly activity, and he has left us several works on both philosophy and meditation. The best known of these are his *Indian Texts on Mahamudra*, a three-volume collection of spiritual songs and instructional texts on mahamudra meditation by the great mahasiddhas of India, and his *Ocean of Literature on Logic*, a commentary on the works of Dignāga and Dharmakīrti. His wondrous abilities are witnessed by the fact that he dictated the latter from memory without recourse to any of the texts or other commentaries. To this day, it remains and important part of the course which nuns and monks follow in their monastic colleges. The first chapter, "Establishing

Validity" is considered especially important because of its discussion of the authority of the Buddha and its treatment of rebirth, because this helps students develop the faith necessary to progress along the path.

I have known and worked with bhikshu David Karma Choephel for more than ten years now and I have great confidence in his ability as a translator. I welcome the publication of his latest translation which will enable foreign students to begin the study of validity. I am certain that it will bring benefit to many.

—17th Karmapa Ogyen Trinley Dorje
9th August, 2015

Foreword

by Khenchen Thrangu Rinpoche

G ENERALLY, WHATEVER actions we do, whether worldly or Dharma, we must first know what is correct and valid and what is incorrect and invalid. Furthermore, if once we know this we engage in unmistaken, unconfused, valid actions, it is definite that in the end we will achieve the proper result. But if we engage in something mistaken, confused, and invalid, we will not achieve a proper result. For this reason, it is important to know the teachings on what is valid and what is invalid.

For this reason, Dignāga and Dharmakīrti elucidated what the Buddha taught in bits and pieces in the sutras in their treatises *The Compendium of Validity* and *The Commentary on Validity*. In particular, the first chapter of Dharmakīrti's *Commentary* "Establishing Validity" explains clearly and in depth the profound and vast intent of *The Compendium's* three lines of homage:

I bow to him who became valid,
The one who wishes to help beings,
The teacher, sugata, and protector.

Later the Seventh Gyalwang Karmapa Chödrak Gyatso commented on Dharmakīrti's intent in his commentary on validity *The Ocean of Literature on Logic.* Additionally, in his general discussions he combined his explanations with the teachings of the Second Karmapa Karma Pakshi in his *Infinite Oceans of Validity.* Thus it is clear and easy to understand. The logic is sharp and easily brings certainty. It has the quality that those with sharp faculties who follow the Dharma will be able to develop a superior certainty not based on others' persuasion and from which others cannot dissuade them that our Teacher the Bhagavan Buddha is valid and that the True Dharma he taught is valid as well.

For that reason, I thought that translating it into English, the universal language of this age, would bring great benefit to people of many different ethnicities living in different lands and countries. When I expressed this opinion to the bhikshu Lotsawa David Karma Choephel, he agreed and went to great effort to translate it. I pray and supplicate that this will bring great benefit to the teachings and beings.

—Khenchen Thrangu Rinpoche

TRANSLATOR'S INTRODUCTION

Karmakavādisiṅhagurubhyām namaḥ

For many, one of the more curious and fascinating aspects of Buddhism is its teachings on rebirth. The idea resonates strongly with some, but for others—especially those who come to Buddhism with a Western background or education—it can be hard to accept. The idea that sentient beings migrate from one lifetime to the next in an infinite cycle runs counter to centuries of Western religion and philosophy; the idea one might have been an animal or something other than human in a past life seems more a joke than a possibility. Rebirth also seems difficult to prove through our own experience. By and large, we do not remember our past lives, we have no way of knowing what if anything will happen after death, and nothing materially links one life to the next. Though there has been some academic and scientific research into rebirth, many people are unconvinced, doubtful, skeptical, or even outright dismissive of rebirth. This is not just an issue for Westerners either. The ancient Indian texts and Tibetan teachings also record numerous stories of people who were skeptical of rebirth or denied it even within cultural contexts where rebirth was generally accepted. But rebirth is central to Buddhist philosophy. As recorded in the sutras and vinaya, the Buddha himself spoke of past and future lives frequently. He taught that the cycle of samsara plays itself out over the course of many lifetimes and that the ultimate goal of buddhahood takes innumerable lifetimes and uncountable aeons to achieve. Without rebirth, neither of those would be possible. Therefore, whether rebirth is true or not is an important issue that Buddhist masters have had to address over the centuries.

Within the Tibetan tradition, the most highly regarded proof of rebirth is Dharmakīrti's long treatment of it in the chapter "Establishing Validity" from his *Commentary on Validity*, which is presented in this book along with the Seventh Karmapa Chödrak Gyatso's commentary on it from *The Ocean of Literature on Logic*. Dharmakīrti discusses rebirth in two long passages that together encompass well over a third of the chapter. Yet for Dharmakīrti, the discussion of rebirth is just a supporting argument in the proof of his main thesis of this chapter: that the Bhagavan Buddha is valid—a reliable authority whom spiritual practitioners can trust to guide them to enlightenment. Intertwined with this is the issue of conventional validity or epistemology: how do we evaluate whether we have trustworthy knowledge or not? As subsidiary arguments in his proof of the Buddha's validity, Dharmakīrti also discusses many other issues, including whether a divine creator exists, the meaning of omniscience, the causes that lead to buddhahood and their results, and the natures of the four noble truths in addition to the logic of past and future lives. Dharmakīrti frames these questions in the context of refutations of ancient non-Buddhist schools, but the issues that he discusses and the way that he deals with them are still relevant to thinkers and spiritual practitioners of today.

Dharmakīrti's words on their own are concise—especially in the *Commentary* as it is written in verse—and do not present his arguments in full detail. This is likely intentional, as many Buddhist philosophical works were intended to be taught from master to disciple, with the master explaining to their disciples orally what was implied or omitted. Later, Dharmakīrti himself wrote an autocommentary on the chapter "Inference for Oneself," and his disciples then wrote commentaries on the other chapters. Thus there began a tradition of written commentaries on Dharmakīirti's works. Over the centuries, many scholars in India and later in Tibet wrote treatises explaining, defending, and reinterpreting Dharmakīrti's works, and interest in his work continues to be strong among contemporary scholars.

Of all the different commentaries that have been preserved or written in Tibet, the Seventh Karmapa's *Ocean of Literature on Logic* stands out on many levels, among them the scope of material it covers, Chödrak Gyatso's reliance the words of Dharmakīrti and his earliest Indian commentators, and his description of how Dignāga and Dharmakīrti's thought fits within the Yogācāra tradition of the Great Middle Way.

Though philosophical in tone, *The Ocean* is not solely scholastic in its intent. For Chödrak Gyatso, as for many Karma Kagyu masters, the ultimate intent of Dignāga and Dharmakīrti's work is to remove the obscurations that prevent us from seeing the union of luminosity and emptiness that is the true nature. In this respect, it is not different from mahamudra meditation.[1] Chödrak Gyatso's *Ocean*, taken together with the other great treatises written by the Karmapas and other Karma Kagyu masters in the fifteenth, sixteenth, and seventeenth centuries, provides the philosophical underpinnings for the meditational practices of the Karma Kagyu school.

THE HISTORICAL BACKGROUND: DIGNĀGA AND DHARMAKĪRTI'S THOUGHT IN INDIA AND TIBET

After the emperor Ashoka adopted it in the third century BCE, Buddhism became the dominant spiritual tradition in India and remained so for several centuries, but it was never the only one. Buddhism coexisted with orthodox Hindu schools, the Sāṃkhya school, Jainism, and other traditions.[2] With the founding of the Nyāya school by the sage Gotama around the second century CE, there developed a set of common terminologies and logical techniques that allowed a period of inter-sectarian debate. Though each sect maintained its own particular views and explanations and characterized terms in its own way, there were enough commonalities to allow for debate on many issues, often grounded in epistemology. As a part of this debate, Buddhist positions came under the scrutiny of different schools—including the Nyāya, Vaiśeṣika, Jain, Cārvāka, and Mīmāṃsaka—making it necessary in the middle of the first millennium for Buddhist thinkers to defend Buddhism against the non-Buddhists' critique. The defense was led first by Dignāga and later by Dharmakīrti. Thus began the study of what would become one of the great topics of Buddhist inquiry—validity or *pramāṇa*.[3]

Traditionally said to be a student of Vasubandhu,[4] Dignāga was a prolific fifth or sixth century master of the Yogācāra tradition. He wrote texts in several different genres, including praises of the Buddha, explanations of Prajñaparāmita sutras, a commentary on a kriya tantra, and a highly regarded commentary on the *Noble Aspiration for Excellent Conduct*. He is most well known for his texts on logic, of which he is said to have written quite a few. Chödrak Gyatso says in *The Ocean* that he wrote 108, though only six are preserved in Tibetan.[5] Later in his life, Dignāga saw that his arguments about epistemology and logic were scattered piecemeal in several different treatises and then wrote the *Compendium of Validity* as well as an autocommentary to restate his positions in a single, coherent text. Dignāga's thought soon became influential among both Buddhists and non-Buddhists alike.

But Dignāga also became a target of criticism from the proponents of several non-Buddhist schools including the Mīmāṃsaka, Vaiśeṣika, and Nyāya. Thus it fell to Dharmakīrti, the seventh century[6] master who was his intellectual heir and most influential interpreter, to defend Dignāga's presentation by writing the so-called "seven treatises"— *The Commentary on Validity, The Ascertainment of Validity, The Drop of Reasoning, Establishing Other Continua, The Drop of Proofs, Examination of Relations*, and *The Logic of Debate*. Like Dignāga before him, Dharmakīrti used vocabulary and logical techniques that were common to non-Buddhist thinkers, and in this respect they can be considered participants in the general Indian philosophical tradition. Yet both used these tools and terminologies primarily to explain teachings that had been given by the Buddha and other Buddhist masters in the sutras, vinaya, and abhidharma, such as the selflessness of the individual, the nature of craving, ego-clinging, past and future lives, and so on.[7] Dharmakīrti's work in particular became especially influential. The extent to which subsequent Buddhist masters adopted his terminology and style of logic—even in discussing topics other than validity—demonstrates his authority within the Buddhist tradition, and the frequency with which he was quoted and rebutted by non-Buddhists (to be defended later by Buddhist commentators) over the next several centuries shows his impact on Indian philosophy in general.

In subsequent generations, several prominent Buddhist masters wrote commentaries on Dharmakīrti's works, explaining in greater detail what had been cryptically concise in Dharmakīrti's own works. They also refuted the rebuttals of subsequent non-Buddhist critics and reinterpreted his ideas in light of their own understanding or aims. Foremost among them for our purposes here (as they are Chödrak Gyatso's primary sources in this chapter) are Devendrabuddhi (dates unknown), a direct disciple of Dharmakīrti who wrote a textual commentary that gives a word-by-word gloss on three chapters from the *Commentary*; Prajñākaragupta (740–800), who wrote *The Ornament of the Commentary on Validity*, a two-volume explanation of the *Commentary*; and Śākyabuddhi (dates unknown), a student of Devendrabuddhi who wrote a sub-commentary on Devendrabuddhi's work.

Despite Dharmakīrti's prominence in India, it was not until the late eleventh century that Tibetans began to take serious interest in Dharmakīrti's work and the topic of validity. Ngok Lotsawa Loden Sherap (1059–1109) translated several texts on validity, including Dharmakīrti's *Ascertainment*, and later Chapa Chökyi Senge (1101–1169) taught it widely and also introduced the style of debate that has now become integral to Tibetan education. But these masters also reinterpreted Dharmakīrti's thought, which has a strong anti-realist bent, to bring it more in line with commonsense conceptions of reality.

The main issue of interpretation revolves around the status of universals—conceptual constructs that are applied to specific things, such as a universal "cowness" that inhabits all individual cows or a "blanket" that is inherent in the threads that are woven together to create it. Several non-Buddhist schools take a strongly realist position and say that such universals have true existence, but Dignāga and Dharmakīrti deny that universals could exist ultimately, even though they are useful on a conventional level of everyday interaction and are thus said to exist relatively or conventionally. In this respect, Dignāga and Dharmakīrti take an anti-realist position on the ultimate level. Yet such a view runs counter to ordinary, commonsense intuition. We see cows as truly being cows and blankets as truly existing; we do not see either a cow or a blanket as being a mere conceptual construct that is projected based on its constituent parts. Thus many later thinkers including Ngok Lotsawa, Chapa Chökyi Senge, and their descendants in the Geluk tradition allow that some commonsense objects and universals may have ultimate existence, thus incorporating a moderate realism into their explanations of Dignāga and Dharmakīrti's thought. The specifics of their ideas (which also vary from thinker to thinker) are too complex to give justice to them in an essay such as this, but their interpretation quickly became dominant in Tibet.[8]

At the end of the twelfth century, the Kashmiri Mahāpaṇḍita Śākya Śrī Bhadra (1127–1225), an author of several works on validity, fled the destruction of Nalanda Monastic University in India by Muslim invaders and came to Tibet, where he would spend ten years teaching and propagating the Dharma. Among his students was the Sakya Paṇḍita Kunga Gyaltsen (1182–1251), who would later become recognized as one of the greatest scholars Tibet ever produced, especially in the field of validity. The Sakya Paṇḍita had previously studied validity, but when he heard Śākya Śrī Bhadra's explanation of Dharmakīrti's texts, he realized that Tibetan presentations of validity with their moderate realism differed significantly from Dharmakīrti's original, anti-realist teachings. He then retranslated *The Commentary on Validity* with Śākya Śrī Bhadra and also wrote his brilliant treatise *The Treasury of Logic*, which gives a systematic presentation of the collected topics from an anti-realist perspective. Though his translation of *The Commentary* soon became standard, the Sakya Paṇḍita's critique of Chapa Chökyi Senge's realist view was not immediately accepted, and it was not until the turn of the fifteenth century that the ideas in his *Treasury* gained much acceptance. At that time, Yaktön Sangye Pal (1348–1414) wrote a commentary promoting the Sakya Paṇḍita's interpretation, and later Sakya commentators such as Gorampa (1429–1489) and Śākya Chokden (1428–1507) wrote several commentaries following Yaktön Sangye Pal's lead. Thus the Sakya Paṇḍita's anti-realist interpretation and his *Treasury of Logic* became the basis for interpreting Dharmakīrti's thought in the Sakya school. This view spread into the Kagyu and Nyingma traditions as well, where the Sakya Paṇḍita's *Treasury* has become a standard part of the monastic curriculum. This is also the intellectual tradition to which Chödrak Gyatso's *Ocean of Literature on Logic* belongs.

Karmapa Chödrak Gyatso and *The Ocean of Literature on Logic*

Among the Karmapas, Chödrak Gyatso was not the first to have a connection with Dharmakīrti and his work. The First Karmapa Dusum Khyenpa (1110–1193) was a student of Chapa Chökyi Senge, though his biographies do not mention whether he studied validity with him.[9] The Second Karmapa Karma Pakshi (1203–1283) wrote a treatise on validity entitled *Infinite Oceans of Validity*, but other than some passages cited by Chödrak Gyatso, this work seems to have been lost and little can be said of its content. The Fourth Karmapa Rolpay Dorje (1340–1383) was also regarded as an expert in validity; the great Kagyu scholar Karma Trinleypa (ca. 1456–1539) says that Rolpay Dorje was the most learned of all the first seven Karmapas in both validity and the middle way.[10] However, it is the Seventh Karmapa Chödrak Gyatso (1454–1506) who became the most widely renowned for mastery of validity, primarily due to *The Ocean*, which is not only the standard Karma Kagyu text on validity but also Chödrak Gyatso's best known and most often studied work.

Though his biographies are not specific about when or with whom he studied validity, it is clear from *The Ocean* that the Seventh Karmapa Chödrak Gyatso was well-acquainted in the Geshe Chapa's reinterpretations of Dharmakīrti's thought as well as with the Sakya Paṇḍita's work and the Indian commentarial tradition. Chödrak Gyatso also had a close connection with Śākya Chokden, the master from the Sakya lineage who had already written about validity by the time they met in 1484. The two had a relationship of equals and spent considerable time discussing various topics, including validity and most especially the Great Middle Way of the Yogācāra tradition—the Shentong view that is the philosophical basis for the practice of mahamudra, the main meditation practice of the Karma Kagyu.

Chödrak Gyatso composed *The Ocean* while staying at Tsaritra—a renowned sacred site in eastern Tibet where many Kagyu masters stayed in retreat—late in 1494 or early in 1495 when he was around forty years of age.[11] Though *The Ocean* is a carefully constructed work, it was not written in an ordinary fashion. Instead, Chödrak Gyatso dictated the entire text while sitting in meditation without referring to any texts at all. As his scribe Dakrampa Khedrup Chögyal Tenpa described:

If there had been anyone other than me to request this of this Lamp of the Three Worlds,[12] it would have been quickly completed, but there was no one, so I asked him to also write this *Ocean of Literature on Logic*. I also was his scribe.

The omniscient lord is completely unlike anyone else. There weren't even any texts on validity near him. He did not look at any books. The whole time his hands were in equipoise, his eyes in a gaze, and his mind in samadhi. Never leaving that state, his wish was to perform his activity in an inexhaustible Dharma rain of teachings and advice, while I sat next to his table holding a blackish pen. When there was a pause and I would ask him to speak, he would merely ask where we were and then dictate in an uninterrupted stream with his eyes in a meditational gaze.

Some of his explanations did not at all match those of present day epistemologists, and these could not penetrate the web of my own partial and supposed intelligence. But when I asked about them, he stopped dictating and said nothing at all. For several days he composed nothing. Then he said to me that I must have confidence in the lama's words and so forth. After that, I did not ask such questions and wrote exactly what he said. He gave such brilliant refutations and such that no ordinary scholarly intellectual would find any opportunity to rebut him if they analyzed even the finest point in a single facet of one of his arguments.

When I asked him to clarify a passage on the calculations of the globe,[13] he gave with certainty all the reasons why it was not so. He then stretched his right hand out a bit into space, said, "I have had such discussions," and smiled slightly. Other than me, no one in his entourage fully saw him stretch out his arm.[14]

The extraordinariness of this feat becomes even more evident upon examining Chödrak Gyatso's *Ocean*, which he himself describes as "unprecedented" in his introductory verses. While there are many commentaries on Dignāga's *Compendium* and each of Dharmakīrti's individual works, there had previously been no other work that comments on so many of them in a single work—*The Ocean* includes commentaries on Dignāga's *Compendium* and Dharmakīrti's three major works, *The Commentary, Ascertainment,* and *Drop of Reasoning*.[15] In his commentary, Chödrak Gyatso introduces the verses from Dignāga's *Compendium* along with glosses and commentary, and then follows them with the explanations from each of Dharmakīrti's different works and his own commentary on Dharmakīrti's words. He also explains the different interpretations given by the major Indian commentators (in this chapter most frequently Devendrabuddhi, Prajñākaragupta, and Śākyabuddhi), but he rarely mentions Tibetan interpretations except to refute those he considers erroneous. His explanations are clear and succinct—the *Ocean's* length comes more from the amount of material it covers than from any long-windedness on its author's part. It is a complex, multi-tiered work, built atop the foundation of Dignāga's *Compendium* and layered with the various strata of Dharmakīrti's three main works filtered through the Indian commentators and Chödrak Gyatso's own interpretation. Even had it been written in a more conventional manner, it would be an impressive intellectual achievement.

Throughout *The Ocean,* Chödrak Gyatso prefaces his explanations of many of the topics addressed by Dignāga and Dharmakīrti with general discussions that give an overview either of the topic about to be discussed or present background information on related issues. Drawing heavily from the works of Dharmakīrti and other masters of the Yogācāra tradition—notably Asaṅga—these general discussions are where Chödrak Gyatso gives his most distinctive synthesis of the various issues. The chapter "Establishing Validity" features ten such general discussions, addressing the characteristics of validity, the purpose of epistemological treatises, the views of non-Buddhist schools, the nature of omniscience, great compassion, the nature of abandonment and realization, selflessness and the three natures, and each of the four noble truths.[16] In both the general discussions and Chödrak Gyatso's gloss of Dignāga and Dharmakīrti's texts, we can see what would become the hallmarks of the commentaries written by the great Kagyu masters of succeeding generations such as Karma Trinleypa, the Eighth Karmapa Mikyö Dorje, and Pawo Tsuklak Trengwa: a heavy reliance on the texts of the Indian tradition and an unwillingness to brook what are viewed as distortions introduced by other masters.

After writing the work, Chödrak Gyatso taught it and gave the oral transmission several times to various masters of his day, including Pawo Tsuglak Trengwa and Śākya Chokden. Chödrak Gyatso gave Śākya Chokden a copy of the text and asked him to proofread it, and the two masters spent some time in discussions focused on the profound issues it raises.[17] According to Chödrak Gyatso's biography, when Śākya Chokden later wrote his own works on logic and validity, he followed the Karmapa's explanations so closely that it is said that the two masters shared the same mind stream.[18]

Though *The Ocean of Literature on Logic* was immediately recognized as an important work, for the first few decades after its composition there were only a few looseleaf, handwritten copies of its two volumes. By the time of the Eighth Karmapa Mikyö Dorje (1507–1554), the pages from these copies had been scattered and many from the last two chapters were lost. As Mikyö Dorje said, "Disciples of lesser intelligence and great laziness were unable to grasp these treatises with a discerning intellect, and the proper compilation of the second volume was compromised."[19] At the suggestion of Karma Trinleypa, a student of the Seventh Karmapa and teacher of the Eighth, Mikyö Dorje collected the remaining pages, which he compiled and edited, and then printed in a woodblock edition that was used to teach in the Karma Dratsang Leksheyling monastic college. Unfortunately, many pages from the original were missing and this edition was thus incomplete. Though it included Chödrak Gyatso's entire explanation of Dharmakīrti's *Commentary*, the commentaries on the *Ascertainment* and *Drop of Reasoning* were incomplete, missing pages especially in the last chapter. However, the first chapter "Establishing Validity" translated here has been preserved in its entirety.

Later Situ Chökyi Jungne (1700–1774) used Mikyö Dorje's incomplete edition as the basis for another woodblock edition, which was then used in the preparation of a third woodblock print prepared at Palpung Monastery in Dergye, eastern Tibet, in 1934 at the request of Situ Pema Wangchok Gyalpo (1886–1952). This last edition is the basis for all the modern editions available, including the editions used for this translation.

Despite the unfortunate early history of the physical text, *The Ocean* has had an enduring influence. It has been taught and its reading transmission passed down through the generations to the present day.[20] In this era, it is the main text used for the study of validity in the monastic colleges of the Karma Kamtsang. It has also influenced masters from other traditions, most particularly Śākya Chokden and the nineteenth century Nyingma master Ju Mipham, who is said to have considered *The Ocean* to be the greatest of all the early commentaries on Dharmakīrti's work and used it as the primary source for his own commentary.[21]

Scholars from all of the traditions recognize *The Ocean* as an important work and debate it to this day, so it can be considered part of a living scholarly tradition.

An Overview of the Chapter "Establishing Validity"

This book presents the first chapter of Chödrak Gyatso's *Ocean of Literature on Logic,* which is his commentary on the first chapter of Dharmakīrti's *Compendium of Validity.*[22] That is in turn an extensive explanation of the verse of homage from Dignāga's *Compendium of Validity,* which reads:

> I bow to him who became valid,
> The one who wishes to help beings,
> The teacher, sugata, and protector.

On the surface level, Dignāga's verse praises the Buddha for the qualities he has—his authority, compassion for beings, teachings, qualities of abandonment and realization, and the protection from suffering he offers all sentient beings. But in his autocommentary, Dignāga explains that these verses give the reasons why the Bhagavan Buddha has become valid—that is, why he is a reliable authority. It is, Dignāga explains, because the Buddha had the two perfect causes and the two perfect results. The perfect causes are the perfect intent (the wish to benefit all beings) and the perfect training (here called the teacher). Due to these two causes, he achieved the perfect results: the perfect benefit for himself (the sugata) and the perfect benefit for others (the protector). That is to say, because many lifetimes ago the Buddha cultivated the compassionate wish to awaken to buddhahood in order to benefit all sentient beings, he trained in developing the intelligence that realizes selflessness (the teacher or perfect training). As a result, he achieved the perfect abandonment of all defilements (the sugata) and thus gained the ability to teach the four noble truths unerringly to sentient beings (the protector). Because of all this, he is valid or authoritative.

At first glance, Dignāga's praise might seem peculiar in its choice of epithets (wishing to help beings, the teacher, sugata, and protector) to prove the Buddha's authority, but it is not without precedent in Buddhist literature. A passage in the *Minor Topics of the Vinaya* relates how the Buddha made a similar argument in a conversation with his cousin Nanda:

"What do you think, Nanda? Does the Tathagata speak words that are misleading?"

"No, Venerable."

"Excellent, Nanda, excellent. It is improper for the Tathagata to say words that are misleading and there is no opportunity for it. Nanda, the Tathagata speaks the correct. He speaks the truth. He speaks the Dharma. He speaks suchness. He speaks unerringly. For a long time, the Tathagata has wished to benefit the world. He has wished it happiness. He has wished it accomplishment and happiness. He has known the path, accomplished the path, taught the path, described the path, and completely guided the path. The Tathagata is the arhat, completely perfect buddha, the one with awareness and conduct, the sugata, the one who knows the world, the charioteer who tames beings, the unsurpassable, the teacher of gods and humans, the Bhagavan Buddha."[23]

Here the Bhagavan describes himself as being truthful and reliable—not saying words that are misleading and speaking the correct, the truth, the dharma, and suchness unerringly—for the same reasons presented in the same logical order as Dignāga gives them in his verse of homage. "For a long time, the Tathagata has wished to benefit the world. . ." corresponds to Dignāga's "wish to help beings." The next sentence, "He has known the path. . ." matches Dignāga's explanation of the meaning of the epithet teacher. "The Tathagata is the arhat. . ." matches Dignāga's sugata, and the last five epithets beginning with "the charioteer who tames beings. . ." correspond to Dignaga's protector. Though this passage is not mentioned in any commentary I have seen and it would be mere conjecture to assume that this passage were Dignāga's direct source, it can be said that his homage—both its words and logic—has a precedent in Buddhist scriptures and thought.

Dignāga's argument for the authority of the Buddha is so short—a verse of twenty-four syllables in Sanskrit and a short paragraph of commentary giving little more than the broad outlines of the logic—that it seems to invite more questions than it resolves. What does it mean to say the Buddha has "become valid"? What is so special about the bodhisattva's compassion compared to ordinary compassion? Why is the training on the path called the "teacher"? What is the meaning of calling the Buddha a "sugata" and "protector"? How do we know that each step leads to the next and that we can therefore trust the Buddha as an authority? Thus when Dharmakīrti wrote his *Commentary*, he devoted an entire chapter to exploring these questions and responding to any objections that might arise.

Dharmakīrti's explanation takes each of the four qualities of the Buddha presented as evidence of his validity—the wish to benefit others, the teacher, sugata, and protector—and explains them first in the order in which they appear (both in terms of Dignāga's verse and in terms of the progression on the path to buddhahood) and then in the reverse order. Presenting them in order demonstrates how each arises as a result of the previous one. That is to say, compassion—cultivating the wish to help beings until it becomes unbearably strong—leads the bodhisattva to train in the path, which is called by the name *teacher*. Through the training in the path, the bodhisattva is able to eliminate all the obscurations and thus achieve the state of sugata. Because the sugata has the perfect realization, he is able to become the protector and teach the four noble truths without error. Since being able to unerringly guide beings who seek liberation to their desired end is the meaning of validity and the means of doing so is teaching the four noble truths without error, it is therefore possible that he could have become valid.

But this alone does not prove the validity of the Buddha, because the existence of cause cannot prove that a particular result will necessarily occur, just as the presence of a seed does not prove the existence of a flower. Likewise, cultivating compassion motivates the bodhisattva to train in the path, but does not guarantee that he has done so. Thus presenting the reasons in order simply demonstrates that the Buddha's validity is possible, but not that he has definitely become valid. As Devendrabuddhi says, "In this way, one can infer from the previous causes—the wish to benefit beings and so forth—that all the later ones are possible, so it proves that validity is not utterly impossible."[24]

But proving the possibility is not enough for Dharmakīrti; he wants to establish the Buddha's validity beyond doubt. For this reason, he also presents the reasons in reverse order, with each result proving the prior existence of its cause. Thus the fact that the Buddha teaches the four truths unerringly—that he is the protector—proves that he has the qualities of abandonment and realization (the sugata), which are the cause of being able to do so. This in turn proves its cause, that the bodhisattva trained in the path (the teacher), which then proves that he must have cultivated great compassion, the wish to help beings. Thus these four reasons that are both causes and results prove Dignāga and Dharmakīrti's proposition that the Bhagavan Buddha is valid.

Though the outlines of the logic are simple enough, Dharmakīrti is extremely thorough in his presentation of it, addressing many ancillary issues and responding to objections from non-Buddhist opponents. This is one of the aspects of Dharmakīrti's work that can make it hard for new students: understanding Dharmakīrti's logic is difficult without first grasping his opponents' positions and objections. Chödrak Gyatso's commentary provides basic overviews of the non-Buddhist philosophies (usually accompanied by brief synopses of the logic refuting their positions), which should provide enough information for the general reader to understand Dharmakīrti's arguments. A few points have also been supplemented with notes.[25] These discussions also provide some of the most interesting parts of this book—the refutation of a creator god, explanation of the meaning of omniscience, discussion of rebirth, and so forth all occur in response to objections from non-Buddhists. Though many of these points are directed at specific ancient philosophies, they often have analogues in Western thought or even reflect doubts that contemporary readers harbor. Thus, even though Dharmakīrti and his opponents may seem remote, the questions they discuss and Dharmakīrti's arguments remain relevant even today.

Though Dharmakīrti's text is philosophical in its tone, it is not necessarily a purely intellectual exercise, especially if studying it is accompanied by introspection and contemplation of its meaning. We can examine much of what he writes in our own experience. For example, when Dharmakīrti describes the protector as teaching the four noble truths, he describes each of the four noble truths in ways we can evaluate for ourselves. In describing suffering, Dharmakīrti writes that "It is impermanent as it's observed / Occasionally,"[26] and we can look for ourselves to see whether or not this is the case. We can likewise evaluate his subsequent arguments that suffering has a cause and that the cause is craving based on our own experience. Doing so, we can evaluate for ourselves whether or not the Bhagavan Buddha truly is a protector, and then consider the rest of Dharmakīrti's arguments. If we approach this text with a purely external focus, there is the danger that many of his arguments might sound circular. But by relating them to what we can examine for ourselves, Dharmakīrti's arguments cease to seem self-referential and instead become grounded in our own experience.

THE PHASES OF ANALYSIS

Since much of his work centers around refutations of his opponents, Dharmakīrti often frames his arguments in ways that they can understand and takes their assumptions as a basis for his reasoning. Thus he generally presents his arguments not from the perspective of his own ultimate view but from the perspective of a level that his opponents and readers can accept. This allows him to make his specific point without needing to defend more profound positions that would distract from his argument. But it also means that he argues on many different levels within this chapter. He often argues on a level of conventional or relative truth, and occasionally he even provisionally seems to accept a non-Buddhist position for the sake of a specific line of reasoning. When it suits his purpose, however, he will shift to a subtler level of analysis. This willingness to shift positions has given a great deal of fodder to the scholars and commentators in subsequent centuries who have tried to determine what Dharmakīrti's own views are and what school they fit into.

Traditionally, Tibetan scholars have said that Dharmakīrti presents the relative truth according to the Sutra school and the ultimate truth according to either the Mind Only or Middle Way. Though useful in many ways, this is a bit of a simplification,[27] and Chödrak Gyatso does not use this framework. Though Chödrak Gyatso does not discuss it in this chapter, in the second chapter of *The Ocean*, he explains how Dharmakīrti presents his arguments on varying levels to match the capabilities of students who are in different phases of development.

He distinguishes three such phases: the preanalytic phase, the phase of partial analysis, and the phase of thorough analysis.

1. The preanalytic phase is the level of ordinary people who have not yet begun to question the true nature of experience as well as of those people who have begun to question things but follow other, non-Buddhist philosophies. For such people, conventional appearances are real as they appear. In addressing them, Dharmakīrti often argues on the level of the conventional (or relative) truth. This is the level in which he mentions water jugs, potters, and sentient beings who are reborn.

2. The phase of partial analysis is the provisional stage of those who have begun to analyze the nature of reality but not yet arrived at the level of the ultimate truth. For such people, Dharmakīrti often argues on the level of external realism. Although on this level he denies the ultimate existence of jugs, sentient beings, and other coarse, conventional phenomena, he does provisionally accept the existence of the atoms and instants of cognition that are their building blocks.[28] At points, Dharmakīrti also argues on an idealist level where all external phenomena are presented as merely manifestations of mind. This phase should thus not be viewed as a single, cohesive view, but rather a progression over which more profound insights come closer and closer to the ultimate truth, though they have not yet arrived there.

3. The phase of thorough analysis is the realization of the Great Middle Way. At this point, the analysis is complete and the view is of the true nature, the ultimate truth.

In this chapter, Dharmakīrti mostly argues on the levels of the conventional truth and external realism—the preanalytic phase and phase of partial analysis—moving back and forth between them as suits his rhetorical needs. The phase of thorough analysis—the view of the Great Middle Way—is touched on in a few places in this chapter but is otherwise not explicitly mentioned here. Often Dharmakīrti will make an argument on a deeper level of analysis but provide an analogy on the conventional level where it will be more easily understood (though this should not be misconstrued as implying that he thinks that conventional analogies are somehow real on the higher levels). Further-

PHASES	LEVEL OF ANALYSIS
Pre-analytic	Conventional
Partial analysis	External realism
	Idealism
Thorough analysis	Great Middle Way

Figure 1: Phases and levels of analysis in Dharmakīrti's work

more, Dharmakīrti does not seem overly concerned with making a thoroughly consistent, ironclad presentation on many of the levels that appear, particularly in the phase of partial analysis, and a seemingly definitive statement made on one level of analysis may be undercut on a slightly higher level a few verses later.[29] Because of this, it often seems difficult to ascertain exactly what Dharmakīrti's own positions are.

What is Dharmakīrti's reason for refusing to be pinned down to any single level of analysis or to any single, definitive position? Likely it is because the primary purpose of his text—as described by Chödrak Gyatso—is not so much to present Buddhist ideas as to refute opponents' incorrect positions and thus clear away any misconceptions in his readers' minds. Therefore he needs to present his arguments on levels that his opponents and readers can accept. Just looking at Dharmakīrti's text confirms that his primary objective is refutation: the stanzas that present a Buddhist position are far outnumbered by the many that refute non-Buddhist ideas.[30] (This should not be taken to mean that Dharmakīrti does not present Buddhist ideas. In fact, he does give clear, succinct presentations of many topics, notably the natures of the four noble truths.) As Chödrak Gyatso says:

> In this way, after the wrong views of eternalism and nihilism and the erroneous paths have been disproven through logic, one will enter the right view and unmistaken path. This is the special purpose of treatises that teach the characteristics.[31]

Were Dharmakīrti to argue on the level of his ultimate view, his opponents would not be able to accept his refutations because they would diverge too far from conventional experience. Thus he must argue on lower levels of analysis that are profound enough to refute his opponents' wrong views yet still close enough to ordinary perceptions that the opponents can accept them. In this way, Dharmakīrti can gradually lead them to more subtle and profound understandings. His intent is therefore not to construct a thorough, consistent epistemology or ontology on each level of analysis but instead to create a plausible enough presentation on the lower levels to convince his audience and guide them to a higher level. Indeed, if it were possible to create a consistent presentation on the lower levels there would be no need for a higher level because the lower level would explain everything satisfactorily. It is precisely because there are necessarily gaps and inconsistencies in the lower levels that more profound analysis becomes necessary. As a verse found in a few sutras and cited in several treatises says,

> And if the faculties were valid
> Who would do anything with the noble path?[32]

That is, if our ordinary perceptions were truly valid, there would be no need to engage in listening, contemplation, and meditation to achieve more profound levels of understanding.

The conventional and the levels on the phase of partial analysis are based to varying degrees on the dualistic, ignorant delusion of clinging to the apprehending mind and the apprehended phenomena as separate and somehow real. This is the sphere in which ordinary beings operate, and it is impossible for all but the most exceptional of individuals to suddenly cast off ignorance and gain a deeper realization of the nature of reality. Therefore, beings need to be guided gradually from a deluded conventional understanding through the gradually more refined but still provisional stages—the stages traditionally called the Sutra school and Mind Only—to reach a definitive realization of the true nature.

DHARMAKĪRTI'S VIEW OF THE ULTIMATE

But what Dharmakīrti considers to be the true nature is a question that has led to great debate over the centuries. He is generally identified as part of the Yogācāra tradition, and many scholars explain that this means his ultimate view is that of the Mind Only school. But Chödrak

Gyatso has little patience for such talk—he describes such a view here as "merely the laziness of confusing Idealism for the Yogācāra Middle Way." For him, as for most masters of the Karma Kagyu, Yogācāra is not the particular set of tenets of the Mind Only (Idealist) school, as many Tibetans would have it, but a lineage of teachers that began with Maitreya, Asaṅga, and Vasubandhu and later included both Dignāga and Dharmakīrti as well as many other Indian masters. Though these masters did of course teach from a Mind Only perspective in some treatises or passages, it would be a mistake to say the Mind Only is their ultimate view. If merely occasionally teaching the Mind Only perspective made one a proponent of the Mind Only, then as many Kagyu texts including this one argue, the Shakyamuni Buddha would also be a Mind Only teacher because he also taught Mind Only tenets in many sutras. Instead, Chodrak Gyatso and other Kagyu masters view Yogācāra masters such as Asaṅga, Vasubandhu, Dignāga, and Dharmakīrti as teaching a Middle Way philosophy—later called the Shentong or "other empty" view—that is not fundamentally different in its view of the ultimate nature from the Middle Way taught by Nāgārjuna and his followers, which is often called the Rangtong or "self-empty" view. Chödrak Gyatso describes the distinction between the two traditions of Asaṅga and Nāgārjuna as primarily one of emphasis. Asaṅga and his followers emphasize luminosity—the "wisdom that realizes the self-aware, self-knowing mind"—whereas Nāgārjuna and his followers emphasize its lack of a nature, the aspect of emptiness. But that clear luminosity and the emptiness are not separate in any way, so there is no difference in the actual nature of what these two traditions teach; there is only a difference in the emphasis and the words used to explain it. As Chödrak Gyatso says:

> In teaching the ultimate suchness, there is no distinction at all between the two great traditions, because the clear essence of mind has been emptiness from the very beginning, and that emptiness has abided as the character of clarity from the very beginning.

Chödrak Gyatso calls this tradition the Great Middle Way of the Yogācara and places Dignāga and Dharmakīrti firmly within it, stating that the "final intent of their texts including *The Compendium of Validity* and the seven treatises fits within and falls within the textual tradition of the Yogācāra." He addresses the reasons for saying their ultimate view is the Middle Way in greater detail in the second chapter "Perception," but he does take up the question in this chapter, notably in his general discussions.

The clearest expression of the Great Middle Way view in the root verses of this chapter is Dharmakīrti's famous couplet that encapsulates the essence of its view: ·

> The nature of the mind is luminous;
> The stains are adventitious.[33]

These two lines have become renowned as a description of the ultimate nature and are often cited in treatises describing buddha nature and mahamudra. But they are not the only evidence of a Middle Way view in this chapter. Chödrak Gyatso's close disciple Karma Trinleypa writes that Chödrak Gyatso cites Dharmakīrti's description of the truth of the path as characteristic of a Middle Way view because it presents the truth of the path as being the same as the truth of cessation:

> Furthermore, in the chapter "Establishing Validity,"
> The truth of the path that directly realizes the nature
> Is said to be the same as the truth of cessation.
> Therefore, this is a text of the Middle Way tradition,
>   he [Chödrak Gyatso] maintained.[34]

What Karma Trinleypa is referring to is Dharmakīrti's description in verse 216 of how the wisdom of the path—here called the view of emptiness—is exclusive of delusion and the faults:

> Because the view of emptiness is exclusive
> Of that, it's proven to be exclusive of
> The faults that have that as their nature.

Because it is exclusive of delusion, when the wisdom of the path arises, delusion simultaneously ceases. This cessation of delusion—emptiness—is not separate from the wisdom of the path that views emptiness, and thus the truths of the path and cessation are unified. The wisdom of the path that realizes emptiness is itself emptiness (cessation), but that cessation is also wisdom by its nature. This position is characteristic of the Middle Way—the lower schools deny that wisdom is empty and assert that it exists in the ultimate truth.

The point of all of this is not so much whether Dharmakīrti's own personal view was actually Middle Way or not; we as ordinary people separated from him by the distance of fourteen centuries have no way to definitively know. What is important is that when viewed as part of the tradition of the Great Middle Way, Dharmakīrti's texts can help us understand the philosophical basis for meditational practices such as mahamudra, as Kagyu masters from the time of Chödrak Gyatso and Karma Trinleypa onward have often said. Regarded in this way, Dignāga and Dharmakīrti's works then cease being merely intellectual but instead become part of the path by which we can, to paraphrase Dharmakīrti's verse of homage, clear away the net of thought and gain the vast and profound bodies of a buddha ourselves.

THE MEANING OF VALIDITY

Over the course of this chapter, Dharmakīrti addresses various issues of interest—whether there is a creator god, the nature of omniscience, how compassion can develop exponentially, the nature of the four noble truths, and so forth—and Chödrak Gyatso adds a few topics in his general discussions as well. For the most part, the text presents these clearly and they do not need further explanation here. However, a couple—the meaning of validity and the topic of rebirth—that could benefit from some additional explanation will be discussed in the next few pages.

Even in the opening verses, it is clear that Dharmakīrti uses the term *validity* on different levels. Often he uses it in an epistemological sense as to how to determine whether a cognition is valid or not, but he also uses it to refer to the authoritativeness of the Bhagavan Buddha. As Chödrak Gyatso highlights (following a distinction found in Dharmakīrti's *Ascertainment* as well as in Prajñākaragupta's *Ornament* and other commentaries), from the very outset there is the tension between the usage referring to the ultimate validity of a Buddha and the usage referring to the conventional validity that is the means to achieve that ultimate validity. Because Dharmakīrti uses the term *validity* in this manner with different but related meanings, there has been a great deal of discussion in the commentarial literature as well as in contemporary academic sources about what he actually intends by the word.

In trying to understand what the word *pramāṇa* means (or its Tibetan translation *tshad ma* in the context of the Tibetan canon), it is helpful to look at how the word is used in the wider context of Buddhist literature, particularly in the vinaya where technical terms are often used in a historical narrative context that illuminates not just their technical meaning but their general usage and diction. The word *tshad ma* appears three times in historical passages in *The Topics of the Vinaya*,[35] where it has the sense of a statement being authoritative or reliable. For example, a passage describing the reaction of the early Śākya princes to the sage Kapila's advice to marry their half-sisters reads, "'The sage's words are valid (*tshad ma*),' they thought. . ."[36] In such narrative contexts, the word *valid* means authoritative and worth heeding, and applies primarily to words. This is similar to one usage of the word *pramāṇa* by non-Buddhist sects that assert the Vedic scriptures are verbal validity because they are "not of human origin," a notion that Dharmakīrti refutes briefly here and at greater length in other chapters of his *Commentary*. Yet though he denies verbal validity, Dharmakīrti does seem to accept this sense of the word as meaning authoritative, in particular in reference to the Bhagavān as ultimate validity. Because he has perfected the qualities of abandonment and realization through cultivating compassion and training in the path, the Buddha is said to be valid—that is, an authoritative, reliable guide.

Yet much of the time, Dignāga and Dharmakīrti use the word *pramāṇa* on the level of epistemology and conventional validity. This usage of the term seems to come from their participation in the pan-Indian pramāṇa tradition and shared systems of logic that started around the second century with the founding of the Nyāya school. From this time onward, there were lively inter-sectarian debates, and each school posited its own criteria for and classification of validity, though there was enough common ground among the schools that they could use it as the basis for their debates.[37] For most of the non-Buddhist schools, it refers to the means of knowledge—the perception, inference, scriptures, and so forth that lead to knowledge, which is considered result of the valid.[38] But Dignāga, Dharmakīrti, and their followers take a more restrictive view of validity. For them validity (at least on the conventional level) must be cognition itself, not the means to knowledge: the means of knowing—the pramāṇa—and its resulting knowing are essentially two simultaneous aspects of the same cognition, as Dharmakīrti describes in his chapter on perception. As Dharmakīrti says here, "The valid is an undeceiving mind."[39] Thus on this epistemological level, Dharmakīrti rules out anything other than cognition (such as scriptures, the sensory faculties, and so forth) being considered valid.

Additionally, for Dharmakīrti the valid must "dwell in the ability to function,"[40] or to dwell in *arthakriyā*, a Sanskrit term he uses with different meanings in different contexts. In the chapter on perception, he uses it in the sense of causal efficacy, but here it has the sense of attaining a goal or aim: the valid enables an individual to encounter an entity as it is apprehended. Chödrak Gyatso explains:

> The meaning of *undeceiving* is that the individual is able to encounter the entity as the valid cognition itself indicates. This is called by the term *undeceiving*. It means nothing other than that it makes an individual comprehend the object without error by way of producing recognition that realizes the way the object is.

Additionally, Dharmakīrti only considers undeceiving cognitions that engage real things (here called specific characteristics,[41] which on the level of external realism refers to atoms and instants of cognition) to be valid, not those that engage conceptual projections such as universals (that is, some sort of "jugness" or "cowness" that would inhabit specific vessels and bovines and make them into jugs and cows). This is because only specific characteristics can fulfill aims—actual water can slake thirst while a concept of water cannot. As Dharmakīrti says:

> Cognition that knows the unknown specific
> Characteristics is intended, since
> One analyzes specific characteristics.[42]

In this way, Dharmakīrti's approach is typically concrete and pragmatic: any description of real or unreal must be based on specific experience, not conceptual projections.

And yet such a characterization of validity can only operate on a lower level of analysis, for a cognition that engages without deception an external object such as fire can only be considered valid on levels where the independent existence of such external objects is not directly challenged. Thus at the end of the first chapter of his *Ascertainment*, Dharmakīrti makes a distinction between such valid cognitions— which he calls conventional validity—and ultimate validity, which is the eventual result of contemplation and meditation:

> . . . in relation to being undeceiving about the conventional, it [conventional validity] is valid here. This here is in all respects a description of the nature of conventional validity, because others are deluded about it and the world is thus deceived. By becoming familiarized with the intelligence produced by contemplation, one is separated from confusion of misunderstanding and manifests ultimate validity, which cannot be turned back from the stainless.[43]

That is to say, ordinary beings misunderstand what validity is and thus treat things that are not valid or authoritative even conventionally— the faculties, Vedas, and so forth—as if they were and then perform actions such as animal sacrifice that will only create more suffering for themselves and others. When taught conventional validity, however, they can contemplate it and develop a view that accords with the true nature, the four noble truths. By meditating on this, they will free themselves from confusion and achieve nirvana, the stainless ultimate validity. In this manner, distinguishing between conventional and ultimate validity can be seen as one aspect of the different phases and levels of analysis described above, and conventional validity becomes a part of Dharmakīrti's method for gradually guiding beings to progressively more profound insights.

Though Dharmakīrti does not explain this distinction in this chapter, Chödrak Gyatso does bring it into his analysis of Dharmakīrti's text, explaining several of these verses in terms of both ultimate and conventional validity. In doing so, he brings out yet another meaning of the Sanskrit *arthakriyā:* the function or *artha* that the Buddha fulfills is the twofold benefit (*artha*) for self and other. As Chödrak Gyatso says:

Due to his perfect intent, he performs all temporary and ultimate benefit for wanderers. Because of the cause of the perfect training of the path, he dwells in the ability to achieve that function of benefiting and is proven to be the protector who never deceives.

Thus for Chödrak Gyatso, the Bhagavan himself is the ultimate validity: he has achieved the perfect abandonment and realization of the sugata and thus fulfilled the ultimate benefit for himself. At the same time, as the protector who teaches the path without deception, he has achieved the ultimate benefit for others.

DHARMAKĪRTI'S ARGUMENT FOR REBIRTH

Of all the various issues that Dharmakīrti covers in this chapter, the one for which it is most famous is his proof of rebirth and reincarnation. This is not merely among contemporary academics. For centuries, Dharmakīrti's defense of rebirth has been celebrated and studied in India and Tibet within a social context where belief in rebirth is the cultural norm. Dharmakīrti's discussion of the logic and supporting arguments occur in two long passages that together account for well over a third of the chapter—113 of 287 stanzas.[44] From the length and depth of his arguments, it is clear that this is just as important an issue for Dharmakīrti as it has been for later scholars.

The reasons become clear upon looking at the context for the proof. Dharmakīrti first addresses the issue in support of his assertion that the cause of achieving buddhahood is cultivating compassion over many lifetimes—a standard Buddhist position dating back to the many occasions when the Buddha spoke of past and future lives recorded in the sutras and the vinaya. Dharmakīrti returns to the topic of rebirth a second time to defend his position that "Suffering is the samsaric aggregates"[45] against the opponents' assertion that there is no samsara where beings come from one lifetime and go on to the miseries of the next. These are two key points of Buddhist thought: without rebirth, the achievement of buddhahood would be impossible, and striving for it would be pointless as well since sentient beings would cease to exist after death and thus be automatically released from any suffering whether they had done any spiritual practice or not. In other words, without rebirth there could be neither samsara nor nirvana, and there would be little need for Buddhism.

But accepting rebirth is difficult for many who have received a Western education. In the materialistic viewpoint that has the ascendancy in the sciences, education, and mainstream media, there is little room for such things as rebirth or afterlife that are difficult to physically measure and quantify. An infinite cycle of rebirth also seems strange to those Christians and others who posit an eternal afterlife. Thus many people these days are skeptical at best about rebirth, and the idea that humans "have a brief tenure on Earth, bracketed by infinities of nothingness,"[46] resonates strongly for many. Even among the Western Buddhist community, there are some well-known authors who deny rebirth and attract a sympathetic following, and it is not uncommon for people to say one can be Buddhist without accepting rebirth. Perhaps this skepticism is for the best. People who read the viewpoints of the proponents and opponents, contemplate the matter, and decide for themselves will come to greater certainty than they would if they unthinkingly accepted rebirth as truth or fiction without really questioning their own beliefs and cultural biases. And those biases may just as easily be those of someone educated in a materialist, scientific environment as those of a person steeped in Buddhism and talk of reincarnation since birth. Thus arguments such as Dharmakīrti's are important for us in the twenty-first century as well—not so much to convince us but to provoke the contemplation that will bring us to greater understanding.

In many treatises, rebirth and karma are described as extremely hidden objects, beyond the sphere of ordinary perception or inference. Such objects are often said to be essentially a matter of faith that need to be accepted based on scriptural authority, but Dharmakīrti does not assert that in this chapter. Instead, Dharmakīrti presents an argument based upon the principles of cause and result, implicitly taking the position that rebirth can be proven logically and therefore known through inference.

The crux of Dharmakīrti's argument is that the mind and matter both arise out of substantial causes of their own kind, and therefore any cognition, including the first cognition of this life, must have been preceded by an earlier one. Here *substantial* and *substance* do not necessarily mean material or physical but can also refer to the immaterial natures of phenomena such as cognition. Matter and cognition have very different substances—one physical and the other not—and thus they are considered fundamentally different in kind. Thus the body and mind cannot be each other's substantial causes.

In Dharmakīrti's presentation, everything that arises has a substantial cause that interacts with various supporting conditions to produce a result. For example, when a lump of clay is made into a pot, the clay is the substantial cause and the various factors that influence its production—the potter, the wheel, the implements, and so forth—are all conditions that affect the finished pot but are different in substance from the clay. Likewise, each instant of cognition has a substantial cause (the previous instant of cognition) that is of the same substance as well as various conditions (the sensory faculties, the object of cognition, and so forth) that affect it but are not of the same substance. Thus the body cannot be the substantial cause of mind because it is different in substance—it is material, not mental—though it can affect cognition by way of being one of its conditions, such as its object.

Additionally, Dharmakīrti follows the general Buddhist principle that all composite phenomena, such as mind or physical matter, are impermanent, arising and perishing in each moment. Each moment of matter acts as the substantial cause of the next moment of matter. Likewise, each cognition acts as the substantial cause of the next cognition, which arises in the following instant. Since every moment of cognition must have a substantial cause, the very first cognition in a given lifetime must have also have a substantial cause, and that would have to be the last cognition of the previous lifetime since it cannot arise without a cause—out of nothing—or out of only physical causes.[47] Therefore for Dharmakīrti, the previous life is proven. As he says in verse 166:

Nonconsciousness is not the substantial cause
Of consciousness, so it is also proven.

As a corollary to this, Dharmakīrti also argues that just as it can be seen that each cognition in this life has the power to produce the next cognition, so too must the consciousness at the time of death also have the capability of producing the next consciousness, which is the first consciousness of the next stage of existence.[48]

Dharmakīrti's argument comes down to the dualistic idea that the mind and body have separate continua, at least on a conventional, commonsense level.[49] For this reason, the main objections Dharmakīrti addresses are those of the Cārvāka school, which (much like materialist scientists and philosophers of today) asserts that consciousness arises from physical causes, the four elements of earth, water, fire, and air. Starting from verse 39d, Dharmakīrti devotes most of the first passage on rebirth to rebutting this position, examining logically the relation between mind and the body. He explains why the mind cannot be a quality of the body, the same in substance as the body, or a result of the body. By demonstrating this, he establishes that the mind and body must have separate substantial continua.

Though he asserts that continua of the body and mind are separate, Dharmakīrti does not argue that they are so radically separated that they have no affect upon each other. Instead, he argues that the body and mind also coexist as cooperating conditions for each other—conditions that are different in substance from the substantial cause but that work together with it to produce a result. For example, decisions we make in our minds cause our body to do things, and physical changes in the body can affect our mental state as well. In particular, changes in the body can be an internal object of cognition. As he says in verse 77:

> Increases of desire and such from thriving
> And such are sometimes born from pleasure or pain.
> They're from the presence of internal objects—
> The balance of the elements and so forth.

Dharmakīrti elaborates on this explanation later in the second passage in which he discusses rebirth. He addresses whether the mind and specific mind states arise out of physical causes, such as anger arising from imbalances in the three humors of bile, phlegm, and wind, or from afflictions such as desire produced by the sight of an attractive person. For Dharmakīrti, though such physical events can affect the mind by way of being an object that is perceived, they do not *necessarily* entail changes in the mind and are thus proven not to be substantial causes of the mind. If they were the substantial cause of mind, then such changes in the humors would necessarily create changes in the mind. Instead, they are merely cooperating conditions for the next instant of cognition.

Thus the body and mind have separate continua that nonetheless are linked and affect each other. Because they are substantially separate, they initially come from different sources—the body from the parents' sperm and ovum (the father's sperm and mother's blood according to traditional treatises) and the mind from the previous life. Likewise, after the moment of death the physical body becomes a corpse, and the mind goes on to the next lifetime. This is illustrated in Figure 2.

Yet such a relationship between body and mind can be difficult for people in contemporary societies with modern educations to accept. In recent years, the dominant voice in articles and books about neuroscience, psychology, and consciousness has been the materialist viewpoint that consciousness is an epiphenomenon of the brain or its neural networks. Correlations have been observed between certain emotional states or cognitive processes and activity in particular parts of the brain, leading many to conclude that the activity in the brain either is consciousness or causes it in some manner. However, exactly how that electro-chemical activity would become subjective awareness is still unsolved; this is often called the "hard problem" even by the proponents of this argument. So widespread is the literature promoting this materialist view that many people accept as a proven fact that consciousness is a manifestation of the brain, disregarding the reality that the hard problem has not yet been solved, which leaves a rather large hole in the materialist argument. And if the materialist view were indeed proven fact, Dharmakīrti's argument for past and future lives would not stand.

But that materialist belief is not unanimous, and there are scientists and thinkers who argue that the correlation of brain activity and certain types of awareness is neither proof positive of a causal connection between the two nor confirmation that they are somehow the same in identity. Instead, they may perhaps just "provide evidence for the

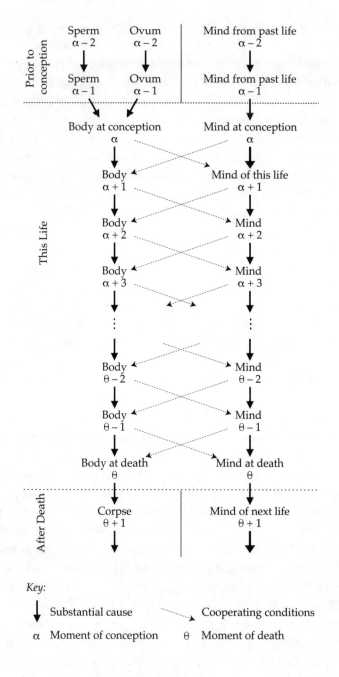

Figure 2: Relationship of body and mind according to Dharmakīrti

role of neuronal networks as an intermediary for the manifestation of thoughts."[50] Indeed, several have noted that there is not necessarily a correlation between brain activity and consciousness. There are many instances recorded in medical literature of people who have had cardiac arrest and whose brains show none of the activity usually correlated to consciousness by materialists (even as measured by an electro-encephalogram in some studies[51]) and yet upon being resuscitated, report subjective experiences that entail consciousness such as near-death or out of body experiences. Many survivors have described in accurate detail events that happened while they were technically dead, which could not occur if there were no consciousness. A large enough number of survivors of cardiac arrest report such experiences—varying sources report that up to fifteen percent have them[52]—that they cannot be written off as an anomaly.[53] Regardless of the content of such experiences, there merely being a continuum of experience in situations where there is no brain activity shows that consciousness can occur independent of brain activity and thus cannot merely be a byproduct of it. And if this is so, then Dharmakīrti's argument that there must be past and future lives because consciousness has its own continuum of substantial causes merits serious consideration.[54]

In the final analysis, whether such arguments are convincing for any given individual comes down to their own experience and analysis of the issue. Though Dharmakīrti's arguments—whether about rebirth or about the authority of the Buddha—are philosophical on the surface level, individuals can test them by looking at their own minds and seeing how one cognition gives rise to the next, how physical sensations affect their minds, how cognitive events in the mind also have an effect on their bodies, and so forth. Regarded in this way, Dharmakīrti's logic becomes a tool for individuals to honestly examine themselves and their own experience to come to certainty on their own about such important issues as past and future lives as well as the nature of the Buddha's authority.

TRANSLATION METHODOLOGY

In approaching this translation, it quickly became apparent that *The Ocean* is a work whose multiple layers—Dignāga's opening verse,

Dharmakīrti's brilliant commentary, and Chödrak Gyatso's explanations of both—are interleaved with each other. Each of these layers is a
distinct work that has a separate author with a separate voice, and ide-
ally each should be approached on its own terms, to whatever extent
that is possible. Due to my training in Tibetan and the Karma Kamtsang
tradition and since these texts have been kept alive by Tibetan tradition,
this translation is to a large degree filtered through the lens of Tibetan
translations and commentaries, though I have tried to examine the
available Sanskrit materials to the best of my abilities.

The deepest stratum (though the thinnest if measured by quantity)
is Dignāga's homage along with his own explanation of it in his autocommentary. This text survives in two Tibetan translations, one by
Vasudhararakṣita and Genyen Senggyal found in the Dergye Tengyur
and the other by Kaṇakavarman and Depay Sherap from the Narthang
Tengyur. The original Sanskrit has been lost, but enough fragments
identified over the years have survived as citations in commentaries
and other texts that several scholars have prepared retranslations of
the Sanskrit from the Tibetan or reconstructed it based on the available
fragments. For this translation, I have referred to Ernst Steinkellner's
2005 reconstruction of the first chapter of the *Compendium* as well as
to the two Tibetan translations. Since *The Ocean* cites from the Dergye
Tengyur translation, this is the translation mentioned in citations here,
even though many scholars consider the other Tibetan translation to
be superior.

History has been kinder to the Sanskrit text of Dharmakīrti's *Commentary*, a few complete copies of which were found in Tibet, and modern editions of it are available. In addition, the Sakya Paṇḍita Kunga
Gyaltsen's translation is deservedly recognized as a paragon of faithful translation. In preparing the English translation of this chapter of
The Commentary, I have compared the Sakya Paṇḍita's translation with
the Sanskrit as well as with the commentaries by Devendrabuddhi,
Śākyabuddhi, and Prajñākaragupta that are available in the Tibetan
Tengyur. Devendrabuddhi's commentary in particular has been helpful, not only because it is a word-by-word explanation of Dharmakīrti's
text but also because it uses a different Tibetan translation of the root
verses, giving an alternate window on the original. In examining these
sources, I have located about a dozen minor discrepancies between

the Tibetan and the Sanskrit original, which are noted in the text of the chapter. (Several of these could have been due to typographical errors introduced into various editions over the centuries.) The goal of this process has been to translate Dharmakīrti's work—to the greatest extent possible—without the filter of Chödrak Gyatso's interpretation so that this translation will be useful to scholars and translators from various traditions.

One important aspect of Dharmakīrti's *Commentary* is that it is written in metered verse, and on examination it is clear that Dharmakīrti took a great deal of care with his language. Likewise the Sakya Paṇḍita's translation is also in verse. Thus in translating the text, I have also attempted to render it in verse, though I have allowed myself more freedom in prosody than either Dharmakīrti or the Sakya Paṇḍita and there are many irregularities. The intent is that the rhythms of the words in the ear help the meaning stay in the mind, though whether this indeed happens is for the reader to decide.

The uppermost layer in this book is Chödrak Gyatso's text from *The Ocean*. For convenience I have primarily used an electronic version of the text, but I have also checked questionable passages against scans of the original woodblocks and other editions. There are a few passages that are unclear or nonsensical in the available editions. Most of these have been resolved by comparing the text with Chödrak Gyatso's sources, Devendrabuddhi and Prajñākaragupta; by checking other sources, particularly those in the Tengyur and Ju Mipham Rinpoche's commentary; and by consulting various Tibetan scholars. These passages are noted where they occur.

One difficulty translators, scholars, and readers all face is the lack of standardized translations for logical and Buddhist terms. Many translators have translated various Indian and Tibetan texts on logic, and different sets of English terminology for standard logical terms have developed. While some terms seem to have become more or less standard, there is considerable variation for others. Though at the outset of this project my intention was to pick one existing set of terminology as the basis for this translation, it soon became apparent that each set of terminology has its own strong and weak points. Thus I decided to take what I felt were the clearest terms from the various texts I have read and combine them here. Some explanations of my choices are given in notes on the first appearance of the term; others I hope will be evident enough from the context.

Attempting a large translation of an important text such as this involves more chutzpah than wisdom for someone whose study of validity has been incomplete at best, and I have only done so because Khenchen Thrangu Rinpoche asked me to. Any errors contained in this book are solely the products of my own pride and ignorance, and for them I beg the pardon of those with greater knowledge of this vast and profound topic.

—David Karma Choephel

A Note on the Numbering of Verses

T<small>HE</small> <small>VERSES</small> of Dharmakīrti's text are numbered sequentially as they appear in this translation. When cited in the notes, verses in this chapter are referred to merely by their number (e.g. Verse 186); verses from other chapters of *The Commentary* are indicated by a Roman numeral indicating the chapter and an Arabic number indicating the verse (e.g. ii.182). The chapter order is as given by Karmapa Chödrak Gyatso, so the chapter on inference for oneself is numbered as the third chapter. Unless otherwise specified, verse numbers given in the notes refer to verses from *The Commentary*.

Thus the numbering in this translation differs from the numbering given in Steinkellner's *Verse-Index of Dharmakīrti's Works*. Though it would have been good to match his system, that was unworkable for two reasons. First, Steinkeller orders the chapters beginning with the chapter on inference for oneself whereas Chödrak Gyatso places it first. Thus following Steinkellner's enumeration would have meant that this translation would be internally inconsistent. Second, Steinkeller assigns numbers to two lines that appear after 133b of this chapter in some but not all versions of the root and in a few commentaries. The root in the Dergye Tengyur does not include these two lines, nor does *The Ocean*, and they do not appear in this translation (except in a note). If the two lines were numbered here, many complete sentences or thoughts would start and end in the middle of stanzas. But when the stanzas are numbered as they appear in the Dergye Tengyur, the meaning fits better with the stanzas.

When verse numbers are cited in the notes, they are cited first with the numbering according to *The Ocean*, with Steinkellner's numbering in parentheses.

A Brief Introduction to
Indo-Tibetan Logic

DHARMAKĪRTI IS RENOWNED as a master logician, and so it should be no surprise that this chapter is built around logical arguments and reasoning. However, the Indo-Tibetan way of reasoning and structuring arguments differs from the Western way, and without a brief introduction to its basics, people who have never read texts such as this might become confused by the terminology and reasoning. Thus this brief introduction is intended to provide newcomers enough of a basic understanding of logic so as to be able to understand Dharmakīrti's and Chödrak Gyatso's arguments. It is not intended to be a thorough study of logic, as that is neither necessary for a basic understanding of this chapter nor within the scope of such a short introduction.

The logic is described here as it is taught in the Tibetan tradition, which developed out of the Indian style of logic and debate established by Dignāga, Dharmakīrti, and their followers. As in Western logic, propositions are proven through syllogisms (*prayoga, sbyor ba*), though the form and presentation differ. Generally, a syllogism consists of four parts: the subject (*dharmin, chos can*), predicate (*dharma, chos*), evidence (*liṅga, rtags*), and analogy (*mthun dpe*). For example, in the classic syllogism "Sound, the subject, is impermanent, because it is produced, like a jug," the subject is sound, the predicate is being impermanent, the evidence is it being produced, and the analogy is a jug. The combination of the subject and predicate is called the proposition (*pakṣa, phyogs*). The evidence is also sometimes called the reason (*hetu, gtan tshig*), and these terms are often used interchangeably.

THE THREE MODES

In order to evaluate whether the evidence proves the proposition or not, the relationships of the evidence to the subject and predicate must be examined. This is done through what are called the three modes (*trirūpam, tshul gsum*): the propositional property (*pakṣadharma, phyogs chos*),[1] entailing pervasion (*anvayavyapti, rjes khyab*), and reverse pervasion (*vyatirekavyapti, ldog khyab*). The propositional property describes the relationship between the evidence and the subject (despite its name, which might suggest it is the relationship to the entire proposition), and the two pervasions describe the relationship between the evidence and the predicate, as shown in Figure 3. In order for evidence to be considered correct, all three modes must be fulfilled. Indeed, this is the characteristic[2] traditionally given for correct evidence: evidence that fulfills the three modes.

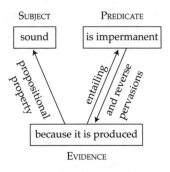

Figure 3: The three modes in a correct reason

For the propositional property to be fulfilled, the evidence must be recognized as present in the subject. For example, being produced is a property of all sound, so the propositional property in this sample syllogism is fulfilled. If on the other hand the evidence is not necessarily present in subject or if the debaters do not both recognize it, the propositional property is not fulfilled. For example, in the syllogism "sound, the subject, is permanent because it is produced by effort," the propositional property is not fulfilled because being produced by effort is not present in all instances of sound, as in Figure 4. (The sound of thunder requires no effort, for example.) In such cases, the evidence is said to be *not proven* or *not established* (*ma grub pa*). Thus when it says in the chapter that the reason (or evidence) is not proven or not established, it means that the propositional property has not been fulfilled.

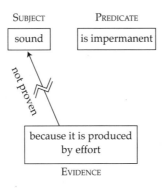

Figure 4: Unproven evidence

The two pervasions ascertain whether the evidence is necessarily present within all instances of the predicate. The entailing pervasion means that the predicate is entailed (*anvaya, rjes su 'gro ba*)[3] by the evidence—that is, in our example that being produced necessarily means being impermanent. This is evaluated by ascertaining that all instances of the evidence (being produced) are included in the similar class (*mthun phyogs*) of the predicate (the set of everything impermanent). If there is any instance of the evidence that is outside the similar class, then the entailing pervasion is not fulfilled. That is to say, anything that is produced—jugs, cars, anxiety, and so forth—must be impermanent for the entailing pervasion to be fulfilled.

The reverse pervasion is evaluated in the opposite manner: it means that everything that is not the predicate (being impermanent) is necessarily also not the evidence (being produced). In other words, everything that is permanent (that is, not impermanent) must also not be produced. In the text, this is called *reverse entailing* (*vyatireka, ldog pa*). It is evaluated by ascertaining that there are no instances of the evidence in the dissimilar class (in our example, the set of everything permanent). Logically, this is the same as the entailing pervasion—it is merely a question of whether it is determined in a positive direction or a negative direction. Thus the reason why there are the two pervasions is because there are cases where it is difficult to ascertain the entailing pervasion but easier to evaluate the reverse pervasion and vice versa. When the two pervasions are fulfilled, the evidence is said to *pervade*, or alternately the evidence is said to be *determinate*.

For example, in Figure 5, the area inside the circle represents the similar class, the area outside the circle represents the dissimilar class, and *e* represents instances of the evidence. Here the entailing pervasion is ascertained (fulfilled) because all of the instances of *e* are inside the similar class. The reverse pervasion is also ascertained because there are no instances of *e* in the dissimilar class—that is, outside the similar class. Thus this is an example of the evidence pervading or alternately of the evidence being determinate.

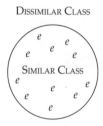

Figure 5: All evidence in the similar class

In Figure 6, however, the entailing pervasion is not ascertained because not all instances of *e* are within the similar class. The reverse pervasion is also not ascertained because there are instances of *e* in the dissimilar class. Thus this is an example of the evidence not being determinate.

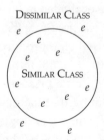

Figure 6: Not all evidence in the similar class

For example, in the syllogism "sound, the subject, is blue because it is produced," the propositional property is proven because being produced is ascertained as always being present in the subject. However, the pervasions are not determinate because not everything that is produced (red jugs, for example) is blue, and there are things (red jugs) that are not blue but are produced. Thus the evidence in such a syllogism is not determinate, as shown in Figure 7, and the proposition is not proven.

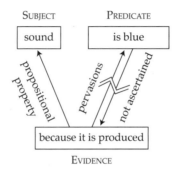

Figure 7: Evidence not determinate

ANALOGIES

Even if all three modes are logically fulfilled, a syllogism is still not considered proven unless both debaters validly recognize that they have been fulfilled. Thus a method to help bring about that recognition is necessary, so it is normal in Indian logic for a syllogism to include an analogy—an opponent who is at first unable to recognize the logic with regard to the subject in question might recognize it when given an easily understandable analogy. For example, an opponent who is unable to recognize the impermanence of sound may well recognize that jugs are produced and thus impermanent. By making the analogy of sound to jugs, the opponent can then be brought to understand that sound is also produced and therefore impermanent.

Because analogies are considered crucial for bringing recognition of the three modes, they are integral to the syllogism, and if the analogy is fallacious then the entire syllogism is considered unproven. Thus there are several instances throughout this chapter where Dharmakīrti refutes an opponent's argument by attacking the analogy, notably in his refutation of the existence of a creator god. In addition, the analogies he provides for his own propositions give him an opportunity to display his own wit.

TYPES OF EVIDENCE

When the evidence fulfills the three modes and there is a valid analogy, the evidence is said to be correct. There are said to be three types of correct evidence: evidence of nature, evidence of a result, and evidence of nonobservation. The first two prove that a phenomenon exists or that it has a certain predicated property, and the last is used to prove the nonexistence of a phenomenon or predicate.

1. Evidence of nature is a reason where the evidence and the predicate of the proposition share the same character. For example, in the syllogism "Sound, the subject, is impermanent because it is produced, like a jug," the predicate being impermanent has the same character as the evidence, being produced. Since the evidence and predicate are thus related by having the same character, the evidence thus entails the predicate. The logic of the first half of Dharmakīrti's chapter, presenting the reasons in order, is based on a series of such reasons of nature in that the presence of a cause proves the capacity to produce a result, as such a capacity is the nature of a cause. Thus the cultivation of loving-kindness proves that there is the capacity to achieve its result— the training in the path. The training in the path in turn proves there is the capacity to gain its result—the sugata—and the sugata proves that there is the capacity to attain the state of the protector. That protector—unerringly teaching the natures of the four noble truths—is the meaning of validity, and thus validity is established from the protector.

2. Evidence of a result is a reason that proves the prior existence of a cause by reason of the existence of the result, just as the presence of a flower proves the prior existence of its cause—a seed. The logic of the second half of this chapter is based on a sequence of such reasons: the ability of the Bhagavan Buddha to protect beings from samsara by teaching the nature of the four noble truths unerringly proves the prior existence of the sugata—his qualities of abandonment and realization. That in turn proves the prior presence of its cause—the training on the

path—which then proves the prior existence of its cause, the cultivation of loving-kindness.

3. Evidence of nonobservation is used to prove the nonexistence of a phenomenon by reason of it not being validly observed. An example of such evidence is the syllogism, "Rabbit horns, the subject, do not exist, because they have never been validly observed, like pink elephants."[4] Dharmakīrti discusses such reasons at length in the chapter on perception, but he does use this type of evidence in this chapter as well.

This short introduction should give readers enough to grasp the basic logic of this chapter. Of course, a thorough study of types of evidence (*rtags rigs*) would require far more study and debate; it is an integral part of a traditional Tibetan monastic education that cannot be given its full due in so few pages. However, there are several books on this topic available, as well as classes in it at various institutes, universities, and Dharma organizations, so readers who wish to study it more should look for such resources.

Acknowledgements

————◆————

Since even before I began to work on this project, Khenchen Thrangu Rinpoche has supported me in all the ways that have made this work possible. First he allowed me to study in his monastic college, the Vajra Vidya Institute, where I had the good fortune to study this chapter in 2003. Since that time, he has provided me with everything I have needed both for my livelihood as well as for my dharma practice. Completing this translation seems but a small offering in comparison to his great kindness.

During the process of translation, I also had the support and assistance of the faculty of the Vajra Vidya Institute in Namo Buddha, Nepal, and Sarnath, India, in particular Khenpo Sherap Phuntsok, who answered many questions and helped me resolve several difficult passages in the text. Special thanks are due to Damien Jampa Dorje of Palpung Sherap Ling monastic college, who reviewed the entire manuscript and clarified many points with khenpos from Palpung Sherap Ling. I am grateful to Michele Martin for her support, especially for her invaluable assistance during the writing of the translator's introduction. The publication of this book is made possible through the support of Ms. Margaret Lee. I appreciate not just her assistance with this project but also her great generosity to many Dharma projects.

PART 1

Establishing Validity

The First Chapter of *The Ocean of Literature on Logic,*
Which Collects the Rivers of All the Explanations of Validity
Explained by Way of The Compendium of Validity, the Seven Treatises,
and the Entire Literature on Logic

by the Seventh Karmapa Chödrak Gyatso

In Tibetan: *Tshad ma kun las btus pa sde bdun dang rigs pa'i gzhung mtha' dag gi sgo nas bshad pa/ tshad ma rjod par byed pa thams cad kyi chu bo yongs su 'du ba rigs pa'i gzhung lugs kyi rgya mtsho zhes bya ba/*

In English: *The Ocean of Literature on Logic, Which Collects the Rivers of All the Explanations of Validity Explained by Way of* The Compendium of Validity, *the Seven Treatises, and the Entire Literature on Logic*

I.

ESTABLISHING VALIDITY

I prostrate to Manjushri, the master of speech.

> Never deceiving beings, he is always loving.
> Not obscured toward anything knowable, he knows and teaches.
> He is the sugata and protector of all worlds;
> I bow to him who has become a valid being.

> Their bodies, suns of wisdom, banish the gloom of ignorance
> And shine the light of loving deeds on beings everywhere.
> To the guardian who relieves beings with gentle melodies
> And regent protector Ajita, I always bow and prostrate.[1]

> Discerning the validity that was taught
> So eloquently by him who became valid himself,
> Dignāga, Dharmakīrti, and their descendants
> Composed the texts on logic; to them I bow.

> In this unprecedented *Ocean of Literature on Logic*,
> I shall bring into one all of the rivers that convey
> The valid meaning taught by the incomparable teacher
> Renowned in the three worlds as the valid authority.

> Many in the Noble Land and amidst the snow mountains
> Have written explanations of each text on reasoning.
> Within this single volume, I'll explain the words and meaning
> Of all of them—*Compendium*, seven treatises, and
>   commentaries—

Without the fault of saying either too much or too little,
Not skewing the meaning of the texts, and without any error.
I'll teach them as they are by the power of the Victors
And their children; it is otherwise not the sphere of intellect.

From the power of the blessings of the Manjushri, the wisdom *kāya* who knows everything known to all the victors directly and without obscuration and yet appears in the form of a child of the buddhas, I shall explain *The Compendium of Validity*, a treatise the Buddha prophesied and allowed, in combination with Master Dignāga's own commentary, the seven treatises, and all the other literature on logic.

This has two topics: first, the necessity for composing the texts on logic and their commentaries, and second, the actual explanation of the texts and commentaries that have that purpose.

First, the necessity for composing the texts on logic and their commentaries

His great compassion lacks any peer in all world realms and is unrivaled anywhere. As he has abandoned all the obscurations of unknowing, his eyes of wisdom penetrate every mandala of knowable phenomena—none left out—so he knows and sees the capabilities, faculties, and predilections of all sentient beings. He is the lord and valid authority for all wanderers including the gods, *ṛiṣhis*, and those known as sages and teachers to non-Buddhists. This Bhagavan Buddha himself displayed infinite infinitudes of bodies appropriate to infinite infinitudes of sentient beings, turning infinite infinitudes of wheels of Dharma that are undeceiving about the temporary and ultimate benefit in the languages of all the infinite infinitudes of wanderers so that they clearly and unerringly know the undeceiving true meaning they had not known before.

These teachings were given—depending upon each individual student—as the guiding meaning, definitive meaning, literal words, implicit words, with an ulterior intention, or as cryptic explanations. The great master Dignāga saw that their meaning was difficult to realize.

So that students could easily realize it and dispel any uncomprehension, misconceptions, doubts, or so forth by way of logical reasoning, it is renowned that he realized all the scriptures of the sugata through the three kinds of validity and then composed one hundred and eight treatises on validity including *The Gateway to Logic* and others. When he saw that the meaning was fragmented among the individual words and texts that communicate it, he thought to make them into a single work and wrote this *Compendium of Validity*.

As the Bhagavan said in a sutra:

> Just as the wise examine gold
> By heating, splitting, and rubbing it,
> Examine my words fully, bhikshus—
> Do not accept them from respect.[2]

For example, when discriminating people seek gold, they inspect gold that is easy to examine by burning it, gold that is somewhat difficult to examine by splitting it, and gold that is extremely difficult to examine by rubbing it. Similarly, Master Dignāga clarified the sutras that teach the evident and are easy to comprehend by analyzing and resolving them through perception. He clarified the sutras whose meaning is somewhat hidden and difficult to realize by analyzing and resolving them through inference proceeding from the power of facts. He clarified the sutras whose meaning is completely hidden and extremely difficult to realize by analyzing and resolving them through the inference of authority. He then composed the treatise *The Compendium of Validity*, which explains the intent of all the Buddha's scriptures through logical reasoning. However, its words signifying that are few and weighty while the meaning signified is deep and vast, so it was not within the sphere of most people considered wise and learned.

With the compassionate wish to help such people, the glorious Dharmakīrti, who was renowned as an emanation of the bodhisattva Samantabhadra, fully and unerringly comprehended the intention of composing the *Compendium* and then wrote seven treatises which explain its intent. Of these, three are like the body: the long treatise *The Commentary on Validity*, the middle-length *Ascertainment of Validity*, and the short *Drop of Reasoning*. The other four are like elaborating branches: *Establishing Other Continua*, which elaborates on the chapter on perception; *The Drop of Proofs* and *Examination of Relations*, which elaborate on the chapter on inference for oneself; and *The Logic of Debate* which elaborates on the chapter on inference for others.

Second, the actual explanation of the texts and commentaries that have that purpose

I will now explain *The Compendium of Validity* according to the valid explanations in the seven treatises and other authoritative Indian commentaries. To begin, the explanation of the long treatise, *The Commentary on Validity*, has three sections:

I. The branches composed by the translators to begin the translation, II. The nature of the treatise that was translated, and III. Activities to complete the translation.[3]

I. The branches composed by the translators to begin the translation. This has two topics: A. The title of the treatise and B. The translators' prostration.

A. The title of the treatise. This has two points: 1. The translation of the title and 2. Explaining the meaning of the title.

1. The translation of the title

In the Indian language: *Pramhnavārttikakārikā*

In Tibetan: *tshad ma rnam 'grel gyi tshig le'ur byas pa*

In English: *The Commentary in Verse on Validity*

"India" is the name of the Noble Land; it is the original name. Among the many languages found there, in Sanskrit the name of this treatise is *Pramāṇavārttika Kārikā*. The reason for mentioning the Indian language is to show that the source of this dharma is venerable and to recollect the kindness of the translators.

When translated into Tibetan, *pra-* can have many meanings, including light, first, best, individual, and so forth. Here it is used in the meaning of *first*. *Māna* means to measure. *Vārttika* means commentary. *Kārikā* means verses. Here, this is a meaning translation. "First measure" is translated as *validity*, so it is called *The Commentary in Verse on Validity*.

2. Explaining the meaning of the title

Adding the prefix *pra-* to the root *māna* gives "first measure," meaning that among cognitions, the first measure is valid, it is said. The characterized, ultimate validity, is never deceptive, and that which characterizes, conventional validity—perception and inference—is temporarily not deceptive with regard to the engaged object, so they are valid.

With *The Compendium Sutra of Validity*,[4] which teaches those two types of validity, the name of the topic is given to the work, hence *validity*. *Sutra* means that it condenses a profound and vast meaning with few words. Since it is compiled from the scriptures of the Bhagavan as well as the author's own and others' texts on logic, it is called a *compendium*. Thus the title is given in terms of the manner in which it is taught.

Since the *Commentary* explains that work and comments on it at length, it is called *The Commentary on Validity*; it is titled in terms of its function. It is set in verses called *vaktram pathya*, a variant of the eight-syllable *anuśaṃsa* meter, so it is the *Verses*. One should also know the reason and necessity for giving a title.

B. The translators' prostration

I prostrate to the noble youthful Manjushri.

Since he is elevated far above the levels of ordinary individuals, listeners, self-buddhas, and the seven impure levels, he is noble. His body, speech, and mind have long been free of the harshness of nonvirtue and have the softness (*mañju*) that always protects each and every sentient being with great loving-kindness. He also has the glory (*śrī*) of indivisible emptiness and great compassion and a youthful manner as if the age of sixteen. The translator bows, saying, "I prostrate to him with my three gates in order to complete the translation, pacify obstructions, and be in harmony with the conduct of exalted individuals."

II. The nature of the treatise that was translated. This has three topics: A. Virtue in the beginning: the homage and pledge to compose, B. Virtue in the middle: the meaning of the text, and C. Virtue in the end: completing the composition.[5]

A. Virtue in the beginning: the homage and pledge to compose. This has two points: 1. The homage, and 2. The pledge to compose.

1. The homage

> 1.   He's cleared away the net of thought
> And has the profound and vast bodies.
> I bow to him who shines the light
> Of the All-Good over all.

This has three points: a. A summary, b. The purpose, and c. The meaning of the text.

a. A summary

This stanza states all the qualities of greatness of the perfect Buddha's bodies: the cause, the perfect intent and training, and the result, the perfect benefit for self and the perfect benefit for others.

b. The purpose

This stanza of homage describing the qualities of the Buddha was written as an introduction so that the glorious Dharmakīrti could bring himself into harmony with the conduct of great beings and so that others—students—could hear of the perfect Buddha's qualities of the greatness and develop faith and respect for him.

c. The meaning of the text. Following Śākyabuddhi's commentary, this has three points: i. Explaining it in terms of the four kāyas, ii. Explaining it in terms of the three kāyas, and iii. Explaining it in terms of the *Compendium's* homage, where the meaning lies.

i. Explaining it in terms of the four kāyas

As it says in *Distinguishing the Two Truths*:

> The mind and mental factors of three realms
> Are concepts with the aspect of projection.
> That these are only the cause of bondage. . .[6]

The host of thoughts of dualistic perception of apprehended and apprehender—the mind and mental factors on any level of the three realms of samsara—are the net that binds any being who has them to samsara. When such adventitious stains as those and their imprints have been made into phenomena that will no longer arise, the dharma nature from which they have been cleared away is the essence kāya. Inseparable from that dharma nature, which is free of adventitious stains, is the wisdom of the buddha, but that is not within the sphere of others, so it is the profound dharmakāya. The appearances of that same wisdom to noble bodhisattvas and to various pure and impure students are respectively the vast body, the sambhogakāya, and the vast deeds, the nirmāṇakāya. He who possesses these four kāyas is the all-good. The light of his deeds—the activity that brings students to a support for the path,[7] onto the actual path, and to the results of the path—radiates over all, appropriate to the students' capabilities.

In order to quell obstacles to the composition of the *Commentary* and complete the two accumulations—the favorable conditions—as well as bring myself into accord with the conduct of the great beings, I, glorious Dharmakīrti, prostrate to him.

ii. Explaining it in terms of the three kāyas

With the antidotes, he has cleared away and conquered forever the net of thought that binds one to samsara along with their imprints. This indivisible expanse and awareness is the essence kāya. Its appearance to bodhisattvas who dwell on the levels in particular—not to listeners and self-buddhas—is the profound sambhogakāya, and what vastly teaches various pure and impure students is the nirmāṇakāya. He who has those three kāyas is the all-good. I, Dharmakīrti, bow to him and to the lights of his activity that shine over all.

iii. Explaining it in terms of the *Compendium's* homage, where the meaning lies

I prostrate. To whom? To the Bhagavan, who has become valid. How did he become valid? you ask. Through the perfect cause and result. The cause is the perfect intent and training. The result is the perfect benefit for self and others.

The perfect intent is the great compassion that wishes to protect beings from the result, suffering. Motivated by this, he taught wandering beings who are bound to samsara by the net of thoughts that cling to the two selves, which are in turn contained within the cause—the origin that is karma and the afflictions—their antidote, the path of realizing selflessness, just as he himself had realized it directly and thus cleared away those bonds. This is the perfect training. The intent and training respectively are the causes of the protector, the benefit for others, and the sugata, the benefit for oneself. The phrase *clears away* teaches the training explicitly, whereas the intent is taught implicitly. The word *and* is a conjunction between the earlier and later.

The results of those two causes are the two perfect benefits. The benefit for oneself includes abandonment and realization. The former is the dharma nature, which has twofold purity.[8] Since that is the sphere of the buddhas' wisdom only, it is profound. The meaning of *su-* or "bliss" is that he has the perfect abandonment, the essence kāya. The meaning of *gata* or "gone" is the perfect realization, the dharmakāya, which he has because he has directly realized the vast object, the nature of phenomena as well as all knowable phenomena, through the vast conscious subject, the two wisdoms that know the nature and variety of all phenomena. Thus the first couplet teaches the sugata, the perfect benefit for oneself that is these two.

Since he has that kāya that is benefit for himself, at all times he performs for all sentient beings benefit or excellence that is never contaminated with anything that is not excellent, and he perfects all kinds of excellence without interruption, so he is called *good*. The sambhogakāya and nirmāṇakāya designated by this name radiate the light rays that destroy the darkness of the two obscurations by turning in accordance with students' capabilities the wheels of Dharma that teach the path he himself has seen. The latter couplet teaches the perfect benefit for others, the protector. This undeceivingly brings students to newly know what they had previously not known, the four truths and so forth, and accomplish their temporary and ultimate benefit. Therefore he is valid.

The protector that performs the benefit of students comes from the cause of perfect intent. The sugata, who is able to accomplish the benefit, comes from the cause of perfect training. The *Amarakoṣa*[9] explains "All-Good" to be an epithet for the Buddha.

2. The pledge to compose

2.   Attached to the vulgar and lacking strong intelligence,
           most people
        Not only take no interest in the fine explanations,
        The stains of jealousy goad them to ire.
        Therefore I have no thought that this will be of help to
           others,
        But from long training of my mind in the fine explanations,
        To rouse enthusiasm, I feel joy for this.

Most Buddhist and non-Buddhist people who imagine themselves learned are attached to and fixate on vulgar actions and vulgar treatises that teach erroneous views and conduct. Because of this, even were they to hear the fine explanation, the *Compendium*, they would reject it. This is the fault of being like a pot with a leaky bottom. Since they lack the strength of intelligence to distinguish fine explanations from bad, they take no interest in the fine explanations of the *Compendium* and so forth because they consider them to be bad teachings; they will not even listen to it. This is the fault of being like an overturned pot. Not only do they have those faults, since their minds do not remain impartial, the stains of jealousy toward Master Dignāga and other authors of fine teachings goad them to ire. This is the fault of being like a poisoned pot. These three faults make one an unsuitable vessel. As is said in the *Four Hundred Verses*:

> A listener who is straightforward, intelligent,
> And interested is described as a vessel.[10]

In contrast to this, most people lack intelligence, lack interest, and are not straightforward. Seeing that people thus have the three faults, therefore I, Dharmakīrti, have no thought that this *Commentary* will be of great help to others who have the three faults just described. But if I explain the meaning of the points in this *Compendium* that are difficult to comprehend, it is also possible that it will be of great benefit to those people who do not have the three faults. Therefore in order to rouse enthusiasm in them to primarily listen to and contemplate the *Compendium* and to realize it, I feel joy to compose this commentary on the *Compendium*, and thus I shall write it.

What is the cause of being able to write this? you ask. For a long time, I, Dharmakīrti, have trained and familiarized my mind through listening and contemplation of the fine explanations in the *Compendium*. Because of having intelligence—the substantial cause of realizing its meaning without error—and the compassion of wishing to benefit others—the cooperating condition—I will compose this.

This meaning is also clearly stated in the *Ascertainment of Validity*:

> It's he with a glorious stainless mind to whom
>   The Noble One appeared, supporting him.
> And yet these fools with worldly intelligence
>   Don't clearly understand his weighty words.
> Although his service to the world has flourished,
>   They criticize him out of ignorance.
> As they will take a meaningless rebirth,
>   I'll clarify his method with compassion.

Similarly, the *Drop of Reasoning* says:

> Right knowledge precedes the accomplishment of all benefits
> for beings, so I am writing this in order to teach it.

The words of these pledges to compose from the *Commentary, Ascertainment,* and *Drop* implicitly teach the topic, necessity, vital necessity, and connection. *The Compendium of Validity* and its topic—right knowledge and that which is associated with it—are the topic of the *Commentary, Ascertainment,* and *Drop.* The *Commentary* and so forth are that which communicates that topic, and so the link between the texts and their topic is the connection, which is taught through the meaning. Engaging these through listening and contemplation engages *The Compendium of Validity,* whose meaning will be realized without error, and that is the necessity. The vital necessity is to reach the result, becoming a valid being. Without the earlier, the latter will not arise, proving that the methods and what they produce are connected.

B. Virtue in the middle: the meaning of the text. This has two topics: 1. The links between the chapters, and 2. Explaining the text of each chapter.

1. The links between the chapters

Master Devendrabuddhi explains that if one were to match the order of the *Compendium,* it would make sense to put the chapter on establishing validity first. However the chapter on inference for oneself is explained first because the glorious Dharmakīrti's *Autocommentary* says, "Distinguishing the actual from what is not depends upon inference, but there are misconceptions of that. Thus I will present it."[11]

Master Prajñākaragupta and his followers explain that this citation merely presents the reason for writing the *Autocommentary* on the chapter on inference for oneself; it does not teach that the root text of the chapter on inference for oneself is first. Therefore, they refute Devendrabuddhi, saying he confused even the order of chapters and explain that this chapter on establishing validity is the first.

There is no contradiction between the two traditions. An autocommentary was written about the chapter on inference for oneself, so the text of that chapter is placed first out of necessity, but that does not contradict the purpose of writing the *Compendium,* and explaining establishing validity first in accord with the order of the *Compendium* also does not contradict glorious Dharmakīrti's intent.

In actuality, it is thus: By virtue of the chapter on inference for oneself having an autocommentary, it is first in the volume, but the order in which the treatise was written matched the *Compendium,* so saying that the chapter on establishing validity is first is Dharmakīrti's intent. Therefore, to explain it in accord with the topics in the *Compendium*, the first of the four chapters is "Establishing Validity." Next is "Perception," followed by "Inference for Oneself," and lastly "Inference for Others." The examination of analogies and false analogies is explained in depth in the chapter on inference for others, and the examination of exclusions is taught in the chapter on inference for oneself. The examination of false refutations is explained in detail in *The Logic of Debate*, so there is no fault of any chapter being omitted.[12]

2. Explaining the text of each chapter. This has four topics: the explanation of the *Compendium's* introductory sections, the homage and pledge to compose; the explanation of the *Compendium's* chapter on perception; the explanation of the *Compendium's* chapter on inference for oneself; and the explanation of the *Compendium's* chapter on inference for others.

The explanation of the *Compendium's* introductory sections, the homage and pledge to compose. This has two topics: First, the homage and second, the pledge to compose.

First, the homage. This has two topics: I. Presenting the passage from the *Compendium* to be explained, and II. The detailed explanation from the *Commentary* of the *Compendium's* meaning.[13]

I. Presenting the passage from the *Commentary* to be explained

> I bow to him who became valid,
> The one who wishes to help beings,
> The teacher, sugata, and protector.[14]

Because of the perfect causes and results, the Bhagavan became ultimately valid. What are the perfect causes? What are the perfect results? you ask. There are two causes: perfect intent, the great compassion that wishes to benefit beings, and perfect training, teaching the path to others. The perfect results are the sugata, the benefit for self that is perfect abandonment and realization, and protector, the perfect benefit for others that teaches the four noble truths. I prostrate to him, the Buddha who has perfected the two benefits.

From the autocommentary on the *Compendium*:

> At the opening of the chapter, in order to instill respect there is a statement of praise for the Bhagavan who has become valid through the perfect causes and results. The causes are the perfect intent and training. . . and the results of wishing to help others are the perfect benefits for self and others. The perfect benefit for self is the sugata, which has three meanings: impressiveness, like a person's fine form; irreversibility, like having cured a contagious disease; and completeness, like a vase that has been completely filled. These three meanings are for distinguishing the perfect benefit for self as superior to non-Buddhists who are free of attachment, to learners, and to non-learners. . . As he accomplishes the perfect benefit for others, he is the protector. Since he has such qualities, I prostrate to the teacher.[15]

II. The detailed explanation from the *Commentary* of the *Compendium's* meaning. This has three sections: A. Explaining the meaning of the *Compendium's* homage in order, B. Explaining the homage in reverse order, and C. Explaining the reason for praising the Bhagavan as being valid.

A. Explaining the meaning of the *Compendium's* homage in order. This has two sections: 1. Overview, and 2. Detailed explanation.

1. Overview. This has two topics: a. A brief teaching of the result, validity, and b. Explaining how that result arises from a cause.

a. A brief teaching of the result, validity. This has two topics: i. The characteristics of validity, and ii. Establishing that the Bhagavan, who has those characteristics, is valid.

i. The characteristics of validity. This has two topics: (1) General discussion; and (2) The meaning of the text.

(1) General discussion. This has two topics: (a) A general presentation of characteristics, the characterized, and the basis for characterization; and (b) Explaining the characteristics of validity in particular.

(a) A general presentation of characteristics, the characterized, and the basis for characterization

The Vaiśeṣikas say that the substances of jugs, blankets, and so forth cannot separately characterize their own essence, which is other. However, universals, qualities, actions, and so forth characterize the essence of a separate substance by way of separate traits. Therefore the characteristics and the characterized are separate in substance, they say.

That is not the case, because the substances of jugs, blankets, and so forth—which are not separate from their own essence—cannot be distinguished as separate by way of universals, qualities, and so forth. In addition, the features such as universals and qualities that establish the substances as separate would also need to be established. If those were also established by way of other separate features, it would be an infinite regress.

Most Kāpilas and Sāṃkhyas say that fire is characterized by heat and burning that is the same in substance as itself. Therefore, the characteristics and characterized are the same substance. That is not the case, because one would be unable to distinguish them in substantial phenomena, saying "This is the characteristic" and "This is what is characterized."

You might propose that they are not separate in substance, but their isolates are separate.[16] Separate isolates are conceptual designations, so they are not the same in substance, but phenomena that are the same substance do not appear to thoughts, so they cannot even be established as separate isolates. Therefore saying they are the same substance with separate isolates is a conceptual designation; in actuality, it cannot be established.

Therefore characteristics and the characterized are not established as either a single substance or as separate substances. As it is said:

All the conventions of the object
And agent dwell in such a way.[17]

This explains that all that is known and all that makes it known are merely conceptual designations.

Therefore the presentation of characteristics and characterized is thus: That which is the appearance to thought of an aspect of an object such as hot and burning, wet and liquid, and so forth is called its characteristic.[18] One fixates upon just that as the specific characteristic and considers it the essence of the object. Conventional expressions such as "fire," "water," and so forth, which are by nature verbal universals, are called the characterized. This is because when a mere verbal universal such as the expression "fire," "water," or so forth occurs as the object of the intellect, one wonders, "What is its nature?" and looks for the characteristics that characterize it. Therefore, the characteristics and characterized appear separate to those who do not know the connection between the name and the entity, but when one knows the connection between the name and the entity, they appear as if they are not separate in essence. Additionally, for those who do not know the connection between the name and entity, the characteristics characterize the name itself, but that is unnecessary for those who know the connection, and so they do not function to characterize.

Characteristics free of the three faults of non-pervasion, over-pervasion, and impossibility properly establish the connection between the name and the entity and are therefore faultless characteristics. However, characteristics which have any of the three faults are unable to establish the connection between the name and the entity.

Well then, if characteristics have another characteristic, that would also require another characteristic and it would be endless. If they do not, wouldn't it be unnecessary for the characterized to have characteristics? you ask. The characteristics are objects such as hot and burning. When they appear as objects to the intellect, one does not search for what their characteristics are, but it is possible that instead one might search wondering, "What is the name of this?" Therefore characteristics do not require another characteristic.

The characterized is the name, and the characteristics are the entity of that name, so the name and entity are not necessarily always observed at the same time. For that reason, one does not autonomously know without being taught that the characteristics are the entity of the characterized.

If people who do not know the name and entity of fire are physically burnt by hot and burning sandalwood, they search for what its name is. At that point, someone who knows the connection between the name fire and the entity heat and burning uses the hot and burning sandalwood as the basis for characterization. When he characterizes it as fire and explains, "Since it is hot and burning," they can learn connection between the name fire and the entity heat and burning in relation to the heat and burning of sandalwood.

Therefore the connection between characteristic and characterized is projected conceptually and then posited, but it cannot be proven in actuality. Thus it cannot be seen with perception that the characteristics and characterized exist separately. As an analogy, in a house with only a single pillar, that which performs the function of supporting a beam[19] and the pillar are not seen as separate through perception. Therefore, one should know that the characteristics and characterized are separate and that their connection is a phenomenon that appears in thought even though it does not exist.

(b) Explaining the characteristics of validity in particular

Validity is a type of cognition, so first the characteristic of cognition: awareness of an object. This is because the *Commentary* explains, "The quality of consciousness—apprehending / An object. . ."[20]

Well then, all nonconceptual misapprehensions such as the sensory cognition of a white conch appearing yellow would not be cognitions, because there is no awareness of an object, you say.[21] It is not so that all nonconceptual misapprehensions have no object in all cases, because ultimately all cognitions are perception of their own essence. This is because it says in the *Compendium*:

We assert that thought as well is self-aware.[22]

The *Commentary* also says:

Therefore all are perception of that.[23]

Therefore we agree to the consequence that the sensory cognition of a white conch appearing yellow is not a cognition in relation to the yellow it apprehends because in relation to the yellow, it is not aware of any object at all, whether its own or another essence. However, with regard to the aspect of yellow, it is awareness of the object, because it is self-aware direct perception of that.[24]

Some Tibetans propose that clear awareness is the characteristic of cognition, but that has this fault: either all thoughts would not be cognitions of their natural or engaged object, or they would be clear awareness.[25] But, you say, they are clear awareness of their own essence, so there is no fault. Well then, this clear awareness can characterize all thoughts merely as cognitions of their own essence but is unable to characterize them as cognition of other objects. Therefore that characteristic would have the fault of non-pervasion. If you say that in one respect, all thoughts are perception of their own essence, they would also be perception of their object and apprehended object.

To classify cognition, there are two: valid and invalid mind. As for the first, a right cognition that autonomously determines[26] its object is called valid. The characteristic that characterizes it is an awareness that is initially undeceiving toward the object it has determined. The *Commentary* says, "The valid is an undeceiving mind." Similarly, the *Ascertainment* and *Drop of Reasoning* say, "In engaging the entity they have determined, they are undeceiving in performing a function."[27]

The meaning of *undeceiving* is that the individual is able to encounter the entity as the valid cognition itself indicates. This is called by the term *undeceiving*. It means nothing other than that it makes an individual comprehend the object without error by way of producing recognition that realizes the way the object is.

Well then, a cognition that perceives the light of a gem as the gem is confused, but it would be undeceiving toward the gem, because it makes the individual encounter the object that it indicates, the gem. If one replies that it is not proven,[28] then there would be no difference between perceiving the light of a lamp as a gem or the light of a gem as a gem in terms of whether or not one can get the gem, you say.

Those two are similar in not directly getting the gem, but there is a distinction as to whether or not they function as the cause for another condition that could get the gem. Therefore the cognition that perceives a gem's light as a gem does not function to get the object it discriminates—the gem—because a gem is not obtained in the object it discriminates as a gem, and it does not discriminate the gem—the object that is later obtained. Thus it is confused about the object. However, because of it, when someone at the door to the treasury, for example, discriminates the light of a gem and enters to get it, they do find a different object, the jewel in the back of the treasury.

Here there is this doubt: Do the two lines "The valid is an undeceiving mind" and "Or that which clarifies the unknown meaning" each teach a distinct, complete characteristic of valid cognition, or do the two teach one characteristic? To examine this, Master Devendrabuddhi says that initial undeceiving cognition is one characteristic of valid cognition, and awareness that clarifies an unknown object is a second.[29] With regard to this, the *Treasury of Valid Logic* says:

> If two characteristics define it,
> The characterized becomes two as well.[30]

This fault does not apply to Master Devendrabuddhi, because "initial undeceiving cognition" and "awareness that clarifies an unknown meaning" are in meaning not different characteristics. Otherwise Master Dignāga would also be at fault for explaining in *The Gateway to Logic* that the characteristic of a proposition is asserting a thesis, while also explaining in the *Compendium* that the characteristic has five facets in the passage that begins "Only the essence, oneself. . ."[31]

Master Prajñākaragupta says that initial undeceiving awareness is the characteristic of conventional valid cognition, and awareness that clarifies an unknown object is the characteristic of ultimate valid cognition. The cognition of nondual experience that is the object of the nobles' self-aware discriminating wisdom is clearly experienced, and it is both ultimate and valid, so it is ultimate valid cognition. Conventional valid cognition is the valid cognition of dualistic appearance of apprehended and apprehender in the mind streams of ordinary individuals, he opines.[32]

That is incorrect: Because ultimate valid cognition is initial undeceiving awareness, it would become conventional valid cognition, and since conventional valid cognition is also awareness that clarifies an unknown object, it would become ultimate valid cognition.

Some say that the earlier and later lines combined teach the one characteristic of valid cognition. That is also not the case, because before the line "Or that which clarifies the unknown meaning" the faults of non-pervasion, over-pervasion, and impossibility have already been refuted.

The purpose and necessity for the master[33] to give two characteristics for validity is this: the Śaivas assert that Īśvara is permanent, self-arising validity. In order to refute that, he states "clarify the unknown meaning" to teach that our Bhagavan is endowed with the valid cognition that clarifies previously unknown meanings. This is because through the power of his meditation, our teacher came to newly know that which he had not known before when he was an ordinary individual—the nature of the four truths—and is therefore a valid being. Teaching this demonstrates that the Bhagavan is superior to the Īśvara whom the Śaivas propose as permanent, self-arising validity, because they do not assert that Īśvara newly knows the previously unknown suchness. Stating "undeceiving" cannot dispel such a misconception, because they assert that Īśvara is undeceiving as well.

The earlier is in terms of eliminating incompatible types. It logically establishes that valid cognition is undeceiving and, because it is also commonly known, also teaches the characteristic that matches common consensus. The latter is in terms of eliminating misconceptions. It teaches the characteristic that matches the etymology, as *pramāṇa* means "first measure." Thus recognizing either one can characterize validity.

To classify validity in terms of its essence, there are two: validity ascertained from itself and validity ascertained from another. In terms of how it engages the object, there are two: perceptual and inferential validity. These are explained at length in each of the texts, so I think this is enough; I shall not write more here.

. Secondly, the characteristic of invalid cognition is an awareness that is deceiving toward the object it determines. To classify it, the master of logic Chapa[34] and his followers explain that there are five types of invalid cognition: assumptions, appearance without recognition, subsequent cognition, misapprehension, and doubt. With regard to this, the *Treasury of Valid Logic* says:

> Assumption, appearance without recognition,
> Subsequent cognition, misapprehension, and doubt.[35]

This presents it as the opponent's position. Then it says:

> Assumptions never depend on evidence.
> They are merely positions and become doubt.[36]

Additionally:

> If appearance without recognition
> Were not valid, all perception
> Would not be valid, because recognition
> Has been refuted for all perception.[37]

And:

> Perception is nonconceptual and present.
> Subsequent cognition is remembrance of the past.
> Their object, tense, and manner of perception are exclusive.
> How could they possibly have a common basis?[38]

Having refuted that, it presents its own position:

> Uncomprehension, misconception, and doubt
> Are the three opposites of valid cognition.[39]

With regard to this, it is true that assumption and subsequent cognition are not different from uncomprehension and that there is no common basis between perception and subsequent cognition. However, it is not definite that all perceptions engage present objects because that would contradict his own position that in perception that is awareness of entities, the apprehended object is past at the time of the perception itself. Uncomprehending mind is the basis for classification, so it is not logical for it also to be one of the classifications. If you classify uncomprehending mind, there are two, doubt and misapprehension, but doubt and misapprehension would become other than uncomprehension. Therefore all invalid cognitions are definitely one of the two, doubt or misapprehension.

Well then, subsequent cognition would not be invalid cognition because it is neither doubt nor misapprehension, but it is recognition, you say. What is this subsequent cognition? It is fixating on earlier and later objects as the same by reason of similarity or connection. This is hardly doubt; it is misapprehension. All cognitions that are not supported by evidence are only doubt. The great treatise *The Reasoned* says that all thoughts that are not supported by evidence cannot eliminate points of suspicion, so they are only doubt.[40] This is also stated in the *Ornament.*

But the cognition recognizing sound as impermanent that arises following perception or inference that apprehends sound as impermanent is the subsequent cognition, you say. Whatever name you give that recognition, it is solely valid, because it newly recognizes the object it knows based on a reason or evidence.

But isn't it apprehension of an object that was apprehended by its substantial cause, the preceding valid cognition? you say. It is recognition through the power of its substantial cause—the preceding valid cognition—merely that sound is impermanent, but it does not recognize whether or not that is the object of the valid cognition that is its substantial cause.

If that is so, all fallacious reasons would be contradictory or indefinite because all invalid cognitions must be one of the two, doubt and misapprehension, you say. Contradictory and indefinite reasons have the property of the proposition. Unproven reasons lack the property of the proposition. Thus there is the distinction as to whether or not there is the property of the proposition, and you yourself have acknowledged that doubt and misapprehension are uncomprehending mind only. Therefore how is this comparable? If you were to categorically state, "It follows that all fallacious reasons are unproven reasons because all invalid cognitions are lack of comprehension," you would have no response to any of the three circles.[41]

(2) The meaning of the text. This has two topics: (a) Explaining the characteristic of validity in accord with common consensus, and (b) Explaining the characteristic of validity in accord with its etymology.

(a) Explaining the characteristic of validity in accord with common consensus. This has three topics: (i) The actual characteristic, (ii) Refuting that it would have the three faults, and (iii) Therefore, there is a purpose to the treatises on validity.

(i) The actual characteristic

When Dignāga praises the Bhagavan as having "become valid," what is the logic that proves he is valid? you ask. To explain:

> 3a–c   The valid is an undeceiving mind.
> To dwell in the ability to function
> Is undeceiving.

Since he is endowed with the superior undeceiving mind that directly knows the nature and variety of all phenomena, it is proven that in the nature of how things are, he is able to perform the function of liberating all sentient beings from samsara. This is the logic that establishes the Bhagavan as the undeceiving valid source of refuge.

Alternatively, the Bhagavan is valid because without deceiving sentient beings, through the power of cultivating the great compassion that wishes to benefit all beings, he has himself become the sugata, abandoning the two obscurations and realizing the nature. He taught the method to achieve this, the paths to higher states and true excellence,[42] and has the superior mind endowed with the ability to protect beings from the impediments to that. Due to his perfect intent, he performs all temporary and ultimate benefit for wanderers. Because of the cause of the perfect training of the path, he dwells in the ability to achieve that function of benefiting and is proven to be the protector who never deceives.

To correlate that actual validity to be accomplished to the conventional validity that accomplishes it: the unmistaken eye consciousness that perceives form is the basis for characterization which is characterized as valid, since it is a mind that is initially undeceiving toward form. How is it undeceiving? you ask. It realizes just as it abides that form dwells in the ability to function, so it is undeceiving toward that object.

(ii) Refuting that it would have the three faults. This has three points: A. Rebutting the fault of non-pervasion, B. Rebutting the fault of over-pervasion, and C. Rebutting the fault of impossibility.

A. Rebutting the fault of non-pervasion

If you say the pervasion does not include verbal validity[43] because that is not proven undeceiving, to explain:

> 3c–d   Verbal is as well,
>   Because it indicates intention.

> 4a–c   The validity of a verbal expression
>   Is that the object of the speaker's action—
>   The meaning—appears to the intellect,

The verbally produced inference that realizes Devadatta has a mind from the evidence of his speaking, as well, indicates the object of inquiry—that Devadatta, who has an intention toward the engaged object, has a mind. For that reason, it is proven undeceiving with regard to its engaged object: it proves that the signified meaning—the object of the speaker's action of speaking—appears to the intellect. The verbal expressions that signify are asserted to be a proper valid proof of that.

If that is so, then that signifying speech also becomes proof of the signified meaning, you say. To teach that that is not the case:

> 4d   Not consequent to the suchness of the meaning.

Things that are the signified meaning are not the cause of that which signifies them, and expressions that signify are not a result that is consequent to the signified object, either. Instead, they refer merely due to a wish to speak. For that reason, for some bases, speech that signifies is mistaken in establishing its signified object.

B. Rebutting the fault of over-pervasion

If undeceiving cognition were the characteristic of validity, it would include the thought apprehending form that arises following a direct perception of form. That is overly pervasive, so it is a fault, you say. To explain:

> 5ab   It grasps the apprehended, so we don't
> Accept the relative.

We do not accept that the thought apprehending form that is a relative mind arising following the perception of form, the subject, is undeceiving with regard to form, because it merely grasps and fixates on the earlier and later as the same with regard to the object apprehended by the valid cognition that is its substantial cause.

C. Rebutting the fault of impossibility

Well then, the eye faculty and so forth are not established as undeceiving cognition, but they are asserted as valid, so there is the fault that the characteristic is impossible in the basis for characterization, you say. To teach that the eye and other faculties are not valid:

> 5b–d   The mind is valid,
> Since it is the main factor in engaging
> The things to be accepted and rejected,

> 6a–c   Since due to separate aspects of the objects,
> The mental realizations are thus separate,
> Because if there is that, there must be this.

Initial undeceiving mind is valid, and the eye and other faculties are not valid. The distinction between them is this: it (the initial undeceiving mind) is the primary factor or cause in engaging or turning away from the objects that are things that beings accept and reject, whereas the eyes and so forth are not. In initial undeceiving cognitions, minds with the aspects of blue, yellow, and so forth objects are separate, so the blue and yellow realized by minds that apprehend blue and yellow are also separate. If there are those separate blue and yellow, there must also be these separate aspects of blue and yellow.

(iii) Therefore, there is a purpose to the treatises on validity. This has two points: A. General discussion, and B. The meaning of the text.

A. General discussion

If initial undeceiving cognition is the characteristic of valid cognition, is valid cognition ascertained as undeceiving from itself or from another? In the first case, no one at all would be ignorant of the characteristics of valid and invalid cognition, so treatises that teach the characteristics of validity would be pointless. In the second case, a valid cognition that ascertains itself as valid would need another to ascertain it. That latter one would also need yet another to ascertain it, so it would be endless. For that reason, in the end nothing would be ascertained as undeceiving, you say.

Cognitions are not always categorically ascertained on their own or categorically ascertained by another. Some cognitions are ascertained on their own and some are ascertained by another. Self-aware perception is always ascertained from itself, because cognitions are not deluded with regard to experiencing their own essence, and the experienced part is the object of self-awareness.

Why are they not deluded? you ask. Delusion toward some objects by way of erroneous misconception of the object comes from not experiencing in vivid clarity that object's own particular essence. For example, the eye consciousness might not experience the particular essence of fish scales in vivid clarity, and so the misconception of the fish scales as silver occurs. There is no cognition that does not experience its own essence in vivid clarity, because if there were, it would follow that it is not cognition. Thus there is not any person at all who misconceives of the essence of cognition as not being experience or has doubts about it. For this reason, Dharmakīrti says, "Its own essence is known from itself."[44]

"If that is so, it is illogical that the Kāpilas[45] could imagine that pleasure and pain are material," you say. Out of strong fixation for their own philosophy, they do not designate experience as mind and instead imagine it to be material. But without experience, there would be no misconception, because they experience in vivid clarity being sated by pleasure and tormented by pain. Therefore it is only necessary to prove the designation of pleasure and so forth as cognition to the Kāpilas; there is no need to prove the entity.

Inference is also solely ascertained from itself, because its very nature is ascertainment.

Sensory perception is twofold: appearances of function and perception that instigates engagement. The former is like, for instance, the perception of seeing the color of fire or water that clearly knows the ability of the engaged object to produce a particular result, such as burning, cooking, washing, drinking, or so forth. This is solely ascertained from itself, because it clearly sees the power of its engaged object to produce its particular result. As is said in *The Reasoned*:

> In ascertaining ability, inference and perception of appearances of function are solely from themselves.[46]

Perception that instigates engagement is twofold: habituated and confusable. In the former, there are no impediments to recognizing the engaged object, such as internal or external causes for confusion, unsuitable lighting, and so forth. The favorable condition—the object—is present, and one has seen the object more than once and has been repeatedly habituated to the term for it, as in the perception that clearly sees one's own awareness. This is ascertained from itself, because, as just said, the impediments are absent and the favorable conditions are complete. As said in *The Reasoned*:

> Some perceptions that instigate engagement are only from themselves: those which after eliminating all confusion and doubt comprehend the features of the nature.[47]

The confusable is perception that, because of some external or internal sources of confusion, produces doubt that prevents the recognition of its particular engaged object. All such cognitions recognize their engaged object later through perception of the appearance of function or inference, based on reasons that are unmistaken with regard to the engaged object, so they are only ascertained from other.

What are such perceptions? you ask. They are perceptions such as the perception apprehending the color of fire that produces doubt that wonders whether that is fire or a pile of *kiṃśuka* flowers.[48] Later there is perception that sees that blazing red one had seen perform the function of burning, cooking, or so forth, or from seeing some reason that is unmistaken toward fire such as smoke, one recognizes it as fire validly without deception.

Well then, is the engaged object attained through the first perception, which produces doubt, or by the second, which produces recognition? In the first case, the later perception would not be valid, and in the second case, the first would not be valid, you say.

Independent of the later, the first alone cannot attain the engaged object, as it merely produces doubt that is uncertainty between the two alternatives as to whether the object is or is not fire. One cannot attain the fire through such doubt, because a person cannot achieve any object that rests on the two alternatives of being or not being fire. Independent of the earlier, the later alone also cannot attain fire. The earlier produces doubt, and then a person who wants fire will engage that object. Once they have engaged it, by force of the proximity of fire, a perception that perceives the nature of the fire with vivid clarity will arise. Recognition occurs by force of that, and the fire is attained by force of the recognition. In this way, the earlier produces the recognition indirectly, and the latter produces recognition directly. Thus the two produce the recognition together, completing the action of valid cognition. For this reason, both are solely valid.

Until recognition arises, the earlier is not valid because the action of validity has not been completed. Later, when recognition has arise, it has ceased and its essence is no longer present, so in ultimate truth it is not logical for it to be valid. However, when recognition has later arisen, it is merely termed "valid." It is in these terms that "Validity is from conventions"[49] is said.

Beginner's perception is such as the perception of seeing a gaur[50] for the very first time. Perception apprehending a sound while one's mind is especially fixated on a beautiful form is inattentive perception.

The *Treasury of Valid Logic* says of this:

> The two awarenesses of object, self-awareness,
> And inference are ascertained from themselves.
> Beginner's, inattentive, and
> Confusable are ascertained from another.[51]

However, beginner's perception is not always ascertained from another. For example, if the perception of a gaur for the very first time produces the doubt, "Is this an ox or gaur?" it would be ascertained from another. But if because of proximity to a gaur one sees with vivid clarity the particular nature of the gaur and recognizes it as one saw it, the perception is solely ascertained from itself even without labeling it with the name "gaur."

Inattentive perception does not become confusable perception ascertained by another that is not realized, because that is not ascertained through its own power but by way of producing an exaggeration or doubt, and exaggeration and doubt do not transcend the external and internal causes of confusion explained above.

B. The meaning of the text

6d   Its own essence is known from itself.

7ab   Validity is from conventions, and
                 Treatises are to eliminate delusion.

There are some valid cognitions whose own essence is known as undeceiving from themselves, but there are also some valid cognitions that must recognize their essence as undeceiving from reasons that establish conventions. Thus treatises that teach the characteristics of validity are written to eliminate the delusion of those who do not know the terms for validity ascertained from self such as self-aware perception and inference. Thus the treatises that teach the characteristics of validity are not pointless.

(b) Explaining the characteristic of validity in accord with its etymology

Is initial undeceiving awareness the only characteristic, or is there another? you ask. To explain:

7c   Or that which clarifies the unknown meaning.

Not only as above, the Bhagavan is endowed with the valid cognition that newly clarifies and makes directly known that which was previously unknown when he was an ordinary individual—the nature of the meaning of the four truths. Thus he is proven valid.

This is what is illustrated. It can be correlated to what illustrates it, analogous validity. For example, an unmistaken eye consciousness that apprehends form clarifies the previously unknown meaning, the entity of form. Such is also valid cognition. The word *or* means "not only initial undeceiving awareness." Both are characteristics whose meaning is not different.

To analyze this, "unknown," "meaning," and "clarifies" respectively eliminate relative cognition, nonconceptual mistaken cognition, and physical faculties from being valid.

Others say:

7d   "Following realization of its essence,

8a   Consciousness of the universal is gained."

If that which clarifies the unknown meaning is the characteristic of validity, then following realization of its (form's) essence, a consciousness that apprehends the universal of form would logically be gained as a valid cognition, because it newly knows a previously unknown universal, you say. To explain:

8b–d   Cognition that knows the unknown specific
          Characteristics is intended, since
          One analyzes specific characteristics.

The consciousness which apprehends the universal of form does not become valid, because the intent is that the cognition that knows the previously unknown specific characteristics only is valid, so the consciousness which apprehends the universal is not accepted as valid. This is since all people who want results analyze only the specific characteristics of the engaged object and then engage it.

ii. Establishing that the Bhagavan, who has those characteristics, is valid

9a   The Bhagavan endowed with those is valid.[52]

Because the Bhagavan is endowed with those two characteristics of validity (initial undeceiving awareness and that which clarifies unknown meaning), the Bhagavan is proven to be valid.

To correlate this to the actual validity to be accomplished: From the cause of the perfect intent, the wish to benefit all beings without deception, the Bhagavan taught the temporary paths to higher states and the consummate paths to true excellence, thus acting as their protector from the lower realms, existence, and the lesser.[53] Such paths were previously unknown, but through the teacher—the perfect training—he makes clearly known to his disciples the sugata that he knew first. Thus since he possesses both of the characteristics of validity, the Bhagavan is established as validity itself.

From the *Ornament*:

> These two characteristics appear undiminished in the Bhaga-van because he makes beings see the path to the higher realms and to enlightenment and liberation as he taught it, and because he teaches the suchness not seen by Viṣṇu, Īśvara, and so forth.[54]

b. Explaining how that result arises from a cause. This has two topics: i. Actual, and ii. Refuting the proposition that a permanent Īśvara could be valid.[55]

i. Actual

9b–d   It says "became" in order to refute
         That he did not arise. Thus based on the means
         To achieve that, it's logical he is valid.

In order to refute the misapprehension that he did not arise out of the perfect causes and instead might be permanent, self-arisen validity, it says "became" in the homage to the *Compendium*. Thus the result, validity, is based on the means to achieve that, which are the causes, superior intent and training, and it is logical that he is valid.

ii. Refuting the proposition that a permanent Īśvara could be valid. This has two topics: (1) General discussion, and (2) The meaning of the text.

(1) General discussion. This should be known as it appears in Rinpoche Karma Pakshi's *Infinite Oceans of Validity*. It has two topics: (a) Presenting the opponent's views, and (b) Refuting them.

(a) Presenting the opponent's views. This has two three points: (i) The characteristics of Īśvara; (ii) The positions of the Vaiśeṣikas, who assert his scriptures; and (iii) Presenting the positions of the Naiyāyikas.

(i) The characteristics of Īśvara

Īśvara has eight qualities: (1) he is subtle, (2) he is light, (3) he is worshipped, (4) he is the owner, (5) he controls, (6) he goes everywhere, (7) he possesses all desires, and (8) he dwells joyfully and happily. Respectively, these mean (1) he creates and destroys the worlds of sentient beings; (2) he creates and destroys the worlds of the environment; (3) he is worshipped by all spirits; (4) he creates and destroys both environments and their inhabitants; (5) he has the power to benefit or harm all spirits; (6) he accomplishes everything mentally; (7) he makes the qualities into everything desired;[56] and (8) those who wish for the high realms and liberation listen to him. To describe those qualities in brief:

> He who is subtle and single arises, dwells, and exists.
> He creates and destroys all of this.
> A powerful lord who confers boons, the god who is worshipped,
> He creates the qualities and achieves great peace.

> There is no knowledge of this creator
> And the self has no power over its pleasures and pains.
> If summoned by Īśvara, one is born
> In the abyss or in the higher realms.[57]

Also:

One achieves liberation by meditating on Īśvara.
Subtle and very fine, he created all the Vedas.
Meditating on dhyana, he is the object of the yogis' dhyana,
Those who wish for peaceful bliss always meditate on Īśvara.[58]

(ii) The positions of the Vaiśeṣikas, who assert his scriptures

The Vaiśeṣikas assert six categories of the nature of the knowable: substance, quality, action, universals, particularity, and inherence.

There are nine substances: earth, water, fire, air, ether, time, direction, self, and mind. They assert that the first four, which are impermanent and have action, are not all-pervasive.[59] The three of ether and so forth are all-pervasive. Most Vaiśeṣikas assert that they have many actions, but there are a few who assert that time is a cause and therefore has action. They say:

Time gathers many beings.
Time makes the elements ripen.
Time makes the sleeping wake,
Time is difficult to transcend.[60]

It is also explained:

An ocean moat and triple defenses
With soldiers, rākṣasas, jewels made by yakṣas,
And their treatise *Immeasurable Śukra* decline.
The rākṣasa child also declines by force of time.[61]

The self is permanent and goes everywhere. It is what commits virtuous and unvirtuous actions. It has no mind itself, but is asserted to be connected to the mind. The mind has activity, so it is not all-pervasive, they assert.

The qualities of those substances are the twenty-five of color and so forth. The five of color, sound, scent, taste, and touch are qualities of the four elements and space. Thirteen—the five awarenesses of visual awareness and so forth, pleasure, pain, desire, aversion, effort, merit, nonmerit, and formation—are qualities of the self. The seven of number, size, individuality, conjunction, disjunction, remoteness, and non-remoteness are qualities of time. The total is twenty-five.[62] Some of these are permanent, and some are impermanent.

There are five actions: lifting, placing, contracting, extending, and going. There are two universals: pervasive and temporary universals. Particularities are temporary, such as the opposite of ox or horse. Inherence is the meeting of cause and result, they say.

Regarding the formation of the world, they assert that when the universe was empty, the partless atoms of the four elements existed distinct from one another, and that Īśvara emanated the world out of these. Later, driven by the force of the dharma and non-dharma performed by beings, the atoms of the four elements adhered. Out of that there formed the light and moving mandala of air. On top of that formed the continuously swirling water. On top of that, the great mandala of earth. On top of that, there formed the great mass of fire that blazed, fully blazed, completely blazed, and blazed in a single flame. Within that, out of Maheśvara's mere wish, there was the great, clear and radiant egg of Brahma. It ripened and shook, and from within it arose Brahma with four faces and matted locks on a lotus. As he is the progenitor of the world, he creates everything there is to arise, and the world forms and abides. They assert that brahmin caste was born out of Brahma's mouth, the kṣatriya from his shoulders, the vaiśya from his thighs, and the śudra castes from his feet. They say that they do not know for the time being whence the outcastes were born.

They assert that there are five types of relations: the relation of dispersion, such as fire and smoke; the relation of conjunction, such as fire and form; the relation of inherence, such as fire and the possession of form; the relation whose characteristic is inherence in conjunction, such as the form of fire and form that has smoke; and the relation whose characteristic is conjunction in inherence, such as fire and the conjunction of the form that has smoke.

They say there are three types of validity: the validity of intuition,[63] perception, and inference.

(iii) Presenting the positions of the Naiyāyikas

Although the Naiyāyikas mostly agree with the Vaiśeṣikas, they assert that there are four types of validity: perception, inference, close evaluation, and verbal. They assert that perception is a thought that recognizes a nearby object. The superior cognition that observes qualities is valid cognition; the superior cognition that focuses on substance is the result of valid cognition, they say.

As they assert that atoms, time, and so forth are permanent, they do not accept that composites are momentary, and since they say that the self and Īśvara are creators, they also do not accept that all phenomena are selfless.

(b) Refuting them. This has two points: (i) Refuting the Vaiśeṣikas, and (ii) Refuting the Naiyāyikas.

(i) Refuting the Vaiśeṣikas

When one analyzes atoms, dividing them into directional parts destroys them, so it is impossible for them to become a coarse object. If a coarse object were a substance that is a whole without parts, hidden parts and colored parts would be the substance that is a whole that is not hidden or colored, so they would not be hidden or colored.

If direction and time were different substances than the four elements, the four elements of earth and so forth would not have any direction such as east or time such as the past. If they were not different substances, earth and so forth would have direction and time as do coarse impermanent objects, so they would also be impermanent. Then how could they be permanent? Also a permanent Īśvara could not be a cause that produces results—sentient beings—sequentially, and if he produced beings sequentially, he could not be a permanent entity.

If valid cognition meets its object and then apprehends it, does it apprehend it through direct or indirect contact? In the first instance, valid cognition apprehending form and sound would be impossible; in the second, the eye consciousness would also perceive scent and so forth.

Additionally, if male brahmins are born from Brahma's mouth, female brahmins would also be born from there. In that case, because they are both born from the same place, brahmins would take their sisters as brides. This would contradict the Vedas, which state that the act of copulating with mothers and sisters degrades the caste, so they will be born in hell.

(ii) Refuting the Naiyāyikas

This should be known from the chapter on perception.

(2) The meaning of the text. This has four topics: (a) A general refutation of permanent validity, (b) Refuting that Īśvara created the world after previously thinking of it, (c) Refuting that Īśvara is the cause of the world and its inhabitants with an absurd consequence, and (d) Refuting that if the Bhagavan is valid, he should know all hidden objects.

(a) A general refutation of permanent validity

The Śaivas say that Īśvara is permanent, self-arisen validity, so he is the supreme validity. To explain that this is not logical:

10a–d　　There is no permanent validity.
　　　　Validity is knowing existing things.
　　　　Knowables are impermanent and thus
　　　　That is unstable.

There is no permanent validity itself, because validity is asserted to be knowing knowable objects that exist as things. Those objects—knowable phenomena—are impermanent, and thus that subject—valid cognition—is also unstable.

In that case, validity is impermanent, but Īśvara who possesses validity is permanent, you say. To teach that this is not logically tenable:

10d　　　　　　　　　　It is illogical

11a–c　　That what arises sequentially be born
　　　　Out of the permanent. Dependence is
　　　　Untenable. He has no effect at all.

Because it is illogical that phenomena that arise sequentially from a cause be born out of a permanent Īśvara, because it is untenable that a result depend upon a permanent condition, and because he (Īśvara) has no effect on the result at all, a permanent Īśvara is not valid.

Well then, Īśvara is impermanent, but he is self-arisen validity, you say. To explain:

11d   Even impermanent, there's no validity.

Even if Īśvara were impermanent, he would not be self-arisen validity, because there is no valid cognition that proves him to be self-arisen validity.

(b) Refuting that Īśvara created the world after previously thinking of it. This has three topics: (i) Overview, (ii) Detailed explanation, and (iii) Summary.

(i) Overview

The Śaivas say:

12ab   · "At rest until engaged, distinctive shape,
           Performs a function, and so forth."

The entire universe with its environment and inhabitants was created after a being had previously thought of doing so, because it is at rest until engaged, like an ax; because it has a distinctive shape, like a palace; because it performs a function, like a battle ax; and so forth—they say they have other reasons as well.

To teach the response to that:

12b–d   These prove
           Our own position, the analogy
           Is not established, or else they breed doubt.

We also assert that mere thought precedes the environment and beings, so these prove our own Buddhist position, because we assert that all worlds arise out of volitional karma.[64] Alternatively, if this is to prove a permanent Īśvara created it, the analogy is not established, because a permanent Īśvara himself is not proven. Or else the reasons are present in the dissimilar class, so they breed doubt about the reverse pervasion: since Īśvara himself is at rest until engaged, has a shape, and performs functions, he would also have been created by Īśvara.

(ii) Detailed explanation. This has five points: A. Refuting by examining shape and so forth, B. Refuting through an absurd consequence; C. Rebutting that it is a false refutation of a similar effect; D. Refuting it because similar words are not suitable as evidence; and E. Teaching how this logic also refutes other assertions.

A. Refuting by examining shape and so forth

Do you present distinctive shape as the evidence or just shape? To explain that the first would be logical:

13.   The way a shape or so forth is conforms
           To whether or not there's someone in control,
           And any inference that one might draw
           From that is proven to be logical.

The way a shape or so forth is conforms to whether or not there is someone, a person, in control through effort, and any inference that one might draw from that—proving that a palace was made by a person—is proven to be logical evidence that fulfills the three modes.
   Others say:

14ab   "It's proven for a different thing because
           The word's the same; there is no difference."

In the second case, it is proven that Mount Meru as well is made by a being as it is established that things that are different from Mount Meru and so forth are made be a being. This is because it is the same as a palace in being described by the word *shape*, so they are not separate as mere shape, they say. To explain:

14cd   The inference is not logical; it's like
         Inferring a fire from a light-colored substance.

Not being different in merely having a shape is not logically correct evidence for inferring that Mount Meru was made by a being, because the pervasion is indeterminate. For example, it is like being unable to prove the existence of a fire from a light-colored substance.

B. Refuting through an absurd consequence

15.   Otherwise, since the vases and so forth
        A potter makes are alterations to
        The shape of clay, it also would be proven
        That termite mounds were made by him as well.

Otherwise if the pervasion were not indeterminate, since the vases and so forth that a potter makes and termite mounds are both similar in being alterations to the shape of clay, it also would be proven that termite mounds were made by him (that potter) as well.

C. Rebutting that it is a false refutation of a similar effect

In that case, if mere shape is given as evidence, criticizing it by looking at a distinctive shape is a false refutation of a similar effect, you say. To explain:

16.   We assert a similar effect is claiming
        A fault of being separate, since in proving
        The effect through the general (as it entails
        The thesis), the related is separate.

The evidence *being produced* is validly recognized as the propositional property and as evidence with the entailing and reverse pervasions of the predicate of the thesis that sound is impermanent. For this reason, the effect entailed by both sound and a jug—merely being produced in general—is also correct evidence that proves sound to be impermanent. However, because the sound and jug to which it is related are separate, a sound's being produced is not entailed by a jug, and a jug's being produced is not entailed by a sound. Therefore we assert that analyzing the particulars as separate and claiming there is a fault—saying that being produced is not evidence that proves sound to be impermanent—is a false refutation of a similar effect. This is because it is a rebuttal that criticizes the presentation of merely being produced (which is able to prove sound impermanent) as evidence after examining a particular being produced.[65]

In this context, the mere shape that is presented as proof is unable to prove the thesis. Therefore refuting it by saying there is a fault after analyzing the particular merely through having shape is not a false refutation of similar effect.

D. Refuting it because similar words are not suitable as evidence

Others may ask, what is the reason why mere shape is not suitable as proof? To explain:

17.   Seeing that a verbal universal
        Is established in an instance of a type
        Is not a logical proof. It's as if speech
        And so forth would be horned because they're "cow."

Seeing that the mere verbal universal "shape" refers equally to Mount Meru and to establishing that an instance of the type having shape—the shape of a palace—is proven to have been created after its creator previously thought of it is not a logical proof that Mount Meru was created after its creator thought of it, because the pervasion is indeterminate. It is just as if one were to say that speech, direction, and so forth would be horned because the word *cow* can refer to them; the pervasion would be mistaken.

Therefore, to teach that the word *cow* can refer to any meaning:

18.   Since words depend on the intended meaning,
        There's nothing to which they may not refer.
        If their mere presence could establish the object,
        Everyone would accomplish everything.

Since all words are used merely in dependence on the meaning a being intends, there is nothing to which words such as "cow" may not appropriately refer. If it were otherwise and the mere presence of the word that signifies it could establish the signified object, everyone (all beings) would accomplish everything (all their desired aims) without effort.

E. Teaching how this logic also refutes other assertions

> 19. This also analyzes the Kāpilas
> And so forth: "Since impermanent and so forth,
> It has no mind, et cetera. If its bark
> Is peeled it dies, and thus it has a mind."

This logic that demonstrates that proving a word does not prove the meaning can also be used to analyze and refute the arguments of the Kāpilas, Nigranthas, and so forth that since awareness and pleasure are impermanent, have arising and perishing, and so forth, they have no mind, are not illness, et cetera; or that since if its (a trees') bark is peeled, it dies, and thus it has a mind.

It follows that arising and perishing, the subject, is not correct evidence that proves that awareness and pleasure have no cognition, because your meaning of the words is not established with regard to the subject in the respondent and presenter's common perception.[66] Similarly, with dying when the bark is peeled, the word *dying* is established, but the meaning is not established as a common perception.

(iii) Summary

> 20. If the thing's essence has not been established,
> When the logic is proven, though that is not proven,
> It does not interfere with particulars,
> Like sound's that is supported upon space.

If the essence of the thing taken as evidence is not established in relation to the subject in the common perception of the two debaters, merely proving the word does not become correct evidence. When the meaning of the evidence's logic is proven in the common perception of the two debaters, though that (the mere word) is not proven, it does not interfere with the subject itself proving the particulars. For example, in relation to sound, the being produced that is supported upon the quality of space permanence is not proven, but being produced would be correct evidence that proves sound to be impermanent.

To give an example of this:

> 21.   Although not proven verbally, if the thing
>   Is proven, it's established, for example,
>   As Buddhists explain to the Aulūkyas
>   That the material and such are proof.

Although the evidence may not be proven verbally in both debaters' common perception, if the evidence's entity that is a thing is proven in their common perception, the proposition property of that evidence is established. For example, because the Aulūkyas[67] assert that atoms are permanent, Buddhists explain to the Aulūkyas that atoms, the subject, are impermanent, because they are material, because they are obstructive, and because of other such correct proofs.

The Buddhist assertion that the meaning of *material* is tactile objects such as atoms of the four elements and so forth is not established as the name *material* to the Aulūkyas. The Aulūkyas' assertion that the meaning of *material* is the measure of substance that is not non-pervasive is not established as the name *material* to Buddhists. However, the meaning, tactile objects—atoms of the four elements and jugs—is established in the common perception of both Aulūkyas and Buddhists, so it becomes a correct proof.

Therefore, to teach that the object taken as the evidence must be unmistaken with regard to the predicate of the thesis:

> 22.   And if that is mistaken or so forth,
>   Even if the word is not mistaken,
>   It should be known to be a faulty proof
>   Because a thing is proven by a thing.

If that object taken as evidence has a mistaken relation to the predicate of the thesis, an unproven propositional property, or so forth, even if the name or word is not mistaken, it should be known to be a proof that has faults, because the thing that is the predicate of the proposition must be proven in relation to the subject[68] by that which is the thing taken as the evidence.

To give examples of how even if the word is not mistaken, evidence is faulty if the object is mistaken:

> 23. In proofs like "Since it goes, it's horned" or else
> "It has a hand, so it's an elephant,"
> The meaning of the terms is common parlance,
> But it is not the meaning that's intended.[69]

When expressions such as "Since it goes, this cow is horned" or "Because it has a 'hand,' this elephant calf is an elephant" are used in proofs, the words may not be misleading when used as proof but the meaning is, so the evidence becomes faulty. The meaning of these terms "going" and "having a hand" refers to "horned" and "elephant" in common parlance only but do not refer to the intended meaning— horned and elephant—by force of actual things.

(c) Refuting that Īśvara is the cause of the world and its inhabitants with an absurd consequence. This has three points: (i) The consequence that causes and non-causes would be the same, (ii) Refuting the analogy of there being no difference, and (iii) Summary.

(i) The consequence that causes and non-causes would be the same

To teach that a permanent Īśvara who is the cause of the entire world and all its inhabitants would have also to be a cause:

> 24. Just as that entity is the cause,
> In the same way, then, at the times
> It's not the cause, why do you assert
> It is the cause, not not a cause?

You Śaivas, just as that entity Īśvara is the cause that creates the universe, in the same way, then, at the times when the universe is being destroyed, Īśvara himself would not be the cause of destruction but the cause of its creation, because Īśvara is permanent without any distinction between earlier and later in creating the universe. If it were otherwise, why or by what reason do you assert that the Īśvara at the time of creating the universe is the cause that creates the universe but not also assert that he is not a cause during other periods? It is logical you would, because there is no distinction between that and his nature at the time of the destruction of the universe.

If you say the pervasion is indefinite:

25.   If Caitra's wound is related to a weapon,
    His healing to medicinal herbs and such,
    Why would you not think that something unrelated
    Such as a tree trunk were itself the cause?

If the wound on Caitra's body occurs in relation to a weapon and the healing of Caitra's body is related to medicinal herbs and such, including mantras, then at that time, if a permanent Īśvara were the cause that produces Caitra's wound and healing, why wouldn't you think that something unrelated to the production of wounds and healing such as a tree trunk as well would itself be the cause of Caitra's wound and healing? It follows that you should.

Therefore, just as a tree trunk is not proven to produce of Caitra's wound or healing, similarly Īśvara is not proven to create the universe. To teach this:

26.   Unless there is a difference in nature,
    It also is illogical to function.
    Since permanents have no reverse entailment,
    The power, too, is difficult to detect.

It also is illogical for Īśvara, who abides with no difference in his nature between when the universe is perishing and other phases, to function to create the universe. Why? you ask. Since a permanent Īśvara has no power to entail anything either positively or in reverse to affect the universe,[70] and since the power to produce the universe is also difficult to validly detect.

If you say the pervasion is indeterminate, to explain:

27.   If you should think that something other than
                  Those which when they are present, it occurs
                  Would be its causes, then for everything
                  Causes would be an infinite regress.

If you should think that something—an Īśvara who has no power to affect the universe positively—other than those causes by which it (the universe) occurs when they are present as a positive effect on it, whereas the universe is prevented when they are absent, would be its (the universe's) cause, the causes of production for everything (all results) would be an infinite regress, because there would be no valid cognition disproving that things with no capacity to affect positively are causes.

(ii) Refuting the analogy of there being no difference

Well then, even though there is no distinction from the times when he is not creating the universe, Īśvara is the cause of the universe. As an analogy, it is just as how a seed—the cause of a shoot—is not different when the soil and so forth are not assembled, but it is still the shoot's cause, you say. To teach that such an analogy is illogical:

27.   If the nature of the soil and so forth
                  Transforms in the production of a shoot,
                  They are the cause. This is because if they
                  Are properly done, the difference is seen.

If the soil and so forth transform into the nature of a cause in the actual production of a shoot, they are the shoot's cause. This is because if they (the field and soil) are properly combined with water and other such conditions, the difference in the results such as sprouts and so forth—goodness and plentifulness—is validly seen.

Others say:

28a–c   "As objects and the faculties assembled
           Aren't different, but are the cause of mind,
           This is like that," you say.

As an analogy, just as the objects—the faculties, attention, and so forth—are not different when separate and not assembled from when they are assembled, but are the cause of sensory minds, this Īśvara is like that—he may not be different from the times when he is not creating the universe but he is the cause of the universe, you say. To explain:

28c–d   It is not so,
       Because there is a difference there as well.

It is not so that there is no difference between the object, faculty, and attention when assembled and when not, because there is the difference there with object and so forth being assembled or not assembled as well as to whether they produce a sensory consciousness or not.

The reason is not established, you say. To explain:

29.   If those, which lacked capacity when separate,
           Do not have a distinctive nature, then
           Assembled they would lack capacity, too.
           So therefore the distinctiveness is proven.

If those (the object, faculty, and attention), which lacked capacity to produce sensory consciousness on their own when unassembled and separate, do not have a distinctive nature when assembled, then assembled, they (the object, faculty, and attention) would lack capacity to produce a sensory consciousness as well. One cannot agree to this, so therefore the distinction between assembled and unassembled object, faculty, and attention in producing or not producing a sensory faculty is proven.

(iii) Summary

30.   Therefore what lacks capacity on its own
           In combination may have qualities.

Those are the causes. Īśvara and so forth
Are not, because there is no difference.

Sensory consciousnesses actually arise from the combination of object, faculty, and attention. Therefore, any one of the object, faculty, or attention on its own lacks the capacity to produce sensory consciousness, but if the combination of object and so forth is complete, they may have the quality to benefit the sensory consciousness. Therefore those (the object and so forth in full combination) are the causes of sensory consciousness. Īśvara, the self, and so forth are not the cause of the universe, because there is no difference between them and the Īśvara at the time he is not creating the universe.

(d) Refuting that if the Bhagavan is valid, he should know all hidden objects. This has two topics: (i) Stating the position, and (ii) Refuting it.

(i) Stating the position

31.   There are those who state, "Validity
          Is knowing hidden objects, but because
          There is not any method to achieve that,
          There is not anyone who would make efforts."

The Cārvākas and Jaiminīyas claim that it is not logical to say:

Thus based on the means
To achieve that, it's logical he is valid.[71]

There are those Cārvākas and so forth who state that this is because if he were a valid being, he would have to know every single hidden object such as the number of insects and so forth or distant objects, but there is not any method to achieve that knowledge, and there is not anyone who would make efforts at such methods.

(ii) Refuting it. This has two topics: A. General discussion, and B. The meaning of the text.

A. General discussion

Is the master refuting here the omniscience of knowing all phenomena? you ask. He is not. There are non-Buddhists who contend that those who do not know the methods to achieve liberation but who do know a trifling hidden object are teachers, so he is refuting them. Omniscient wisdom is extremely remote for those with childish impure minds, so it is inconceivable. Thus he does not examine that here. As it is said:

> Thus analyzing form, et cetera,
> And mind as apprehended characteristics
> Is for those who have impure minds. The yogi's
> Realization is inconceivable.[72]

From *Establishing Others' Continua*:

> The Bhagavan's comprehension of objects is inconceivable because it transcends the objects of knowledge and speech in all ways.[73]

Well then, are ordinary individuals in all aspects unable to examine the object of omniscience? you ask. The manner in which omniscient wisdom engages an object is difficult for ordinary individuals to realize through valid cognition proceeding from the power of facts, and this is said with that in mind. Omniscience can be understood through the validity of authoritative scriptures. As it says in the *Commentary*:

> When moving on to the third area,
> It's logical to accept the treatises.[74]

Well then, how does one understand it from authoritative scriptures? you ask. With regard to this, there is the wisdom that knows the variety of all phenomena—the wisdom that comprehends all phenomena that are included among aspects, signs, and attributes. As is said in the *Middle Length Mother of the Victors*:

> Subhūti, in this way the Tathagata comprehends those aspects, signs, and attributes that are aspects, signs, and attributes that describe phenomena. . .[75]

The wisdom that knows phenomena as they are is the wisdom that knows that the dharma nature of one phenomenon and the dharma nature of all phenomena are inseparable. As is said in the *Great Mother in One Hundred Thousand Stanzas*, "If one knows the long and short of one phenomenon, one will know the long and short of all phenomena."[76] Master Āryadeva also said:

> One thing is the essence of all things.
> All things are the essence of one thing.
> Whoever sees the suchness of one thing
> Sees the suchness of all things.[77]

Some people might think that if both the wisdom that knows the variety of all phenomena and the wisdom that knows all phenomena as they are know all phenomena, then it is not logical to divide them into two wisdoms. However, if they do not, one or the other of them would not be omniscient wisdom. For that reason, I shall explain:

Just as there is no thing coarse or subtle at all that space (which is the sense base of dharmas) does not conjoin, there is no phenomenon at all that the Tathagata's suchness does not conjoin. For that reason, that which is the suchness of one phenomenon is the suchness of all phenomena, and that which is the suchness of all phenomena is the suchness of the Tathagata. This is explained at great length in the *Great Mother in One Hundred Thousand Stanzas*:

> Subhūti, that which is the suchness of form is the suchness of the Tathagata, and the Tathagata comprehends that which is the suchness of the Tathagata. . .

Therefore the wisdoms that know the nature and variety are merely distinguished as separate isolates in students' minds, but in actuality there is no difference because when that very wisdom that knows the suchness of all phenomena knows the dharma nature of all phenomena, it also knows all phenomena, which are indivisible from that:

A single instant of knowing
Pervades the mandala of the knowable.[78]

Therefore the master does not refute omniscience.

Well then, doesn't it say, "We have no use at all for whether / He knows how many bugs there are," you ask.

In regard to that, the Śaivas assert that Īśvara, who does not know the methods to pacify suffering, is a teacher, and since the creator of all pleasure and pain is Īśvara, by pleasing him with animal sacrifices and so forth, one will enjoy the pleasures of heaven. They do not know the distinction between the valid and the invalid, so based on some fallacious logics they accept scriptures that say sacrificing livestock is a method for the high realms and washing in a river is a method for liberation, and they assert that the being who created those scriptures is the teacher.

Additionally, the Cārvāka and Mīmāṃsaka schools say that all outer and inner things merely appear in this world without any cause. They say that there is no full ripening in this life of actions performed in a previous life, no previous and future worlds[79] in which the ripening of actions performed in this life is experienced, no higher realms, no liberation, no omniscience, and so forth, thus denying all extremely hidden phenomena. In the perception of those who make such assertions, valid cognition that engages the power of things does not provide proof of liberation and omniscience, which are extremely hidden objects. They do not accept the authoritative scriptures as valid, so for the time being the wisdom that knows all phenomena is put aside. Instead, merely knowing everything that is necessary is taught here in terms of being needed for those beings who long for liberation.

"How is it that Īśvara and such others do not know what is necessary for those beings who long for liberation?" you ask. Īśvara taught that one must perform animal sacrifices in order to attain the higher realms and liberation, but there is no need to speak of achieving liberation through that—one won't even achieve the higher realms, because it is contradictory for the higher realms to arise from the cause of lower realms. Similarly, the Cārvākas and so forth do not know what is necessary for those who long for liberation, because they teach an erroneous path denying karma, cause, and result. Therefore it is not logical that Īśvara and so forth should be valid authorities for those beings who long for liberation. Someone who has comprehended for themselves without error the nature of the four truths and is able to teach it to others is logically a valid authority, regardless of whether or not they know the insect population or far off objects.

B. The meaning of the text. This has two points: 1. Teaching that knowing the unnecessary is not validity, and 2. Teaching that knowing the necessary is validity.

1. Teaching that knowing the unnecessary is not validity

To teach that we look for a teacher who knows the method to pacify suffering, not one who knows the number of insects and so forth:

> 32.   People who have suspicions of being confused
> By those who, without knowledge, act as teachers
> Will look for someone who possesses knowledge
> In order to act upon their explanations.

> 33.   And for that purpose, they examine
> The wisdom that they need to achieve.
> We have no use at all for whether
> He knows how many bugs there are.

People who want to pacify suffering have suspicions of being confused by those who, without knowledge of the methods to pacify suffering, act as teachers. They will look for someone as a teacher who possesses knowledge of the methods to pacify suffering in order to train in acting ardently upon the methods explained by this teacher who knows the methods to pacify suffering. They do not look for someone who knows the size of the insect population as their teacher. And for that reason, before they will follow him, they examine whether or not a teacher has the wisdom that knows the methods to pacify suffering, which are what they who want peace need to achieve. We who long for peace have no use at all for whether he knows how many bugs there are.

2. Teaching that knowing the necessary is validity

34.   We assert that making known the suchness of
What should be taken up, what given up
Along with the methods is validity.
It is not making everything known.

The teacher who knows everything that is necessary for us makes known what should be taken up (the truth of cessation) along with the method for achieving it (the truth of the path), and the suchness of what must be given up (the truth of suffering that is to be known), along with the method to pacify that (eliminating the origin). We assert that such a one is valid. Someone who does not know the nature of the four truths might make everything known including the number of insects there are, but that is not necessary for those who long for liberation. For that reason:

35.   Whether or not they do see far away,
They should see the suchness that is desired.
If seeing far away is validity,
Come here and let us worship vultures!

Here, whether or not those who know the necessary meaning do know the number of insects seen from far away, they are worthy to be the teachers of those who long for liberation, because they themselves have seen without error the very meaning that is desired by those who long for liberation—what is to be adopted and rejected, the four noble truths along with the method—and have the compassion to teach it to others. If merely seeing far away and knowing the number of insects even without knowing the desired meaning is validity, well then, come here, you Cārvākas and Mīmāṃsakas. Cast aside those who know the methods to pacify liberation and worship far-seeing vultures as your teacher.

2. Detailed explanation. This has two topics: a. The detailed explanation of the perfect cause, and b. The detailed explanation of the perfect result.

a. The detailed explanation of the perfect cause. This has two topics: i. The explanation of the wish to help beings, the perfect intent, and ii. The explanation of the teacher, the perfect training.

i. The explanation of the wish to help beings, the perfect intent. This has two topics: (1) General discussion, and (2) The meaning of the text.

(1) General discussion

If the resultant validity explained in the line, "The valid is an unde-ceiving mind" is explained in the lines "Thus based on the means / To achieve that, it's logical he is valid" to be based upon the preceding perfect cause, then what is the perfect cause? you ask.

This has two topics: (a) Presenting our own tradition, and (b Refuting the extreme of a nihilist view toward cause and result.

(a) Presenting our own tradition

The validity that was the object of the verse of homage explained above is born out of the cause, repeatedly cultivating the perfect intent, the great compassion that wishes to help all wanderers. Because it has the aspect of wishing to free each and every sentient being from the great ocean of suffering, such great compassion has three types: great com-passion focused on sentient beings, great compassion focused on dhar-mas, and nonreferential great compassion. Great individuals come under the power of those three types of compassion and thus develop the wish to liberate sentient beings from the great ocean of suffering. Knowing that no one other than a perfect buddha is able to do that, they develop the superior intent of wishing to truly achieve the state of a buddha, who is a friend for all beings. There is no other method to achieve that than the training of practicing the path.

Practicing the path, as well, is not for anything other than solely the sake of sentient beings, because achieving perfect buddhahood has the resolve of bodhichitta as its root, and the resolve of bodhichitta has great compassion as its root. That compassion, as well, is born out of a focus on suffering sentient beings. It is in these terms that the fearless master Candrakīrti said:

The listeners and mid-buddhas are born from the Sage.
The buddhas are born from bodhisattvas.
Compassionate wishes, a nondual mind,
And bodhichitta are the causes of the victors' children.[80]

From *The Sutra of the Tathagata's Secret*:

"Bhagavan, who has the resolve of bodhichitta?" "Great King, those whose superior intent is not disturbed." He asked: "Bhagavan, whose superior intent is not disturbed?" "Great king, those who develop great compassion." He asked, "Bhagavan, who develops great compassion?" The Bhagavan spoke: "Great king, those who develop the resolve to never give up on any sentient being."[81]

And as it is also said in *The Sutra of Ten Dharmas*:

Child of noble family, here when those who dwell in the family of the bodhisattvas arouse the resolve of bodhichitta, the Tathagata or the Tathagata's disciples encourage and protect them and make them properly uphold it. This resolve for unexcelled completely perfect enlightenment is the first cause of longing for bodhichitta. Arousing the resolve of unexcelled completely perfect enlightenment upon hearing someone praise perfect enlightenment or bodhichitta is the second cause. Recollecting the attitude of compassion upon seeing sentient beings who have no protector, no refuge, and no champion and then arousing the resolve for unexcelled completely perfect enlightenment is the third cause. Seeing the Tathagatas' supremely complete utter perfection, feeling joy, and then developing the resolve of unexcelled completely perfect enlightenment is the fourth cause.[82]

According to this treatise as well, by way of the perfect intent—great compassion that wishes to benefit wanderers—and the perfect training—meditating on the two selflessnesses that destroy the root of samsara oneself and teaching that path to others as well—one achieves the state of a valid being whose nature is the union of the benefit for oneself—the sugata—and the benefit for others—the kāyas of the protector. This is the unexcelled thought of both Lords of Reasoning.[83]

(b) Refuting the extreme of a nihilist view toward cause and result. This has three points: (i) Presenting the Cārvāka tradition, (ii) Refuting it, and (iii) Explaining why it is necessary to refute the nihilist view.

(i) Presenting the Cārvāka tradition

This should be known according to the explanation in *Infinite Oceans of Validity*. The Cārvākas have five kinds of denial: denial of cause, denial of result, denial of unseen objects, denial of validity, and denial of the valid being.

As for the first, they assert that all phenomena have no cause. This is because other than birth, sentient beings are not caused by the accumulation of virtuous or unvirtuous actions, because there is no coming from a past world to this one. Therefore things arise without any cause at all. External assemblies of earth and so forth are unmanifest sentient beings, whereas living creatures are manifest sentient beings—individuals who do not come from another world—because clear awareness comes from the combination of the father's semen, the mother's blood, and so forth. For example, it is just as beer arises out of barley, yeast, and so forth.

They assert that things arise without cause. The rishi Juktopchen[84] and others say:

> That peas are round, that long high thorns are sharp,
> That peacock feathers have such bright designs,
> And that the sun has light and waters flow down hill
> Are not made by anyone; the cause is in their essence.

The roundness of peas is not made by anything else and so forth; all things have no cause, they claim.

As for denying the result: an illusionist whose livelihood was insufficient drew wolf prints at an intersection. He then told the townspeople that a demon called "The Wolf" would eat them all and that in order to prevent this, the townspeople should throw all food and wealth outside and not leave their houses for seven days. Similarly, the learned renunciate Gautama spoke of the terrors of future lives, but those do not exist. Since the mind has a physical nature, when the body passes away, the mind also ceases. Thus there is no future life:

> Enjoy pleasures while you are not dead;
> Once you die, you can't enjoy them.
> Since the body as well will become ash,
> How can there be another birth?
> Alas, that which the learned one has said
> Is just the same as a wolf's prints.

Also:

> Enjoy the beautiful girl well and eat.
> When your great body has passed away, you will not have them.
> This body is merely an assembly.
> What is destroyed and gone will not come back.

Since there are no past or future lives, there are no results of virtue or nonvirtue, they say.

As for denying the unseen, they say that gods, beings in hell, and so forth, which are not in the sphere of perception, do not exist.

As for denying validity, they say that since inference is confused about the object, it is not valid, so only perception is valid.

As for denying the valid being, they say that when the body perishes, the mind also ceases so it is not reasonable to meditate on suchness for many aeons. They also say that since they are not seen with perception, there is no omniscience and no mind that is free of desire.

They do not refute that there is no self who is an agent or that all composites are impermanent. However, they deny that formations arise out of karma and afflictions, that the suffering of death is brought about by birth itself, that one existence is connected to the next, and that one sinks into the great ocean of samsaric suffering. Thus they do not accept that everything defiled is suffering. They say there is no omniscience or mind free from desire, so they also do not accept nirvana as peace.

(ii) Refuting it

Experience proves that cognition is preceded by a previous cognition. Thus a cognition not preceded by a cause is impossible, just as a shoot not preceded by a seed is impossible. Therefore it is not logical to deny the cause.

That mere cognition has the capacity to produce the next cognition is proven by experience. Thus there is no cognition that does not produce a later cognition, just as a lamp that does not produce light is impossible.

If you refute the existence of a valid being just because you do not perceive him, then your eyes, heart, and teeth also do not exist because you do not see them. Proving that omniscience and so forth do not exist because of the evidence that they are not seen and asserting that there is no inferential validity are contradictory.[85] Therefore it is not logical to deny unseen objects, inference, and valid beings.

(iii) Explaining why it is necessary to refute the nihilist view

When one sees the logic that refutes the lack of past or future lives or the lack of a valid being, one automatically realizes that there are future lives and valid beings. People who have realized this are not interested only in the pleasures of this life but also make effort at some things that bring benefit in the next life, because they understand that they have no power to stay in this life alone and definitely must go to the next world.

For example, a person who goes to another country on business may see the other country as nice and pleasant, but when they turn their attention to their children, spouse, and so forth, they think, "I do not have the opportunity to stay in this country forever but must quickly return to my own country." They then strive to acquire in that land the merchandise needed in their own country. Similarly, those who wish to seek out things that will help in the next life should seek the things that help in the next world, the paths to higher states and true excellence. They must look for these from an authoritative individual whom they can believe or an authoritative scripture that will not deceive them about that for which they long. As it says in the *Commentary*:

People who have suspicions of being confused
By those who, without knowledge, act as teachers
Will look for someone who possesses knowledge
In order to act upon their explanations.[86]

Some accept that there is a next world, but do not know how to seek the methods necessary for it. Not knowing the distinction between valid and invalid, on the basis of some fallacious reasonings they accept scriptures that teach live sacrifice as a method to achieve the high realms and bathing on a river bank as a method for liberation, and they accept the individuals who created those scriptures as teachers.

Those who unmistakenly know the characteristics of validity do not proceed merely out of faith in scriptures. Instead, through those scriptures they analyze the teachings about the evident and the hidden through logic based respectively on perceptual and inferential validity to see whether or not they are contraverted. At all times, they examine whether the words of the scriptures' author contradict their own words in earlier or later passages either explicitly or implicitly. As it says in the *Commentary*:

In order to retain them, one engages
In the analysis of scriptures that
Establish logically the seen and unseen
Or do not contradict their own words.[87]

Thus from the evidence of scriptures purified by the three analyses[88] and the authors of such scriptures being comparable, it is logical to assert that scriptures that teach the extremely hidden methods of what to adopt and what to reject for the high realms and liberation and the authors of those scriptures are authoritative sources. From the *Commentary*:

Authoritative words are inference
From universals that are undeceiving.[89]

Such scriptures and authors also teach the unmistaken paths to the higher states and true excellence, saying that by performing meritorious and unmoving karma, one achieves the pleasures of the gods and humans of the Desire realm and of the dhyanas of the higher realms, whereas from performing nonmeritorious acts the suffering of the lower realms arises. Thus those who assert that these are authoritative sources practice what they teach.

Therefore unmistakenly practicing virtue and giving up misdeeds in this life is a benefit one receives in this life from knowing what is taught in the treatises that teach the characteristics of validity. The benefits received in future lives is that by thus doing what should be done and giving up what should not, one leaves future rebirth in the lower realms far behind and achieves the pleasures of the higher states of gods and humans. The ultimate purpose is as described in the *Ascertainment*:

> Cultivating the intelligence produced by contemplation separates one from the confusion of misunderstanding and manifests the ultimate stainless validity.[90]

After thoroughly analyzing with intelligence the nature of things—impermanence, selflessness, and so forth—in external and internal things, one gradually cultivates them. When one has come to the culmination of that training, the ultimate valid cognition achieved as the culmination of the clear appearance of the meaning of selflessness that one cultivated becomes manifest. When selflessness is thus directly realized and ultimate validity becomes manifest, personality view, which has the characteristic of clinging to me and mine, is stopped. Stopping that prevents the causes of rebirth in samsara that follow it, all karma and afflictions. In the end, one achieves the sublime bliss of unexcelled liberation, which is the pacification of all samsaric suffering forever. This is the sublime, utmost purpose.

In this way, after the wrong views of eternalism and nihilism and the erroneous paths have been disproven through logic, one will enter the right view and unmistaken path. This is the special purpose of treatises that teach the characteristics. These treatises are written by those who have the altruistic wish to help the teachings and sentient beings. Those who wish for excellence for themselves and others engage them through listening, contemplating, and meditating.

(2) The meaning of the text. This has two topics: (a) Establishing our own position, and (b) Refuting criticism.

(a) Establishing our own position

When it says, "Thus based on the means / To achieve that, it's logical he is valid" what are the means? you ask. To explain:

36a   The means is compassion. That's from cultivation.

The perfect cause that is the means to achieve the state of a valid being is the cultivation repeatedly over many lifetimes of the great compassion that wishes to liberate all wandering beings forever from the great ocean of suffering. One achieves the state of a valid being from that, so that is the cause by which one achieves that state.

(b) Refuting criticism. This has two topics: (i) Refuting the argument that cultivation over many lifetimes is not tenable, and (ii) Refuting the argument that even with cultivation, omniscience would be impossible.

(i) Refuting the argument that cultivation over many lifetimes is not tenable. This has two topics: A. Presenting the criticism, and B. Refuting it logically.

A. Presenting the criticism

The Cārvākas say:

36bc   They say, "The mind's supported by the body
            So it is not achieved through cultivation."

Compassion and other mental states are results of the body, and all the results of the body are physical qualities. Thus the mind is supported by the body, so when the body perishes, it perishes as well. As an analogy, it is like a wall and mural. For that reason, it (the state of a valid being) is not achieved through the cultivation of compassion for many lives, they say.

B. Refuting it logically. This has two topics: 1. Brief overview, and 2. Detailed explanation.

1. Brief overview. This has two points: a. Refuting that there are no past or future lives, and b. Refuting the assertion that the faculties and so forth arise without depending on their own kind.

a. Refuting that there are no past or future lives

> 36d Not so, since the support has been refuted.

It is not so that compassion and other mental states cease when the body perishes because of being supported by the body. This is since it has been validly refuted that the body is the support for the mind.

How is it validly refuted? you say. To explain:

> 37. When one takes birth, the inhalation and
> The exhalation, faculties, and mind
> Do not arise from just the physical
> Without depending upon their own kind,

> 38a For that would be absurd.

At the time when sentient beings take birth, the inhalation and the exhalation of breath, faculties such as the eye faculty, and the mind do not arise just from the physical body without depending upon previous instances of their own kind, for otherwise there would be the extremely absurd consequence that the elements of earth, water, and so forth would have respiration, faculties, and mind.

In addition:

> 38a–d   What else is there
> Than the capacity to make a link
> That has been seen? There is not anything.
> And due to what would it no longer link?

That inhalation and exhalation, the faculties, and so forth have the capacity to make a link to a subsequent instance of their own kind has been seen previously at the time of taking birth. What else—what extra cause—is there that would later at the time of death prevent linking to a subsequent instance of their own kind? There is not anything. Due to what reason do you assert that the previous instance of its kind would no longer link? It is illogical to assert that.

b. Refuting the assertion that the faculties and so forth arise without depending on their own kind

The Cārvākas say that the faculties and so forth do not arise in dependence on a previous instance of their kind. Though they arise, there is no fault that consequentially the earth, water, and so forth would have inhalation and exhalation, faculties, or mind. Some portions of the elements of earth and so forth lack the seeds for sentient beings, but some earth and so forth can become living beings who have manifestly clear minds, they say. To explain:

> 39.   There is not any portion at all of earth
>   And so forth in which living beings may not
>   Be born from warmth and moisture and so forth.
>   Therefore all by nature is a seed.

There is not any portion at all of the elements of earth and so forth in which living beings may not be born from warmth and moisture, the womb, miraculous birth, and so forth.[91] Therefore all portions of the elements of earth and so forth by nature are seeds of living beings.

Therefore, to teach that the elements of earth and so forth would all become living beings:

> 40.   Therefore, if faculties and so forth were
>   To arise without depending on their kind,
>   Then just as one becomes, so too would all,
>   Because there is not any difference.

Since all elements of earth and so forth are the seeds of living creatures, therefore if the mental mind,[92] faculties, breathing, and so forth were to arise solely from the substantial cause of the physical body made of elements without depending on previous instances of their own kind, then just as one portion of the elements of earth and so forth becomes a living creature, so too would all portions of the earth and so forth become living creatures, because there is not any difference between the elements and the earth and so forth that function as the substantial cause for living creatures.

2. Detailed explanation. This has four topics: a. Refuting that mind is a quality of the body, b. Refuting that mind and body are the same in substance, c. Refuting that mind is a result of the body, and d. Refuting criticism.

a. Refuting that mind is a quality of the body. This has five topics: i. Refuting that the body is the dominant condition for the mind, ii. Refuting through the consequence that a dead body would have mind, iii. Refuting that the body is the substantial cause of the mind, iv. Refuting the assertion that objects that are other and do not affect each other are supporter and supported, and v. Refuting in particular that intelligence and so forth are supported by the body.

i. Refuting that the body is the dominant condition for the mind. This has four topics: (1) The mind does not change after the faculties change, so it should be the support, (2) Refuting that if the body were permanent, it could not be a support, (3) Refuting the reasons why there would be no future rebirth, and (4) Refuting by examining whether it arises from a body that has faculties or that does not.

(1) The mind does not change after the faculties change, so it should be the support. This has two points: (a) Actual, and (b) Refuting that it is contradictory of the Bhagavan's scriptures.

(a) Actual

> 41.   If individual faculties
> Are harmed, there is not any harm
> To mental mind. But if that changes,
> Those are seen to change as well.

If the individual faculties of the eye and so forth are harmed by some other condition, there is not any harm to the mental mind. For this reason, the mental mind is not supported by the body. Thus the body is supported by the mental mind, because if that mental mind is changed by desire, fear, sorrow, and so forth, those faculties of the eye and so forth are validly seen to change as well.

To teach that mental mind is not supported by the body but that the faculties and so forth are supported by the mental mind:

42.   So therefore the support for mind to abide
        And some that are supported by the mind
        Are the causes of the faculties, and thus
        The faculties are from the mental mind.

The mental mind is not supported by the body, whereas the eyes and other faculties are supported by the mental mind. So therefore the support for the continuum of the mental mind to abide and some karmas called volitional that depend on the cause of previous instances of their own kind are the causes of the faculties that arise in the Desire and Form realms. As those are the causes, thus the physical faculties arise from the mental mind.[93]

Additionally:

43ab   If there has been a propeller such as this,
        Later as well there will be such as that.

If the mental mind of a being at the time of death has previously at the time of birth been the propelling cause for such faculties and so forth of the same kind as those faculties and so forth, later as well it will be the propeller for faculties and so forth such as that of the previous phase of taking birth.

(b) Refuting that it is contradictory of the Bhagavan's scriptures

Others say that if mental mind is not supported by the body, that contradicts the Bhagavan saying that mental mind is supported by the body in the *Sutra of Abhidharma*, where he states "Body and mind mutually act upon each other." In order to teach the meaning of this:

43cd   Because its consciousness can benefit,
            The body is explained to support the mind.

The body affects the body consciousness, and its (the body's) consciousness can benefit the mind indirectly. Because of this, it was
explained thus with the intention that the body supports the mind
indirectly.

Others say:

44ab   "In that case, without faculties the mind
            Does not."

In that case, mental mind is supported by the faculties because without the faculties of the eye and so forth, the mental mind does not arise,
you say. To explain:

44b–d   And nor do those without it either.
            Accordingly they are each other's cause,
            So therefore they are mutual results.

Well then, the faculties as well are supported by the mental mind,
because nor do those faculties arise without it (the mental mind) either.
According to that assertion, they (the faculties such as the eye and the
mental mind) acted as each other's mutual cause previously at the time
of taking birth. And if you agree to that, since they function as each
other's cause, so therefore in the next life as well they will be mutually
cause and results. If you agree, that establishes that there are previous
and future births.

(2) Refuting that if the body were permanent, it could not be a support

45a   Sequential is not from the non-sequential.

The sequential arising of the mental mind is not from a body that
does not arise sequentially, because the body would be permanent.[94]

If you say the body may be permanent but produces the mind successively in dependence on conditions, to explain:

45b   Not different and not dependent either.

There is no sequential production of the mental mind in dependence
on the condition of the body, because the body is a permanent phenomenon is not differentiated physically.
    Others say:

45c   If mind were in a sequence from the body,

Previous mental minds arise in succession, and later minds as well
will arise in a sequence from the body dependent on that, you say. To
explain:

45d   Then that would indicate its sequence, too.

Then that would indicate its (the body's) sequence of earlier and
later, because the mental mind supported by the body is proven to have
a sequence of earlier and later.
    To substantiate this:

46.   Earlier moments are the causes
           Of later moments, which had not
           Existed previously, and thus
           It's always seen that they are causes.

At the time of taking birth in the past, earlier moments of the body,
faculties, and mental mind are the causes of later moments of their
own same kind, which had not existed previously, and thus for that
reason it is always—after death and so forth—validly seen that they
(earlier moments of the mental mind and faculties) are causes of later
moments.

(3) Refuting the reasons why there would be no future rebirth

Others say that it is not so that earlier moments of the mental mind,
faculties, and so forth are seen as the causes of later moments prior to
death. It is thus: the mind at the moment of death of a person on the

great way, the subject, does not link to a later mind, because it is a mind of death. As an analogy, it is like the mind of death asserted for arhats. To explain:

> 47ab How would it be contradictory
> For the last mind to link to another mind?

It follows that the last mind of a person at the time of death, the subject, is not correct evidence from the observation of something contradictory that proves that the mind of a being on the great way at the time of death does not link to a later awareness, because how would it be contradictory of logic for it to link to another later mind? It would not be.

To teach that the analogy is therefore not tenable:

> 47cd And why is it that you admit
> The mind of an arhat will not link?

Why or by what reason is it that you Cārvākas admit that the mind of an arhat at the time of death is an analogy that proves that there is no linking to a later awareness, because for you there are no arhats? You might say that even though that is not established, you are proposing it as an analogy since it is explained in the Buddhist school that their minds are liberated, just like a lamp going out. However, if that Buddhist citation is valid, then previous and future lives are proven.[95]

> 48ab Why would you follow a philosophy
> That has not been established validly?

If it is not valid, why would you Cārvākas follow a Buddhist philosophy that has not been established validly in either scripture or meaning and see the mind of an arhat at the time of death as a correct analogy? It is not logical to propose an analogy that has not been validly proven.

The Cārvākas say:

> 48c And if you say, "Because it lacks the causes,"

If you say that the mind of an arhat at the time of death does not link to a later mind because it lacks the causes of that later mind—the body, faculties, breathing, and so forth—to explain:

48d   Why did you not say just that here?

Why did you not say here as correct proof establishing that a person's mind at the time of death does not link to a later mind that just that lack of body, faculty, breathing, and so forth is valid proof? It would have been logical to say so. If you say you agree completely, then it follows that the lack of body, faculties, breath, and so forth, the subject, is not correct evidence that proves that the mind of a being at the time of death does not link to a later mind, because the pervasion is indeterminate.

(4) Refuting by examining whether it arises from a body that has faculties or that does not. This has two points: (a) The actual refutation, and (b) Refuting it with other logic.

(a) The actual refutation

If mental mind arises from the body, does it arise from a body that has faculties or from a body that does not have faculties? In the first case, does it arise from each of the faculties or from all of the faculties combined? If you say it is the former, to explain:

49ab   Since it would apprehend like consciousness,
        The mental's not from one with faculties.

Thoughts in the mental consciousness do not arise directly from the eye faculty, since if they did, they would apprehend forms clearly like the eye consciousness that is supported by the eye, but that is not the case. Therefore the mental consciousness does not arise directly from a capacity with the eye faculty as a dominant condition.

Well then, it arises from all the faculties combined, you say. To explain:

49cd   Since their capacity to produce knowing
             Is separate, not from all together either.

The five faculties of eye and so forth have separate capacities to produce distinct consciousnesses that apprehend their objects of form, sound, and so forth clearly, but do not have the capacity to produce awareness that apprehends all objects clearly. For this reason, a mental mind that clearly apprehends all six of form and so forth, does not arise from all of the faculties combined together. The word either means "not only does it not arise from individual faculties." If it were otherwise, the one mental mind would apprehend all six objects clearly, so it would be pointless to have multiple faculties.

If you say that it is the second case, where mind arises from a body without faculties, to explain:

50a   As those have no awareness, not from others.

As those—the hair, nails, and so forth, which are not faculties—do not produce any awareness as their dominant result, the mental mind does not arise from hair, nails, and so forth that are other than the eye and such faculties.

In that case, mental mind is supported by the body because it coexists with it, like, for example, a lamp and its light, you say. To explain:

50bc   As these have the same cause, they coexist,[96]
          Just like the faculties, like form and flavor.

As these (the mental mind and body) are both propelled by the same propelling karma as their cause and then arise together, the mind and body coexist. However, they do not become supporter and supported just because of that. For example, it is just like the five faculties of eye and so forth, which coexist but are not supporter and supported, or like the form and flavor of sugar, which coexist but are not mutually supporter and supported.

In that case, the mental mind is supported by the body because when the body changes the mind is also seen to change, you say. To explain:

50d   It is affected by way of the object.

If the body changes, it (the mental mind) is affected by way of taking the body as the apprehended object. It is not affected by way of the body functioning as the dominant condition. It is like fainting upon seeing another's blood, for example.

(b) Refuting it with other logic

51.   That which by being present benefits
           Since that is always consequent to it
           Is a cause. Therefore he used the locative
           And said "because this has arisen."

Since that result is always consequent to that which is its cause and because that cause which by being present benefits the result is a cause, therefore when the Bhagavan said, "When this exists, that arises" in the *Śālistambha Sutra*,[97] he used the locative case to indicate a reason and used the ablative case when he said, "Because this has arisen, that arises." This explains the distinction between cause and result. Such a relation of cause and result is not seen between the body and mind.

Here Master Devendrabuddhi says that the body and mind are not established as cause and result because there is no entailment or reverse entailment that the body is first observed in the womb and the mind observed afterward.[98] Prajñākaragupta says that the mind is not the result of the body because it is not always proven to be entailed or reverse entailed by it.[99]

Therefore, although it is possible that the body might merely benefit the mind, it is not the substantial cause. To teach this:

52.   There are, of course, some instances where it
           May benefit the mind's continuum,
           But like a jug and such with fire and so forth,
           Just that alone does not cause mind to cease.

There are, of course, some instances of the time of birth in the Desire and Form realms where by way of directly producing a body

consciousness, it (the body) may benefit indirectly the mind's continuum that follows the body consciousness. However, just that alone
does not make the body the substantial cause of the mind, because the
body ceasing does not cause the mind to cease. For example, fire and so
forth can benefit jugs and such, but putting the fire out does not cause
the jug to cease.

ii. Refuting through the consequence that a dead body would have mind.
This has four points: (1) The actual consequence, (2) Refuting that the favorable conditions are absent, (3) Refuting that impediments are present, and
(4) Rebutting criticism of our position.

(1) The actual consequence

53ab   There would be the consequence that if
           The body remained, the mind would not cease either.

There would be the consequence that if the body—the cause of the
mind—were to remain without ceasing after death, the mind would
remain in the body without ceasing.

(2) Refuting that the favorable conditions are absent

You might say that breathing, which is a requisite for the mind, is not
present in a dead body, so the mind does not remain. To explain:

53cd   There if it's there and under its control,
           So breathing is from it, not it from that.

54ab   Without exertion where would inhalation
           And exhalation of the breath be from?

The inhalation and exhalation of breath is there if it (the mental
mind) is there, and that inhalation and exhalation of breath is under
its (the mental mind's) control. So for these reasons, the inhalation and
exhalation of breath is from it (the mental mind), and it (the mental

mind) is not from that (the inhalation and exhalation of breath). Therefore without mental exertion, where would the power for a person to
inhale and exhale the breath be from? It would not be. Master Devendrabuddhi explains that this is similar to how it is due to a prior wish
that one stretches or bends their arms. The inhalation and exhalation of
breath are also initiated or stopped under the power of a mental wish.
This is a reason of nature.[100]

Therefore if inhalation and exhalation were the cause of mind, the
increase or decrease of the breath would also make the mind increase
or decrease. To teach this:

> 54cd   From them diminishing or increasing,
>   It also would diminish or increase.

If inhalation and exhalation were the cause of mind, from them
(inhalation and exhalation) diminishing or increasing, it (the mind)
also would logically diminish or increase, because the inhalation and
exhalation are the mind's cause. Devendrabuddhi says that it is just as
how a tree increasing or diminishing does not make the great ocean
increase or decrease.[101]

To teach that such logic is the same if the body is the cause of breathing as well:

> 55a   The consequence is the same for them as well.

For them who assert that the body is the cause of respiration as well,
the consequence is the same that the dead body would have respiration, and since that was present, it would have mind. This is because
the body—the direct cause of the breath—is present.

If you say that for us there similarly would be the consequence that
the mind would be present in the dead body because the continuum of
the mind does not cease, to explain:

> 55b–d   It is not similar if the mind's the cause,
>   Because it is asserted other factors
>   That propel remaining are the cause.

We say that the mind itself does not arise from exhalation and inhalation; the previous mind is the cause from which it arises. Because the karma for it to remain in the body has been exhausted, there is no similar fault that there would consequentially be a mind in a dead body. Well then, why is it that the body and mind coexist? you ask. It is because it is asserted other factors—karmas that propel the body and mind to remain together—are the cause for the body and mind to coexist. For that reason, although the body is not the mind's cause, for the time being causes for the mind and body to coexist are not nonexistent.

Devendrabuddhi says:

> Therefore the duration it remains is determined by the force
> of the propulsion. Thus since that does not engage from then
> on, it is not the same.[102]

Prajñākaragupta comments that in saying that we assert that there is another cause that propels remaining, the fault is not the same. Why is that, you ask? The mind has mind as a cause as well. Why is that? you ask. "The reason why it stays" means it remains for a short while. The other cause that propels the mind to remain in the body is the imprints of formations from ignorance, which are the cause, he says.

(3) Refuting that impediments are present

Others say:

> 56ab   "Like wicks and so forth, it has been degraded
> By humors, so the body is not the cause."

Just as wicks and so forth that are sodden with water and so forth cannot produce lamplight and so forth, the adverse condition of the humors of bile and wind creates the impediment of degradation, so for that reason at the time of death there is a body, but the dead body is not the cause of the mind to remain, you might say. To explain:

> 56cd   When death has brought the humors into balance,[103]
> It once again would be brought back to life.

Well then, death also reverses the adverse conditions such as the humors, contagion, poison, and so forth together with death, and the positive conditions are complete in the body. When that occurs, it (the dead body) once again would have a mind and be brought back to life. This is according to Devendrabuddhi.

Others say:

57a–c "But even though a fire might be reversed,
The changes to the wood are not turned back,
And likewise that cannot be brought back either."

But even though a fire—a cause for wood to change—might be reversed, the changes the fire made to the wood—ashes and so forth—are not turned back into wood again. Likewise, even if the cause for the mind to change such as contagion and so forth are reversed, that mind that has been changed by contagion cannot be brought back at the time of death either, you say. To explain:

57d Not so, since remedies can be applied.

It is not so that the body and mind cannot be brought back due to the damage from contagion, poison, and so forth, because since there are methods for medicinal remedies to be applied, they are able to be reversed, according to both Devendrabuddhi and Prajñākaragupta.

To teach that there are reversible and irreversible phenomena:

58. There are some instances where changes made
To certain things make them not rearise.
For other things, they are reversible,
Like fire with wood or gold as an example.

59. The first, even small, is not reversible.
But as with the solidity of gold,
That to which the alterations made
Are reversible will once again arise.

There are some instances where irreversible changes made to certain things make them not rearise. For other things, they (the changes) are reversible. Therefore it is not certain that change is irreversible in all aspects. For example, fire produces in wood the irreversible change into ashes and so forth, but when fire produces the change of melting in gold, the gold once again becomes solid. As for the first (the irreversible), even a small amount of ash made by fire is not reversible into wood. But that body and mind to which the great alteration whose characteristic is death made by contagion, poison, and so forth is reversible will once again be brought back and arise without illness. It is as with, for example, great molten gold that has been melted by fire being removed from the fire and once again becoming completely solid. This is according to both Devendrabuddhi and Prajñākaragupta.

(4) Rebutting criticism of our position

Others say that this contradicts the explanation that some illnesses are incurable. To explain:

> 60.   It's said some illnesses are totally
> Incurable since cures are to find
> Or life has been used up, but if it is
> Solely the humors, none is incurable.

The reason it is said that some types of illness are totally incurable is since the medicine or doctor that cures the illness is hard to find and one cannot encounter it, or since the life propelled by past actions has been used up. This is why they are described as incurable illnesses. But if one finds medicine and a doctor and the propelling karma and life have not been depleted, they are curable. Because you assert that those illnesses are not preceded by past actions or the mind and are produced solely by the humors of phlegm, bile, and so forth, none would be incurable, because the changes in the elements would begin once again. This is according to Prajñākaragupta.

Additionally:

61.   If the causes of deterioration[104] are
Removed by halting poison and so forth
In the dead, or cutting out the bite as well,
Why would they not come back to life?

Poison, disease, and so forth are halted in a dead being's body, or else when a being dies from the bite of a venomous snake, the poison remains in the wounded area of the snake bite, and cutting out that bite removes the causes of dying such as poison while the requisites for living are all present. Thus why would they who have died because of snake bites and so forth not come back to life? They would. Therefore the absurd consequence in "There would be the consequence that if / The body remained, the mind would not cease either" stands.

iii. Refuting that the body is the substantial cause of the mind

62.   Without a change in the substantial cause,
It is not possible to make a change
In what is caused, for instance like a basin
And so forth without changes to the clay.

Without a change of increase or decrease in the substantial cause (the body), which is other, it is not possible to make a change of increase or decrease in the result which is caused, the awarenesses. For instance it is like a basin and so forth that do not change without a change to the clay. Therefore it is not logical that a result could change without change in its substantial cause. To teach this:

63.   It would not be logical for a thing
That is not changed to be the substantial cause
Of something else that does get changed,
Like gaur and oxen and so forth.

It would not be logical for a thing that is not changed at all to be the substantial cause of something else that does get changed. For example, a gaur changes without an ox changing, so the ox is not the substantial cause of the gaur. Water and fire and so forth are similar as well.

To teach that the body and mind as well are like that analogy:

> 64a The mind and body are like that, too.

The mind and body as well are proven not to be the substantial result and substantial cause. They are like fire and water, for example, which do not entail or reverse entail each other and thus are proven not to be substantial result and substantial cause.

Others say that the body and mind are ascertained to always coexist, so they are substantial cause and result, like a torch and torchlight. To explain:

> 64b–d Results that arise from its cause
>   Cooperating coexist,
>   Just as with fire and molten copper.

The body's substantial cause—the fetal stages of mushiness and so forth[105]—act as the cooperating condition of the mind, and the mind also acts as the cooperating condition of the body's substantial cause. The results that arise from that are a single conglomeration, so the body and mind coexist. It is, for example, like when fire melts copper: the fire and the molten copper coexist, but they are not substantial cause and result.

iv. Refuting the assertion that objects that are other and do not affect each other are supporter and supported. This has three topics: (1) The actual logic of the refutation, (2) Rebutting criticism of this, and (3) Summary.

(1) The actual logic of the refutation. This has two points: (a) The reason why it is not tenable for them to be supporter and supported, and (b) The absurd consequence.

(a) The reason why it is not tenable for them to be supporter and supported

> 65a What is and what is not are not supported.

If the mind is and persists, it does not need a support, and what is not and does not persist does not need any support at all. For that reason, the mind is not supported by the body in terms of the body causing the mind to persist. Devendrabuddhi says, "That which does not do anything for something else is not its support, like, for example, Mount Vindhya and Mount Himavān."[106]

Others say:

65bc   If that's not so and the support is the cause
        For it to persist,

You might say that is not so. The body functions as the support of the mind in terms of functioning as the cause for it to persist without perishing after being established, you say.

Well then, is that persistence of the mind that the body creates the same as the mind or different? If you say it is the former, to explain:

65cd   it has no support
        Since that's not other than that which persists.

66ab   If other, it is just the cause of that.
        What is the entity that it has made?

This mind has no support—the body—that makes it persist, since even without the body, that (the persistence) is not other than the mind that persists. In the second case, if you say it is other, then what is the entity of the mind that it (the body) has made persist? It follows it has not made it persist, because it does not produce persistence that is the same in substance as the mind, but is just the cause of that persistence which is substantially other than the mind.

(b) The absurd consequence

66c   Consequentially, it would never perish.

There would be the absurd consequence that it (the mind) would never perish, because the cause for it to persist without perishing—the body—is permanently and stably present.

Others say:

66d "That's from a cause of perishing," you assert,

Well, the body does make the body persist, but that mind perishes from encountering a cause of perishing, you assert. To explain:

67a But there as well, the consequence is the same,

Even if you assert that, does the cause of perishing produce perishing that is a different object from itself, or perishing that is not a different object? In the first case:

Since that's not other than what perishes.
If other, it is just the cause of that.
What is the perishing that it has made?

The consequence is the same. In the second case, a cause of perishing would be unnecessary. Additionally:

67b And what would the cause of persistence do?

And what would the cause that makes the mind persist—the body— do to make the mind persist without perishing? It follows that it does nothing, because the cause of perishing makes the mind perish.
   Others say:

67cd "That makes it persist till it meets the cause
Of perishing."

You might say that without the cause of persistence, it would perish of its own essence before meeting the cause of perishing. Instead, the cause of persistence makes it persist until it meets the cause of perishing. To explain:

67d The nature of things is

68ab To perish. There is nothing to prevent this,[107]
So what would the cause of persistence do?

The mind by its very essence has the nature of perishing. This is present as the nature of things and there is nothing valid to disprove[108] this. For that reason, what does the cause of the mind's persistence—the body—do to make it persist without perishing? It follows it does not do anything. This is according to Devendrabuddhi.

(2) Rebutting criticism of this. This has two points: (a) The analogy is not tenable, and (b) How this refutes other things as well.

(a) The analogy is not tenable

Others say:

68cd   "For instance, like a support for water and
        So forth," you say.

You might say that just as a bowl, for instance, is a support for things such as water and so forth to persist without perishing, the body is also the support for the mind to persist without perishing. To explain:

68d   It is the same for this,

For this action of a bowl as a support for water to remain without perishing, all the consequences of the line "What is and what is not are not supported" are the same. How are they the same? you ask. If water and so forth have their own persistence, they do not need a support, but that which does not have persistence does not need anything as a support. For that reason, water is not supported by the bowl—it is the same.

Thus to teach that a bowl is not a support for the water to persist without perishing:

69a   As when things perish each and every instant,

A bowl is not the support for water to persist without perishing, because water and other such things arise and perish each and every instant. Thus it is not the support for water to persist without perishing.

However, it is temporarily the support for the water not to spill. To teach this:

69b–d   A thing's continuum is thus the cause
         Of it arising, hence that is the support.
         Otherwise it would not be logical.

70.   Because it prevents movement,[109] it is thus
         A support for water and so forth. But why
         Would qualities, universals, or else actions
         That do not move need a support?

A bowl is the cause for later instances in the continuum of the same kind of thing—water and so forth—to arise without spilling in this way, like the earlier instances of that continuum. For that reason, it is the support of water and so forth. Otherwise it would not be logical for a bowl and water to be the support and supported if it were not so that the continuum of water and so forth arose from the bowl. Therefore, because it (the bowl) prevents water from spilling down and produces a lack of falling, and because it (the bowl) is thus a support for water and so forth, it does not otherwise have any other action of moving or going. But why would qualities, universals, or else actions need a support to remain without perishing like water? They do not need one.

(b) How this refutes other things as well

71.   This disallows inherence and
         Causes that would have inherence
         As well as that a kind would dwell,
         Because there is not any support.

This logic that refutes the assertion that other objects that have no effect could be support or supported also dissallows the assertions that there is inherence that makes a relation between mind and body as supporter and supported; that for the body, the self would act as a cause that has inherence with mind; and that a kind would dwell in instances or that predicated features—other already established objects such as white and so forth—would dwell in blankets and so forth because it teaches that there is not any supporter or supported for other already established objects.[110]

(3) Summary

> 72a   If something else were to make a thing perish,

If you say that supported things such as the mind persist by their nature if they do not meet the cause of perishing, but meeting something else that is the cause of perishing makes supported things such as the mind perish, to explain:

> 72b–d   Then what would its cause of persistence do?
> If it still perishes without another,
> The causes of persistence have no power.

Then what would the body—its (the mind's) cause of persistence—do to make the mind persist? It follows that it does nothing, because if it (the mind) still perishes of its own nature without another object that is a cause of perishing, then the body asserted to be the cause of the mind's persistence would have no power to make the mind persist without perishing.

If you say that the reason is not proven, to explain:

> 73.   Everything with support would have persistence,
> And all that arises would have a support.
> Thus for that reason, no thing ever
> At any time would perish.

Everything with support such as mind and so forth would permanently have persistence until it encounters the cause of perishing, and all things that arise from a cause would have the support of a permanent substance that would make them persist without perishing. Thus for that reason, it would follow that no thing such as the mind and so forth would ever perish at any time until encountering the cause of perishing.

Additionally, do all things such as mind perish of their own nature or not? To teach that it would be contradictory in the first case:

> 74ab And if their character is that they perish
> By their own nature, what else makes them stay?

If the character of things such as the mind is that they perish by their own nature, then for that reason what other cause of persistence such as the body and so forth else makes them (things such as the mind) persist or stay? It follows that there is none. In the second case:

> 74cd But if their character is not to perish
> By their own nature, what else makes them stay?

If the character of the mind and so forth is not to perish by their own nature, then what other cause of persistence such as the body and so forth else makes them, things such as the mind, persist or stay? It follows that there is none.

v. Refuting in particular that intelligence and so forth are supported by the body. This has four points: (1) The logic of intelligence and so forth not being supported by the body, (2) The logic of desire and so forth not being supported by the body, (3) Explaining this with an analogy, and (4) Teaching that these two are supported by the mind.

(1) The logic of intelligence and so forth not being supported by the body

> 75. Without an increase or decrease of body,
> There can be an increase or a decrease
> In intelligence, et cetera, due to
> Distinctions in the action of the mind.

The body and intelligence are not substantial cause and substantial result, since without being entailed by an increase or decrease in the qualities of the body, there can be an increase or a decrease in intelligence, loving-kindness, compassion, and freedom from desire, or desire, hatred, delusion, and such due to distinctions in the action of the mind consciousness functioning as the substantial cause.

Devendrabuddhi and Śākyabuddhi both refute that the body is the substantial cause of intelligence and so forth, but Prajñākaragupta refutes that it is the dominant condition.[111]

If you say that the pervasion is indefinite, to explain:

> 76ab   Things that have support, such as the light
>   Of a lamp, et cetera, do not have this.

If something is not entailed or reverse entailed by the increase or decrease of the body, it is pervasively not the substantial result of the body. This is because things that have the support of a physical substantial cause such as the light of a lamp, shoots, shadows, et cetera, do not have have this entailment with the substantial cause of mind, which is not entailed by the increase or decrease of the body.

Others say:

> 76c   "From that as well, there are distinctions in this."

Taking nourishment and so forth makes the body increase, and from that as well it is seen that the distinctions in this (intelligence and so forth) increase. For that reason, intelligence and so forth are entailed and reverse entailed by the increase and decrease in the body, you say. To explain:

> 76d   Not so, since that does not affect the mind.

Since that (the body that is increased by taking nourishment) does not directly affect the mind that is supported by the body as a dominant condition, it does not directly produce intelligence and so forth by way of being the substantial cause. Well then, how is it? you ask. Taking nourishment and so forth directly affects the body and in this way affects intelligence and so forth indirectly only.

(2) The logic of desire and so forth not being supported by the body

Others say that desire arises from the body strengthening and aversion from it weakening, so intelligence and so forth also arise directly from the body. To explain:

> 77. Increases of desire and such from thriving
> And such are sometimes born from pleasure or pain.
> They're from the presence of internal objects—
> The balance of the elements and so forth.

Sometimes when the body is thriving and there is inappropriate attention, desire, hatred, and such arise, but they do not increase solely from the conditions of the body thriving, weakening, and such, because they are born directly from the feelings of pleasure or pain that arise in association with the mental consciousness. The feelings associated with the mental consciousness arise from the feelings associated with the body consciousness. Therefore they (the causes of desire or aversion—the pleasures and pains associated with sensory consciousnesses) arise from the presence of internal objects—distinctions of internal sensations such as the balance or imbalance of the elements and so forth—as the apprehended object.

To teach how this logic also refutes other propositions:

> 78. And this explains how loss of memory
> And such arise from fever and so forth,
> Because the mind born from distinctions of
> Internal objects makes the alteration.

This logic that explains how sensations of pleasure or pain arise by way of the object and not by way of the bodily support explains how loss of memory, stupefaction, distraction, and so forth arise from illness of fever, poisons, and so forth, not from the body functioning as the substantial cause. This is because the mind of the sense faculties born from the distinctions in touch of the internal apprehended objects due to disease, poisons, and so forth makes the mental mind change, and loss of consciousness and so forth arise from that alteration.

(3) Explaining this with an analogy

79.   As an analogy, it is just as
How certain types of individuals
On hearing or else seeing tigers or
Blood and such are stupefied and so forth.

As an analogy, it is just as when certain unstable kinds of individuals with cowardly mental continua are stupefied, become distraught, die, faint, get goosebumps and so forth upon hearing a tiger, hearing of the death of a child and so forth, or seeing blood or terrifying things. This does not arise from the tiger and so forth being the substantial cause. Instead it arises indirectly by way of taking it as the object. Similarly, memory loss and so forth arise from the substantial cause of the previous cognition, so they arise from fever and so forth functioning as an object, not functioning as a substantial cause. For that reason, the body is not the substantial cause of the mind.

(4) Teaching that these two are supported by the mind

80.   Therefore it won't arise without
The mind to whose formations it
Is definitely consequent.
Thus it's supported by the mind.

The body is not the substantial cause of the mind. Therefore it (the later mind that is definitely consequent to the formations of the preceding mind of the same kind) will not arise without that preceding mind as a substantial cause. For that reason, it is supported by the preceding mind functioning as the substantial cause; the body is not the substantial cause. This is according to Devendrabuddhi.

b. Refuting that mind and body are the same in substance. This has three points: i. The actual logic of the refutation, ii. Rebutting criticism about the manner of entering the place of birth, and iii. Merely not seeing them does not prove that past and future births do not exist.

i. The actual logic of the refutation

81.   Just as formations of listening and such,
Formed in the mind, at times are evident
In mind, these qualities would also be
In the body, as it is not separate.

Just as through the power of cultivating them, the qualities of listening and so forth—formations from earnestly pursuing listening, instructions in the crafts, and such, which are formed on the support of the mind—at times are evident in the mind, similarly these qualities of listening and the crafts would also be evident in the body, as it (the body) is not separate from the mind. This is according to Devendrabuddhi.

The *Ornament* says:

> Just as formations of listening preceded by. . . experience (the substantial cause), are not evident during periods of deep sleep but are evident. . . during waking periods, they would also be evident in the body. . . Just as qualities of the body such as darkness are observed by others, why would not the mental qualities of the crafts and so forth also be observed?[112]

ii. Rebutting criticism about the manner of entering the place of birth

Others say that if sentient beings came to the womb and so forth from another birth instead of arising from the great elements, it would not be logical for them to come to an unclean place, and neither would it be logical for Īśvara to send them against their will. To explain:

82.   Those who have attachment to a self
Are not led by another sentient being.
They embrace inferior places from the wish
To obtain happiness and avoid suffering.

It has been proven that those sentient beings who have attachment to a self are not led powerless by another sentient being such as Īśvara. Instead, due to the preceding attachment of wishing to obtain happiness and avoid suffering for themselves, they embrace inferior places such as the womb due to attachment. It is, for example, just as how wasps will take to unclean places or lustful people will embrace the corpse of a woman. This is according to Devendrabuddhi.

Prajñākaragupta says that it is the power of karma that those who are incited by lust perceive even inferior places erroneously and embrace them. For example, it is like a lustful man entering a prostitute's house.

To teach that craving alone is the cause for taking birth:

83.   Craving and the cognition that
    Misconstrues suffering are the bonds
    That cause rebirth. Whoever lacks them
    Is someone who will not be born.

The cognition that erroneously misconstrues inferior places such as the womb, which are suffering, as pleasurable and the craving that wants to avoid suffering and gain happiness bind one to the womb and are the causes of rebirth in the womb. Whoever lacks them, craving and the erroneous cognition, is someone who will not be born in a womb.

iii. Merely not seeing them does not prove that past and future births do not exist

84a   If going and coming are not seen,

The Cārvākas say that going from this life to the next and coming from the previous to the place of the womb are not seen, so therefore there is no being reborn from a between state to the place of the womb. To explain:

84a–d   it is
    Because the faculties are not acute
    That they cannot be seen, as for example
    Those with poor vision don't see wisps of smoke.

You Cārvākas, it is because your faculties are not acute that you do not see it, but that alone does not prove that there is no being reborn from the between state to the womb. As for example, that those people with poor vision do not see a wisp of smoke does not prove that there is no smoke. It is not proven that all beings do not see the between state, because it is seen by those of the same class and the pure divine eye. This is according to Prajñākaragupta.[113]

If you say that the between state is corporeal, so it should be obstructive, to explain:

> 85.   Although they are corporeal, they are subtle.
> Thus some are not obstructive to some things,
> Like water or like mercury with gold.
> It does not not exist from not being seen.

Although they are corporeal, they are subtle and limpid. Thus some bodies of the between state are, like bodies in dreams, not obstructive to some things. For example, it is just as water is not obstructed by clay that has not been fired or gold is not obstructed by mercury. Therefore, it (the between state) does not not exist because of not being seen by you Cārvākas. This is according to Prajñākaragupta.

c. Refuting that mind is a result of the body. This has two topics: i. Refuting that a whole could be a cause, and ii. Refuting that parts could be a cause.

i. Refuting that a whole could be a cause. This has two topics: (1) Refuting that the whole is single, and (2) Refuting criticism.

(1) Refuting that the whole is single

If the body is the cause of the mind, is that body a single element with no parts, or is it multiple with parts? If you say it is the first, to explain:

> 86.   If the arm or so forth were to move, then all
> Would move. Thus contradictory actions are
> Illogical in a single entity,
> So they'd be proven separate, au contraire.

It follows that for a person, the subject, if one limb such as the arm or so forth were to move, then all the limbs would move, because the moving limb and all the other limbs are a singular entity that lacks parts. This pervades because it is illogical that the contradictory actions of moving and not moving could be combined in a single entity. You might say that when the limb is moving, the whole is not, so there is no fault. So it follows that the whole, the subject, is proven to have a separate state from its limbs, because when the limbs are moving, the whole of the person on the contrary remains unmoving.

Additionally:

87.   If one were covered, all would then be covered,
        Or if not covered, all would be visible.
        If one changed color, all would change or else
        It would be realized that it did not change.

88a   Therefore conglomerations are not single.

For a person, the subject, it follows that if one of their limbs were covered by cloth, all the remaining limbs would then be covered by cloth, because the covered limb and the remaining limbs are a single entity that lacks parts. It is like the essence of a jug, for example.

If you reply that although the limb is covered, the whole is not covered so there is no fault, then it follows a person's face that is covered by cloth, the subject, would be fully visible to the eye consciousness that apprehends it just as it was previously when not covered, because the covered face and the uncovered whole are a single entity that lacks parts.

Additionally, for a person, the subject: it follows that if one of their limbs changed color, all the remaining limbs would change color, because the limb whose color changed and remaining limbs whose color did not change are a single entity that lacks parts. Or else it would follow that the portion that changed color also did not change color, because the limb whose color changed and the limbs whose color did not change are a single entity that lacks parts. This would be realized and known.

Therefore the whole—the individual's body—does not exist as a single substance that is a conglomeration of many parts, because it dwells in many substances such as moving, unmoving, and so forth that are exclusive of each other.

(2) Refuting criticism. This has two topics: (a) The dispute and (b) Teaching the response.

(a) The dispute

> 88b–d   You say, "It's multiple. Because there's no
> Distinction from before, because of atoms
> It therefore is not realized."

Some Vaiśeṣikas say it is the second case: a person's body is multiple and has parts. In that way, because just as the atoms previously before being assembled were not an object of a sensory consciousness, later when they are assembled as well they therefore are not realized by the sensory consciousnesses, because there is no distinction in them transcending the faculties and because they are atoms.

(b) Teaching the response. This has four topics: (i) A refutation from the reason not being established, (ii) A refutation from the pervasion being indeterminate, (iii) Refutation from nonobservation, and (iv) Rebutting criticism.

(i) A refutation from the reason not being established

> 88d   It's not proven

> 89ab   There's no distinction, because the distinguished
> Are objects of the faculties; atoms aren't.

The reasoning that there is no distinction between a person's body, a jug, or so forth and the unassembled atoms during the period when they transcend the object of a sensory consciousness is not proven, because the atoms that are distinguished from individual atoms in that they arise with the ability to produce sensory consciousness are the apprehended objects of the sensory faculties. Nor is the second reason (that they are atoms) proven, because the atoms during the period of being assembled in a body or so forth are not called by the convention *atoms*.[114]

To each that this logic also refutes other analogies:

> 89cd   And this disproves as well that they
> Would not obscure, et cetera.

This teaching that the second reason is unproven disproves as well such objections as thinking that if there were no whole that was a single substance, it would follow that they (people's bodies and so forth) would not obscure, obstruct, et cetera, because the individual atoms assembled are non-obscuring and unobstructive.[115] This is to teach the response that such reasons are not proven.

(ii) A refutation from the pervasion being indeterminate. This has two points: A. The actual refutation, and B. Rebutting the response.

A. The actual refutation

> 90.   How could a mix of gold and mercury
> Or so forth or hot rocks or such appear?
> How would the faculties and such, which lack
> Capacity individually, perceive?

How could a mixture of gold and mercury or water and milk and so forth, or alternately hot rocks, hot wood, or such that are mixed with atoms of fire—the subject—appear to the sensory consciousnesses? It follows they would not appear, because there is no single substance of a whole, as particles of incompatible kinds do not compose a substance. Similarly, how would the faculties, object, attention, and such, the subject, produce a cognition that perceives an object? It follows they would not, because there is no whole that is a single substance nor any distinction from those that are unassembled and lack the capacity to produce a sensory consciousness individually.

Others respond to this:

91a   If from conjunction,

Well then, from the faculties, object, and attention there arises a conjunction,[116] and the sensory consciousnesses arise from that, so there is no fault, you say. To explain:

91ab   here the consequence
          Is the same.

Here in this context as well where three conditions produce conjunction, the consequence that the faculties and so forth would not produce a sensory consciousness by way of producing a single conjunction is the same, because there is no difference in it being multiple and lacking substance.

B. Rebutting the response

91bc   And if you say that the conjunction
          Of gold and mercury appears,

Others might say that although the mixture of gold and mercury is not substantial, there is the conjunction that is atoms of different kinds meeting. That is what appears to the sense consciousness, they say. To explain:

91cd   without
          A visible support, how is it realized?

If the support for conjunction—the meeting of atoms of gold and mercury—is not visible by valid cognition, how is it (the conjunction that is the meeting of gold and mercury atoms) realized by a sensory consciousness? It follows that it is not realized.
    Additionally:

92ab   Conjunctions of form, flavor, and so forth
          Are contradictory.

It would be contradictory for drinks whose characteristic is that they are made from a combination of various substances such as juices, molasses, and such to be a conjunction of qualities such as a delicious flavor, a good visual form, smell, touch, and so forth, because those are qualities of a combination of many particles of different kinds that have no substance of a whole. You cannot agree, because terms such as "The drink looks nice" or "The drink is delicious" are seen in the world. This is according to Devendrabuddhi.

Others say about this:

> 92bc   If you assert
> It's attribution,

If you assert that the conjunction is contained in the one substance of the continuum of the flavor and form, so the conventions "the drink's flavor is delicious" or "its form is fine" are made from attributing conjunction to the atoms of flavor and so forth, to explain:

> 92cd   there'd be separate minds.
> How could one say a row is long?

The two flavors of a drink made from various substances and of milk would appear separately to the mind as an essence of flavor and as an attribution, because of the two, one is the essence of the flavor and one is an attribution. As an analogy, it is like spotted and brown cows. Additionally, how could one indicate a long row of birds in formation, designating it by saying it is a long row? It follows one could not, because there is no relation of inherence that is substantially the same as length. This is because length is not contained within any individual bird in which it would have to be contained. This is according to Devendrabuddhi.

*(iii) **Refutation from nonobservation.*** This has four topics: A. Giving the evidence, B. Rebutting that it is not proven, C. Refuting that declension would be impossible, and D. Rebutting that expressions of collection would be impossible.

A. Giving the evidence

93.　　　The essences of number, conjunction, action,
　　　　Et cetera, do not appear to mind
　　　　Separate from the essence of that which
　　　　Possesses them or separate from expressions.

Form and so forth; phenomena such as a number of one and so forth; conjunction with another object; action of lifting, placing, and so forth; declension, otherness, nonbeing, universals, et cetera do not exist as separate substances from the essence of a jug that possesses them or separate from expressions that signify the essence of a substance separately. This is because if they did exist as a separate substance, they would be able to appear, but their essences do not appear to the mind. This is according to Devendrabuddhi.

B. Rebutting that it is not proven. This has three points: 1. Though words and cognition are separate, the object is not definitely separate, 2. Refuting the response, and 3. Refuting that the number of qualities is another object.

1. Though words and cognition are separate, the object is not definitely separate

Others say that the number, conjunction, and so forth of a jug exist as separate substances from the jug, because words and cognition focus on them separately. To explain:

94.　　　Objects of words and of cognitions are
　　　　Projected by thoughts that follow separate things,
　　　　Like qualities and so forth for example,
　　　　Or like the perished and unborn.

The number and so forth of a jug do not appear as separate specific characteristics to words and cognitions that signify the jug's qualities, number, and so forth. This is because they take nominal objects that are projected by thoughts that follow separate things that are isolates, which are the reverse of separate bases for opposition.[117] It is just as cognitions and words such as *one, possess,* and so forth can refer to qualities of form and so forth, for example. Or it is just as how words and cognitions such as singular, dual, plural, and so forth can apply to that which does not exist from having perished or that which does not exist from not yet being born.[118] Therefore the pervasion is indeterminate.

2. Refuting the response

95a   If you propose that here it's nominal,

Others propose that saying a number of singular and so forth for the qualities of form and so forth here is merely applying it nominally as a nickname.[119] To explain:

95b–d   Why would you not assert, then, that the reason
          Because of which you posit that would be
          The cause of those for every entity?

Why would you not assert that the reason because of which you posit that expressions of number and so forth apply to qualities such as form and so forth nominally as nicknames would be the cause of those words and cognitions applying expressions of number and so forth to every entity such as a jug and so forth nominally as nicknames? It follows that you should. This is according to Devendrabuddhi.

Prajñākaragupta explains:

That they have been projected by beginningless thoughts would be the reason, but there is no time when they could be designated things.[120]

Others respond to this:

96.   "They are not nominal in every case.
        The separate features are called principal.
        If that from which it's separate should be absent,
        The separate would not have an object," you say.

In that case, they (expressions such as "the number of jugs") do not refer to all objects[121] nominally, because they can also refer to the object, the number of jugs, as an actual name for the features that are separate from the nickname as the principal. If it were otherwise, expressions such as "number" would refer to the number of jugs and so forth as the principal and to the number of qualities and so forth nominally. What would that be realized from? The expression that signifies the number of jugs and so forth would signify number and so forth separately for signified objects that are not separate, so expressions that signify them with separate expressions would have no object, you say. To explain:

97a–c   Though not an object with another reason,
         Expressions for white and such, number and such,
         As well as conjunction aren't synonymous.

Expressions that signify the number of jugs and so forth are not synonymous expressions, because though the signified object does not have a reason that is substantially other, expressions for the number, action and such of white and such, as well as conjunction are not synonymous expressions, as you yourself have asserted.

3. Refuting that the number of qualities is another object

97d   If those were to have other objects, too,

Others might say that those qualities of white and so forth have qualities that are other separate objects such as number and so forth or conjunction, so it is indeterminate. To explain:

98.   There'd be no distinction between qualities
         And substance. They'd be separate through distinctions
         In isolates, though they're not other objects,
         As in the phrases "not action" and "not substance."

If that were so, there would be no distinction between the characteristics of qualities and substance, because qualities would support other qualities such as number, conjunction, and so forth. Therefore although there is not any other signified object, expressions that signify the number and so forth of qualities such as form would engage word and thought separately, because they would engage word and thought separately through distinctions of their separate isolates. For example, it is just as how the phrases "not action" and "not substance" are asserted to engage by way of separate isolates.

C. Refuting that declension would be impossible

You might say that the number of jugs and so forth are substantially separate because the phrase "the number of jugs" can be declined, just as with the expression "Devadatta's pitcher." To explain:

> 99.   Also expressions signifying things
>   That indicate the number and so forth
>   As separate from that which possesses them
>   Make a distinction from the other features.

Expressions signifying predicated things that indicate the number of jugs and so forth as if they were separate from the jugs that possess them do not refer to the number of jugs and so forth by force of them being separate substances from the jugs. This is because the expression "the number of jugs" merely makes a distinction that excludes the other features of the jugs such as their color and so forth. Therefore expressions that signify the number of jugs and so forth do not indicate that the jugs and the number of jugs are separate substances but indicate that the isolates are separately signified.

> 100.   In certain cases, one might say to those
>   Who want to know just that, without implying
>   Anything else, "that which a finger possesses"
>   As if it were a separate predicate.

Expressions that signify the number of jugs and so forth indicate just the number of jugs and so forth without implying anything else—the other predicated features of the jug—as a mental object to those who want to know just the isolate of the number of jugs among the many features of the jugs such as their color and so forth. For that reason, the number and so forth of jugs is not indicated as separate in substance from the jugs, but is spoken of as if it were a predicate with a separate isolate. For example, in certain cases where one wants to signify merely the predicated feature of a finger's straightness, although the finger and that which it has are not separate substances, the expression "that which a finger possesses" can be used. This is according to both Devendrabuddhi and Prajñākaragupta.

For that reason, the only difference between expressions that signify predicates and expressions that signify subjects is whether or not they exclude other features. The signified are not separate in substance. To teach this:

101.　　"The finger that is possessed" designates
　　　　The selfsame object but it implies all,
　　　　So it is called a phrase that signifies
　　　　The subject. In this way the sign is made.

Expressions that signify predicates and those that signify subjects both comparably designate the selfsame signified object, but since it implies and signifies that it possesses all the features of the finger, the phrase "the finger that is possessed" is called a phrase that signifies the subject. For that reason, that which is signified by the two phrases "that which the finger possesses" and "the finger that is possessed" is not substantially separate, but in order to know in this way whether the signified's other features are thus excluded or not, the combination of signs is made. This is according to Devendrabuddhi.

D. Rebutting that expressions of collection would be impossible
Others might say that there may be no whole, but if the mere assembly of the parts such as flavor and so forth did not exist, then expressions such as "the jug's form" and so forth would not apply, just as the expression "the form's form" does not apply. To explain:

102.　　By eliminating distinctions of the power
　　　　Of form and so forth, the word *jug* refers
　　　　To the exclusion of that which is not
　　　　A cause of a comparable result.

The word that signifies jug is an expression that signifies a collection. The signified jug is a collection of atoms of the eight substances,[122] so the eight substances of the atoms of form and so forth within it producing the individual awarenesses that apprehend themselves is a result of the particular, whereas the combination of the atoms of the eight substances producing the ability to hold water is a result of the general.[123] Therefore by eliminating from being the signified the distinctions of the power of the atoms of eight substances of the jug's form and so forth to produce awareness that apprehends themselves, the word *jug* excludes that which, such as wood and so forth, is not a cause of making it hold water, which is the common result that is comparably entailed by the atoms of the eight substances. For that reason, the word that signifies a jug refers to that which is able to perform the function of holding water, the common result of the jug's atoms of the eight substances.

Therefore, though there is not a single whole, words that call the single result of a collection of many a "jug" are from the wish to signify a single capacity. To teach this:

> 103ab   For that reason, "the jug is form" is not
> An expression with a single referent.

The word *jug* excludes the jug's form as the signified. For that reason, the word that signifies the jug and the expression that signifies the jug's form are not expressions with a single, common signified referent.

(iv) Rebutting criticism

Others say that it is not tenable to say "not an expression with a single referent," because in relation to a jug's features, the word jug signifies a kind.[124]

> 103cd   Therefore this is the difference between
> Signification of kind and of collection.

There is the distinction that in relation to the expression "golden jug," the word "jug" shares a common signified, whereas in relation to the term "the jug's form," it does not share a common signified.

Therefore there is the difference of excluding or not excluding other features between being an expression that signifies kind in relation to a gold jug and being an expression that signifies collection in relation to a jug's form.

Here there are two types of expressions that signify collection: those that refer to many collections and those that refer to one. Those that refer to many are such as the words "jug" and "wood." Those that refer to one are such as the expression "Mount Vindhya" and so forth.[125]

Others might say that because a jug and the jug's form are not separate substances, the expression "the jug's form" would not signify the jug and its form separately. To explain:

> 104.   Saying "the form and so forth of a jug"
> Makes its universal into a part
> And indicates distinctions in its power.
> This proposition also describes others.

A jug and the jug's form are not substantially separate, but it is not contradictory for separate expressions to refer to them, because making the universal of the jug's eight substances—the jug—into a part or distinction and saying "the form of the jug" distinguishes the form of the jug that has the power to produce an eye consciousness that apprehends the form of a jug, which distinguishes it from the form of a pillar and then indicates it. This proposition of pure logic also describes others: in saying "the scent of sandalwood" as well, there is no sandalwood that is a separate substance from the scent, but the sandalwood and scent are indicated separately. This is according to Devendrabuddhi.

ii. Refuting that parts could be a cause. This has three topics: (a) Refuting by examining parts that are assembled and unassembled, (b) Refuting the response, and (c) Rebutting that it is comparable for ourselves.

(a) Refuting by examining parts that are assembled and unassembled

Since a single body is not the cause of mind, you who assert that the body is the cause of cognition must assert that the many parts of the body are the cause of the mind. If that is so, then either the assembly of multiple parts must be the cause, or any single one must be. If you say that it is the first—that all the parts of the body together are the cause of mind—to explain:

105ab   If the entirety should be the cause,
          Then not when even one part is removed.

If the entire assembly of the body were the cause of mind, when even any one part of the body is removed, such as the nose being cut off, then the mental consciousness would not arise in that individual's body, because the assembly of causes would be incomplete.

If you say it is the second case—that any one part is the cause of mind—to explain:

105cd   If each one had capacity as well,
          Then many would occur at the same time.

If each single atom in a person's body had the capacity to produce a mental consciousness as well, then many mental consciousnesses would occur simultaneously from each atom in the body at the same time, because the assembly of direct causes of multiple mental consciousnesses would be complete. This is according to both Devendrabuddhi and Prajñākaragupta.

(b) Refuting the response. This has two topics: (i) It is impossible for breath to be the cause of knowing, (ii) Even if possible, it would not be logically tenable.

(i) It is impossible for breath to be the cause of knowing. This has three points: A. It is untenable for multiple breaths to be the cause, B. It is untenable for a single breath to be the cause, and C. The untenability of the response.

A. It is untenable for multiple breaths to be the cause

Others say that there is no more than one breath. A single breath makes the mind know, so there will not be multiple simultaneous consciousnesses.[126] To explain:

106ab   As they are the same in being multiple,
          The out- and in-breaths aren't determinant.

As they are the same as the atoms that are part of a person's body in being multiple, the out-breath and in-breath do not definitely produce one mental consciousness.

B. It is untenable for a single breath to be the cause

Others say the reason is not proven, because breaths are only one single substance. To explain:

106cd   Even if single, many would manifest,
          Because their causes always would be present.

Even if breaths were one single substance, many earlier and later mental consciousnesses would simultaneously arise manifest in the present, because their (those mental consciousnesses') causes—the body, the inhalation and exhalation of breath, and so forth—would always be present.
   Others respond:

107a   If you say they are not the cause of many,

You might say that although the inhalation and exhalation and body themselves may be multiple, they can only produce a single consciousness at one time; they are not a cause that produces many simultaneously. To explain:

107b   Since there's no difference, not successive either.

The body and breath would not be the cause of many successive consciousnesses either, because there is no difference between the earlier and later in that which does not cause multiple simultaneous consciousnesses.
   Additionally, to teach it is inconclusive that the breath and body are not the cause of only a single consciousness:

107cd   Since multiple objects can be apprehended
            During one breath, no certainty from that.

Since it is seen that even during the duration of one breath, multiple consciousnesses that apprehend multiple objects arise, there is no certainty that only one single consciousness will arise from that duration of one breath.

Others say:

108a   If one mind were to cognize multiple,

You might say that it is not that successive consciousnesses know multiple objects over multiple moments, but that one mind cognizes multiple objects simultaneously, so there is no fault. To explain:

108b–d   That would be simultaneous because
            There's nothing contrary. It would not be
            Successive either, since there's no distinction.

That mind that successively apprehends multiple objects during one breath would apprehend multiple objects simultaneously, because there is nothing validly contrary to it apprehending them simultaneously. This is because it is a mind where there is no distinction in its nature earlier or later. If that were not so, it would not apprehend multiple objects successively either, since there is no distinction of earlier and later moments from the nature of the earlier. This is according to Devendrabuddhi.

C. The untenability of the response

Others say:

109.   If you should think that many instants
            Of respiration that are at times
            That aren't of their own kind should be
            The causes of suchlike cognitions,

Some think that in the permanent body, multiple substances arise sequentially, while the many earlier and later instants of respiration that are at times of not arising from previous instants of their own kind are the causes of suchlike cognitions arising in a sequence of earlier and later, so there is no fault of occurring simultaneously. To explain:

> 110ab   How could they be sequential if
>   They lack a cause to be sequential?

If they (the inhalation and exhalation) lack a cause to have a sequence of earlier and later, how could they arise sequentially? They would not. Others say:

> 110cd   If the cause is the previous instance of
>   Its own kind,

If you say the cause is the previous instance of its own kind, and the body is not the cause, to explain:

> 110d   then the first would not occur

> 111a   Because a similar cause does not exist.

If that were so,[127] then at first immediately after birth in the womb and so forth, breath would not occur anew, because the cause of that breath—a similar previous instance of its own kind—does not exist. If you say the reason is not established, a previous lifetime is proven, but if you agree, then it is proven that the breath is not the cause of the mind.

(ii) Even if possible, it would not be logically tenable. This has three points.

A. Refuting through the consequence that cognitions would arise simultaneously

> 111b–d   If so, they'd certainly be multiple
>   Because the breaths have separate locations.
>   Thus minds would simultaneously arise.

Even if it were so (to state the assertion) that breath were the cause of mind, because the breaths have separate locations of origin from which they arise, they would certainly be multiple, like a herd of livestock, for example.[128] Therefore because the direct cause—the breath—would be a simultaneously present multiple, thus multiple minds would simultaneously arise.

B. Refuting through the consequence that it would not arise if the breath were incomplete

> 112ab   And if though multiple, those were the causes
>   Of a single cognition at one time,

Others say that though inhalations and exhalations may be multiple, those assembled simultaneously at one time are all the cause of a single cognition.

> 112cd   If even one were absent, it would not
>   Arise, as when the breathing is weak and so forth.

At times when the breathing is weak, ceases, and so forth, if even one aspect of the breath were absent, it (consciousness) would not arise, because the entire assembly of all the aspects of breath is its cause. This is according to Prajñākaragupta.

C. Refuting through the consequence that there would be a distinction in cognitions

> 113a   Supposing they were causes as they are,

Supposing others say that they (heavy, weak, long, and so forth breaths) are causes of consciousness just as they are. To explain:

> 113b–d   There'd be a distinction in cognition, too.
>   It is not a result of that if it
>   Does not differ from differences in that.

There would be a distinction in cognition, too, in that it would be clearer when a person's breath became stronger and unclear when there was no breathing, because consciousness is a direct result of breath. Consequentially, it (consciousness) is not a direct result of that breath, because it (consciousness) does not become different by increasing and decreasing from differences in that breath increasing and decreasing. This is according to Devendrabuddhi.

(c) Rebutting that it is comparable for ourselves

Others might say that we also assert that later cognitions arise from earlier ones, so the consequence that many cognitions would appear simultaneously also applies to us. To explain:

114.   The power of consciousness is ascertained,
        So one is the cause of one. Consciousness lacks
        The ability to cling to other objects,
        Because it does not grasp another object.

The power of earlier consciousnesses to successively produce later consciousnesses has been distinctly ascertained, so the causes for multiple to arise simultaneously are not complete. For that reason, the one single previous consciousness is the cause of one single later consciousness of a similar class. Therefore, multiple consciousnesses of a comparable class do not arise simultaneously. The power of the earlier consciousness to produce the later consciousness is distinctly ascertained, because if a consciousness lacks the ability to apprehend blue by clinging to another separate object, it does not grasp another blue object. This is according to Devendrabuddhi.

Others respond:

115a–c   And if the mind were to arise one time
          From the body and afterward to definitely
          Arise from its own kind,

You might say that at first in the womb and so forth, the mental mind arises one time from the body, and afterward later ones definitely arise from earlier ones of their own kind, so multiple minds do not arise at the same time and there is no fault. To explain:

115cd   why is it that
                 The body's capability would cease?

Because the entity of the body is permanent and has the capacity to produce multiple simultaneous mental cognitions at first in the womb and so forth, later why is it that its capability to produce multiple mental cognitions would cease? It would not.

d. Refuting criticism. This has two topics: i. The criticism, and ii. The answer.

i. The criticism

116a–c   If you should say, "It is not the support,
            And for that reason when the body ceases
            The mind alone persists,"

Others say, "In your tradition, the body is not the mind's support, so when the body with the faculties perishes and ceases at the time of death, since it (the body) is not the support of the mind, after death, the mind alone will persist independent of the body."

ii. The answer. This has four points: (1) Refuting it by analyzing the three realms, (2) Rebutting criticism about later cognitions linking rebirth, (3) Presenting the proof that later faculties link rebirth, and (4) Refuting that they are born from causes that are other objects.

(1) Refuting it by analyzing the three realms

Is that in the two realms of Desire and Form or in the Formless? If you say the former, to explain:

116cd   if it is from
                 Acquiring the state of being a cause of that,

117ab   The cause for the continuum of mind
            To stay does not become an element.

The mind of a dying person who will be reborn in the realms of Desire or Form does not abide independent of a body after death, because the prior karma that is the cooperating cause for the continuum of mind to stay in a body acquires the state of being a cause of its result (the next body) becoming a cooperating condition. If it does not become the element of a cooperating condition that produces the body of the next lifetime, the mind alone will persist, as for example with living beings who are born in the Formless realm. Therefore Devendrabuddhi says:

> When because of the last body linking rebirth to the next body, the mind becomes the cooperating cause. Since they cooperate at that time, they coexist. In this way there is no contradiction.[129]

Well then, what is the substantial cause of the body in the next world? To explain:

117cd   The five sense bases of this lifetime are
            The causes that produce another body.

The five sense bases—the five faculties of the eyes and so forth—at the time of death in this lifetime are the substantial causes that produce another (the next) body.[130] Therefore, when one dies in Desire or Form and migrates to Formless and then once again takes birth in Desire or Form, the previous faculties from Desire and Form are the cause, though the actual substantial cause is the seed of the faculties present in the mind of Formless.

(2) Rebutting criticism about later cognitions linking rebirth

Others say that a person's mind at the time of death is not the cooperating condition of the next body and his body is not the substantial cause of the next body because it is not observed to be so. To explain:

118.   In denying that things are its elements
         Or its causation, that they are not observed
         Does not bring certitude, as was explained,
         And faculties and such are inconclusive.

In denying that the mind of a person at the time of death is a thing that is a cooperating element of it (the body of the next birth) or that their body is the substantial cause of the body of the next birth, merely stating as evidence that those are not observed as such is not correct evidence that would bring certitude, as was explained thoroughly in the line, "It does not not exist from not being seen."[131] Additionally, giving reasons such as that the body of a person at death is not the substantial cause of the next body because it is a faculty or because it has hands, or that the mind is not the cooperating condition of the next body because it is mind and other such reasons are not correct reasons, because they are inconclusive reasons that leave doubt about the pervasion they should prove.

(3) Presenting the proof that later faculties link rebirth

119ab   It has been seen that earlier faculties
          Have the capacity for their own kind.

The faculties of a person at the time of death, the subject, are able, if nothing prevents them, to produce later faculties because they are faculties. For example, just as it is it is validly seen that earlier faculties of the eye and so forth in this life have the capacities to benefit subsequent faculties of their own same kind, it is the same here as well.

Others say that the faculties do not have separate natures, so earlier faculties are not causes of later ones, and for that reason, the analogy is not established in the subject. To explain:

119cd   Since change is seen, it is established that
          The subsequent ones will arise as well.

Since it is seen that later faculties change as entailed or reverse entailed by the clarity or haziness of earlier faculties, it is validly established that the subsequent faculties will arise from earlier faculties as well. Therefore, it is not so that the analogy is not established in the subject.

(4) Refuting that they are born from causes that are other objects

120a   If they were to arise from the body,

Others say that they, the five faculties of the eye and so forth in this life, arise from the body, not from previous instances of their own kind. To explain:

120b   The consequence would be as before.

A deceased body would also have faculties, because the consequence would be the same fault as before in the line "Because their causes always would be present."[132]
Others say:

120c   If from the mind,

If you say that these present faculties arise from the mind, so there is no fault, to explain:

120cd   another body
          Would also arise from this same.

The five faculties of another body—that of the next life—would also arise from this same mind, because the five faculties of this life arise from the mind.
Therefore it is proven that the body is not the substantial cause of the mind. To teach this:

121.   Thus it cannot be not so that since the cause
        Is absent, all final cognitions do not link,
        And for that reason we assert
        That proofs like that are inconclusive.

The body is not the substantial cause of the mind. Therefore in saying "All minds at the time of death of ordinary individuals and those asserted to be arhats, the subject, do not link to later awareness, because the cause of linking is absent," the reason is not established, and we assert that proofs like that and "because it is a mind at the time of death" are inconclusive reasons. Thus, not all the final cognitions at the time of death of ordinary individuals and arhats in this life do not link to the next cognition. For that reason, the next world is proven to exist.

(ii) Refuting the argument that even with cultivation, omniscience would be impossible. This has three topics: A. Presenting the criticism, B. Refuting it, and C. Responding to rebuttals of that.

A. Presenting the criticism

122.   If you should say, "Though there may be
         Distinctions due to cultivation,
         It cannot transcend its own nature,
         Like jumping or else heating water,"

Others say that it is not tenable to state, "The means is compassion. That's from cultivation."[133] The reason is that there may be slight distinctions of improvement due to cultivating compassion and so forth, but it (compassion) cannot transcend its own nature to become the essence of omniscience and so forth. As an analogy, people who train well in jumping may well have trained in jumping, and it is possible they might go slightly further, but they cannot jump an earshot, a league, or so forth.[134] Or no matter how much one heats water, its heat does not increase infinitely and it will not catch fire.

B. Refuting it. This has three points: 1. The reason why jumping and the heat of water do not increase infinitely, 2. The reason those are not analogous to love and so forth, and 3. The reason love and so forth especially increase.

1. The reason why jumping and the heat of water do not increase infinitely

123.   Once done, if doing it again depends
         On effort or if the support's not stable,
         Then the distinctions will not multiply.
         If that is so, their natures aren't like that

124.   Because the abilities to benefit those
         Do not have the capacity to effect
         Later distinctions, because the support
         Does not persist in perpetuity,

125ab   And since though they might increase, the distinctions
         Are not the nature.

If whatever one cultivates such as jumping and so forth does not depend upon physical effort, it would be possible for it to increase infinitely. However, jumping again depends on physical effort. Or if the support—the body—is not stable, though one might practice jumping and so forth, the distinctions will not multiply infinitely. If that is so, their natures are not like that of compassion and so forth, which grow stronger and stronger as one cultivates them. This is because the abilities to benefit those (jumping and heating water) do not have the capacity to effect an infinite increase in later distinctions of jumping and so forth without depending upon the body that has been trained. It is also because they both depend upon efforts of the trained body. In particular, it is because the supports for jumping and heating—the body and water—do not persist in perpetuity but instead will be depleted. It is also because although the distinctions might increase somewhat from jumping or heating water, it is not their nature to increase infinitely.

2. The reason those are not analogous to love and so forth

125b–d   Whereas once they're made,
         If they do not depend on further effort,
         Other efforts will create distinctions.

Whereas once cultivation has made distinctions, if they do not depend upon further repeated effort to arise again and are supporter and supported, other later efforts will create distinctions, while jumping and heating water are not like that.

126.   Like fire and such with wood, like mercury,
        Like gold and such, compassion in the mind
        And so forth that arise from cultivation
        Naturally engage upon their own.

For that reason, later instances of compassion, joy, equanimity, and so forth in the mind arise stronger than previous instances of their own kind due to thorough cultivation. This is because after they have been cultivated, they naturally engage upon their own from just the previous cultivation without depending on physical effort, and they grow stronger and stronger. As an analogy, unless there is something to prevent it, fire that burns wood and such naturally engages on its own and burns further without relying on effort until the wood has been consumed. It is like mercury and gold, copper, and such that have been smelted in a closed earthen crucible: their qualities of refinement that have the character of purity do not depend upon a second smelting but naturally engage on their own. This is according to Devendrabuddhi.

3. The reason love and so forth especially increase

127.   Therefore the quality that's born
        Of those arises as its nature,
        Thus subsequent and subsequent
        Efforts produce distinctions.

When it has been cultivated, a quality of the mind such as compassion or so forth does not depend on effort, and its support is stable. Therefore, it is born of the cultivation of those earlier instances of its own kind; it is a quality that arises as the nature of the mind and naturally engages on its own. Thus subsequent and subsequent efforts produce distinctions from earlier ones until the culmination is reached.

To correlate that to the thesis in question:

128.   Because those minds of compassion and so forth
            Multiply out of the preceding seeds
            Of instances of a homogeneous kind,
            If cultivated, where would they stay still?

Because compassion and so forth are cultivated and multiply out of the preceding seeds of instances of their homogeneous kind, for that reason if those minds of compassion and so forth are not deprived of cultivation and there are no hindrances, where—at what limit—would they stay still? They would increase without any limit.

To teach that for that reason jumping is not like that:

129.   But jumping does not come in that same way
            From jumping—strength and exertion are its causes.
            As there's a limit to their capacity,
            Jumping is inherently limited.

Subsequent jumping does not arise from previous instances of its own kind— jumping itself—and increase infinitely in that same way as compassion and so forth, where the later compassion and so forth arise because of previous instances of their own kind. The substantial causes of jumping are the strength and exertion of a person's body, which have a limit to their capacity. For that reason, jumping inherently has a defined limit.

C. Responding to rebuttals of that

Others say that if jumping arises from physical strength and exertion instead of previous instances of its own kind, why wouldn't a person jump as far at the earlier time when they have not trained as at the later time when they have trained, because they also had the strength earlier?

To respond to this:

130.   At first they do not jump as later since
            The body has contrary qualities.
            Once effort gradually eliminates
            Contrarieties, they stay within their strength.

At the very first, people who train in jumping do not jump as they do later during the period when they have trained in jumping, because phlegm and so forth have made the body heavy, which is contrary to lightness. Later, the effort of training in jumping gradually eliminates the contrary bodily qualities of phlegm and so forth. Once the body has no heaviness, they can jump as far as they have the strength to and stay within that, but they cannot jump any further. This is according to both Devendrabuddhi and Prajñākaragupta.

Others say that if compassion and so forth were to increase infinitely by force of cultivation, all beings would have compassion and so forth. To explain:

131.   Compassion rises out of its own seeds.
         If not impeded by contrary factors
         Originating from seeds of their own,
         The mind will become that in character.

132.   And thus the previous cultivation is
         The root of the acuity of further
         Qualities of mind such as compassion,
         Detachment, intelligence, et cetera.

Compassion and so forth, which arise out of their own seeds—previous instances of their own kind—can increase without limit through power of cultivation. However, it is not pervasively so that compassion and so forth increase limitlessly in all sentient beings. It is possible that the favorable condition—continual cultivation—be absent and that the impediments—the contrary factors of hatred and so forth—would prevent it. If there is no impediment by the contrary factors of hatred and so forth, which originate from their own seeds (inappropriate attention and so forth), and the favorable condition of cultivation is not lacking, the mind will become that (compassion and so forth) in character.

Thus the previous cultivation of compassion and so forth is the root or cause for the further later distinctions of the qualities of mind—great compassion, detachment, the intelligence that discerns phenomena, and additionally other mental qualities such joy, equanimity, et cetera—to grow more acute and clearer. Cultivation creates only the clarity; it is not the cause of their arising. This is according to both

Devendrabuddhi and Prajñākaragupta. Therefore, beings have had compassion and so forth since beginningless time, but they have not cultivated it and thus have not been able to increase it limitlessly.

To teach that therefore it is necessary to cultivate the favorable conditions:

> 133ab   A compassionate nature is from cultivation
> As with detachment, desire, and disgust.

Thus as explained, it is from cultivating compassion and so forth that one's nature becomes the great compassion that wishes to fully protect sentient beings from terrible suffering. As analogies, when the mind achieves liberation, one achieves detachment; persons who are thoroughly habituated to desire naturally engage in desire; and individuals who despise the unclean achieve disgust for filth by force of habituation.

ii. The explanation of the teacher, the perfect training. This has three topics: (1) How the teacher arises from compassion, (2) The actual explanation of the teacher, which arises from compassion, and (3) The explanation of why this is called the "teacher."

(1) How the teacher arises from compassion

> 133cd   To drive away suffering, the compassionate
> Apply themselves to training in the methods.[135]

> 134ab   If what is born from method and its cause
> Are hidden, it is difficult to explain it.

Bodhisattvas, who have a compassionate character that has been naturally present since the causal phase, seek to pacify the suffering of other sentient beings. Thus to drive away others' suffering, they apply themselves to cultivating the training in the method to completely pacify suffering, directly realizing the four truths. This is because they wish to unerringly teach those methods that are congruent with the pacification of their own suffering to others. The pervasion is not indeterminate, because for people who engage in the benefit of others, if that which is born from the method (the truth of cessation) and its cause (the methods of the truth of the path) are hidden and not made manifest to oneself, it would remain difficult to explain it (the path) to other students.

(2) The actual explanation of the teacher, which arises from compassion. This has two points: (a) The manner of meditating on the four truths, and (b) The manner in which clear appearances arise from cultivation of that.

(a) The manner of meditating on the four truths

> 134cd   They investigate through scripture and through logic
>   And analyze the cause of suffering,

> 135.   Its nature of impermanence and so forth
>   By way of the attributes of suffering,
>   Because they see that if the cause remains,
>   There's no elimination of the result.

The method to realize the four truths is to examine and investigate through the intelligence born of listening that follows upon scripture, the intelligence of contemplation that follows upon logic, and the intelligence born of meditation that follows upon both. With this, one analyzes whether that suffering has a cause or not; if there is a cause, what its nature is—whether it is permanent or impermanent; what the cause's characteristics are; what makes it increase; and so forth in order to comprehend that the attributes of that suffering itself are impermanent—occasionally arising, increasing, waning and so forth. This is logical because they see and know that if the cause—the truth of origin—remains in this way without being destroyed, there is no method to eliminate the result, suffering.

Therefore, in order to teach that it is logical for those who wish to eliminate the cause of suffering to meditate on its antidote, the path:

> 136.   In order to eliminate its cause,
>   They examine what is contrary to it.

> From realizing the essence of the cause,
> Its contrary is recognized as well.

In order to eliminate its (suffering's) cause, people who meditate on the methods to abandon the origin—the cause of suffering—examine the truth of the path that is contrary to it (the origin). Then the antidotes—the truth of the path—that are the contrary of the origin that is the cause of suffering will be recognized as well, because they have fully realized the essence of the origin, the cause of suffering. It is just as how one who realizes the essence of an illness' cause will also know the medicine that is its remedy.

If you ask what are the causes of the suffering whose characteristic is birth and what dharma is the antidote that is exclusive of that, to explain:

> 137.   The cause is the attachment formed by clinging
> To me and mine whose sphere of experience
> Is the composite. What opposes that
> Is seeing selflessness, exclusive of it.

The cause of suffering is formed by clinging and being attached to me and mine; fixation through craving whose sphere of experience is me and mine is the cause of suffering. The antidote which opposes that clinging to me and mine is the intelligence of directly seeing selflessness, because its focus and aspects are exclusive of it and thus can eliminate it.

(b) The manner in which clear appearances arise from cultivation of that

> 138a–d   From a long time of cultivation
> In many ways with many methods,
> The faults and qualities in them
> Have become evident,

Great beings cultivate for a long time—aeons and so forth—and in many ways the intelligence that realizes selflessness and has the aspect of emptiness with many various methods. From this, the faults to be eliminated and the qualities that are antidotes will become evident to them, the meditators.[136]

Therefore the distinction between the great sages and the listeners and self-buddhas in the extent of their benefit to others is from whether they have eliminated the imprints of the cause or not. To teach this:

138d   and thus

139.   Because their minds are clear, they have abandoned
             The cause's imprints. This is the distinction
             Between great sages, who work for others' weal,
             And the rhinoceroses and so forth.

From the power of meditating for a long time on many methods, they have taken up the antidotes and given up the discards. Thus by force of cultivating many methods, it is very clear in their (the great sages') minds what is to be done and what is to be given up. Because of this, they have abandoned the origin, the cause of suffering, along with its imprints. Thus the great sages are preceded by the excellent intent and training during the phase of the cause, and in this way they work for the vast weal of others and have abandoned the imprints. The rhinoceros-like self-buddhas,[137] listener arhats, and so forth, are not like that, so this is the distinction between them.

(3) The explanation of why this is called the "teacher"

140.   Because it has that purpose, cultivating
             The means itself is said to be the teacher.
             They happen first, before accomplishment,
             And so the two are described as the cause.

Because it has that purpose of being the cause of the perfect teacher in the phase of the result, cultivating the means during the phase of the perfect training itself is said to be the teacher in the *Compendium's* verse of homage, because the name of the result is given to the cause. The reason for this designation is that the distinctive name of the achievement itself indicates the methods for becoming able to teach sentient beings.

For that reason, they (the perfect intent of the wish to benefit beings and the perfect training of the teacher) happen first, before the accomplishment of sugatahood, preceding the result of the sugata which arises from them, and so the two (the perfect intent and training) are described as the cause of the sugata and protector. The actual teacher is not the cause of sugatahood. For that reason, cultivating the methods itself, not anything else, is the teacher. This is according to both Devendrabuddhi and Prajñākaragupta.

The general discussion of the perfect training will be explained in detail below in the section on the four truths, so it should be known from that.

b. The detailed explanation of the perfect result. This has two topics: i. The explanation of the perfect benefit for oneself, the sugata, and ii. The explanation of the perfect benefit for others, the protector.

i. The explanation of the perfect benefit for oneself, the sugata. This has two topics: (1) General discussion, and (2) The meaning of the text.

(1) General discussion. This has two points: (a) What the sugata has abandoned, and (b) Tangentially, what the listener and self-buddha arhats have abandoned.

(a) What the sugata has abandoned

The buddhas' truth of cessation is the ultimate result of removal[138] through the path of realizing the twofold selflessness. It is superior to the detachment of the worldly, the learners, and the nonlearners[139] through three distinctions. What are the three distinctions? you ask. Excellent abandonment, irreversible abandonment, and complete abandonment.

Why is it excellent abandonment? you ask. Because it is worthy of praise by the exalted, it is excellent abandonment. This is because it is abandonment that does not provide the support for suffering to arise in another existence because it is done through the antidote, the intelligence that realizes selflessness, and because that is the antidote for existence. The *Commentary* says:

> Three qualities of abandoning the cause
> Are sugatahood. As it is not a support
> For suffering, it is excellent. It comes
> From seeing selflessness and from the training.[140]

The worldly abandonment that is detachment from lower levels through worldly paths is not excellent abandonment, because it functions as a support for the arising of suffering in other existences and thus is not abandonment worthy of praise by the exalted. Why is it the support for suffering? you ask. It is because such an abandonment is the result of a path that views higher levels as peaceful and lower levels as coarse, and such paths are the cause for birth in the higher levels of Form and Formless. Those levels as well variously have the suffering of change and the suffering of formation. As it is said:

> . . . Are suffering without exception
> Because they have three sufferings.[141]

Why is it irreversible abandonment? you ask. It is because it has abandoned the cause of reversal, all of the seeds of the view of self. As it is said:

> He has abandoned the seeds of the self view,
> And thus he has gone irreversibly.[142]

Non-Buddhist yogis and noble learners such as once-returners do not have irreversible abandonment of their discards because they have not destroyed the seeds of the view of the self, so it is possible for them to regress from their abandonment. It is thus: though they may have temporarily abandoned the afflictions which cause rebirth on those levels, they will once again in some way take birth on those levels. Though they have abandoned some aspects of the afflicted, those will re-arise in their beings. Such is called reversible abandonment. As it is said:

Reversibility is said to be
The rearising of the faults and birth.[143]

For that reason, non-Buddhist yogis' abandonment is reversible. They achieve the samadhis up through the Peak of Existence and temporarily abandon the afflictions up through the sense base of Nothingness, but by power of conditions, they either regress from those samadhis or, even if they do not regress for a time, the propulsion of that unmoving karma is exhausted. Then, just like an arrow shot into the sky whose momentum is exhausted, they will once again take rebirth in the migrations down to the Incessant Hell. This is because they lack the realization of selflessness, so they have not even abandoned the manifest view of the self. As it is said in *In Praise of Superiority*:

Those people blinded by ignorance
Who turn away from your Dharma
May go up to the Peak of Existence,
But suffering recurs; existence is created.[144]

The abandonment of learner once-returners and nonreturners is also reversible, because they have not abandoned the instinctive view of the self,[145] so based on that, it is possible that the afflictions they have abandoned will arise again and they will regress from the result. There is no regression from the result of the stream-enterer, because that is distinguished by the abandonment of the discards of seeing, and all the discards of seeing are rooted in the imaginary view of the self[146] and thus eradicated when the path of seeing is achieved.

The position of the Great Exposition that there is also regression from the result of arhat as well is not tenable, because if that were so, their minds would not be able to be stable toward liberation, and since the arhats have no view of the self, there is no cause for the afflictions to arise. It is illogical to regress from the result of arhat without the afflictions arising.

Why is it complete abandonment? you ask. From cultivating the path for innumerable aeons, there is the perfect culmination of the clarity of the mind toward faults and qualities of the discards and antidotes.

Thus all of the negativities of the three gates without exception have been abandoned. As it is said:

> From a long time of cultivation
> In many ways with many methods,
> The faults and qualities in them
> Have become evident. . .[147]

And:

> All are abandoned through the cultivation.[148]

According to the *Treasury*, "The swiftest in three lives are freed"[149] and "Following / One hundred aeons, a rhino appears."[150] As these say, the listeners and self-buddhas do not meditate for more than three life-times or one hundred aeons. Thus their minds are not clear about the subtlest of subtle faults of the discards or the subtlest of subtle qualities of the antidotes. Therefore they are on their own unable to unerringly teach wisdom to others. As is said:

> Though free of the afflictions and disease. . .
> . . . unclarity in teaching the path remains.[151]

(b) Tangentially, what the listener and self-buddha arhats have abandoned

This is abandonment that eliminates the seeds of the afflicted through supramundane intelligence. There are two types: nirvana with the remainder of the aggregates and nirvana without remainder. The first is the analytic cessation[152] distinguished by the destruction of just the origin that is afflictions through the antidotes.[153] The second is ana-lytic cessation distinguished by the cessation of everything defiled. The vajra-like samadhi abandons the entire origin that is afflictions in a manner that it will not arise again. All other defiled dharmas are abandoned by way of being free of the desire of interest, but not in the manner of not arising again, because as long the arhats have not discarded the formations of life, they are connected to the aggregates of suffering. Once they have discarded the formations of life, the eye and everything else defiled naturally cease at that time, like a fire whose fuel is exhausted, and they achieve the appellation of "passing into the complete nirvana without any remainder of the aggregates." In this way, nirvana with remainder is distinguished by the elimination by the antidote of the origin that is afflictions, and nirvana without remainder is distinguished by the cessation of everything defiled without exception. Therefore the abandonments of the listeners and self-buddhas are the results of removal achieved by the paths that realize merely the selflessness of the individual and the nonexistence of the apprehended in addition to that.[154]

(2) The meaning of the text. This has two topics: (a) The actual sugata, and (b) Refuting criticism.

(a) The actual sugata. This has two topics: (i) Overview and (ii) Detailed explanation.

(i) Overview

> 141ab Three qualities of abandoning the cause
> Are sugatahood.

In the word *sugata*, the syllable *su-* means excellent, and is explained as either abandonment or realization. Of these two, here it is explained in terms of abandonment. Because the Sage, the Bhagavan Buddha, has the three qualities of excellently abandoning the cause of suffering (clinging to self and mine) along with its imprints; irreversibly abandoning it; and completely abandoning it, he is the sugata.

(ii) Detailed explanation. This has three points: A. Excellently gone, B. Irreversibly gone, and C. Completely gone.

A. Excellently gone

141b–d   As it is not a support
For suffering, it is excellent. It comes
From seeing selflessness and from the training.

Here, as the sugata is not a support for suffering and has abandoned and extinguished it, he has gone excellently. For that reason, not being a support for the suffering of taking rebirth in existence is the abandonment of suffering from directly seeing selflessness—the antidote for clinging to a self and mine—and from the training of cultivation.

B. Irreversibly gone

142.   Reversibility is said to be
The rearising of the faults and birth.
He has abandoned the seeds of the self view,
And thus he has gone irreversibly

143a   Since that and truth have separate characters.

Ordinary individuals and so forth have not abandoned the seeds of the view of the self. Thus if there are both birth—the origin of karma—and the origin[155] of the faults of the afflictions such as desire and so forth, that which has been abandoned is said to be reversible. The Bhagavan Buddha has abandoned the seeds of the view of the self, and thus he has gone irreversibly. Why is that? you ask. Since that wisdom that realizes selflessness realizes without error the object, the truth—the meaning of selflessness—its character is to engage aspects and focuses that are separate from and exclusive of the view of the self. Clinging to a self is the opposite of that.

C. Completely gone

143b–d   Though free of the afflictions and disease,
Unskillfulness of body, speech, and mind
And unclarity in teaching the path remain.

144a   All are abandoned through the cultivation.

Noble listeners and self-buddhas have not abandoned all the unskill-fulness of body, speech, and mind, so they skip as they walk with their bodies, chitchat pointlessly with their speech, or do not rest their minds always in equipoise, and thus have neutral mind states. Thus there remain some remnants of the discards. Though that is so, such unskillfulness is not motivated by the afflictions because they are free of the afflictions of desire and so forth as well as afflicted ignorance. As they are free of those, they have the quality of lacking the capac-ity to ever again produce the disease of samsara, suffering. Therefore although they have no afflictions nor anything afflicted, some discards do remain. Because they have not abandoned unafflicted ignorance, their minds are unclear in teaching the path without error, since they have not cultivated it for a long time and in many ways.

The Sugatas have come to the culmination of thorough cultivation of the path that directly sees the two selflessnesses, so they have aban-doned all of the stains of the discards.

(b) Refuting criticism. This has two points: (i) The criticism, and (ii) The response.

(i) The criticism

> 144bc   Some say he has not exhausted all the faults
> Because he speaks and so forth.

Some Jaiminīyas and others say, "Because your Bhagavan speaks and has cognition and so forth, he has not exhausted all the faults. There-fore how can his abandonment be complete?"

(ii) The response

> 144cd   This sows doubt
> About the reversal and is thus mistaken.

Proving the Bhagavan has not exhausted all the faults because of the reason that he speaks sows doubt about the mode of the reversal by merely being not exclusive of the similar class. For that reason, it is thus mistaken evidence.

Thus to examine why they would say complete abandonment is impossible:

145. They think the faults are inexhaustible
      Because they're permanent or else because
      There are no methods or else it may be
      Because he has no knowledge of the methods.

They think and assert that the faults of desire and so forth are solely. inexhaustible because they (the faults) are permanent, because there are no methods to abandon them, or else because even though there may be methods to abandon them, he has no knowledge of those methods. To teach that any of these cases is illogical:

146. They have a cause. The cultivation of
      The cause's antidote extinguishes them.
      His understanding the nature of the cause
      Establishes that he knows that as well.

Because they (the faults of desire and so forth) have a cause that produces them, they are proven not to be permanent. It is also not so that there is no method to abandon them, since cultivating the intelligence that realizes selflessness—the antidote of the cause, which is the fault of clinging to a self and mine—extinguishes all of them (the faults). His understanding that the nature of the cause of all faults is the twofold clinging to a self and mine establishes that he knows that (the method to eliminate them) as well.

ii. The explanation of the perfect benefit for others, the protector

147. The protector teaches the path he has seen.
      He tells no falsehoods as that would be fruitless.
      Because he is compassionate, all the efforts
      He undertakes are for the sake of others.

148a   Thus he is valid.

The sugata, the Bhagavan Buddha, acts as the protector for sentient beings from the suffering of samsara because he unerringly teaches others the very methods or path to pacify suffering just as he himself has seen them. As teaching a wrong path would be fruitless or pointless, he tells no falsehoods to deceive sentient beings. This is because there is no cause for him to teach the path incorrectly as he has abandoned all the faults that are causes for teaching the path wrongly and any lack of knowledge about the object of the path.

You might think that he may know, but he would deceive since he has no love. The sugata does not have any deceptiveness either, because he has great compassion for all sentient beings. Previously during the period he was on the path of learning, all the efforts he undertook toward the path and the methods for extinguishing the afflictions were for the sake of others; they were done to benefit sentient beings.

Because he teaches others unerringly the path to liberation he himself has seen and internalized, the sugata is the protector of all sentient beings. Thus it is logical that he is valid.

B. Explaining the homage in reverse order. This has five topics: 1. Explaining the perfect benefit for others, the protector; 2. Establishing from that the perfect benefit for self, the sugata; 3. Establishing from that the perfect training, the teacher; 4. Establishing from that the perfect intent, the wish to benefit others; and 5. Thus establishing he is valid.

1. Explaining the perfect benefit for others, the protector. The first has two topics: a. Teaching that he is the protector because he teaches the four truths, and b. Explaining the nature of the four truths that he taught.

a. Teaching that he is the protector because he teaches the four truths. This has two points: i. General discussion, and ii. The meaning of the text.

i. General discussion

What is the protector, the perfect benefit for others? you ask. It is the form bodies that unerringly teach sentient beings the temporary paths to the higher realms and the ultimate truly excellent paths. The dharma they teach is the selflessness of the individual and the selflessness of phenomena.

The selflessness of the individual is the sixteen true aspects of the four truths, because the view of the self and the afflictions it causes are abandoned in their entirety by meditating on them properly. What are the sixteen true aspects? you ask. Impermanent, suffering, empty, and selfless are the aspects of the truth of suffering. Cause, origin, production, and condition are the aspects of the truth of the origin. Cessation, peace, sublime, and emancipation are the aspects of the truth of cessation. Path, reasoning, accomplishing, and deliverance are the aspects of the truth of the path.

Because of being dependent on conditions, *impermanent*. Because of being inherently harmful, *suffering*. Because of being incompatible with mine, *empty*. Because of being incompatible with the view of the self, *selfless*.

In the manner of a seed, *cause*. In the manner of arising, *origin*. In the manner of consequence, *production*. In the manner of manifestly establishing, *condition*.

Because the aggregates have been destroyed, *cessation*. Because the three fires are pacified, *peace*.[156] Because there is no hostility, *sublime*. Because of being free of all faults, *emancipation*.

Through the meaning of going, *path*. Through the meaning of being logical, *reasoning*. Through the meaning of completely accomplishing, *accomplishing*. Through the meaning of making one transcend utterly and completely, *deliverance*.

Why are there definitely sixteen aspects? you ask. They are taught to be sixteen as antidotes for sixteen views that are exaggerations or denials. The four of impermanent, suffering, empty, and selfless are respectively antidotes for the views of permanence, bliss, mine, and self.

As antidotes for the view that proposes there are no causes, the view that there is a single cause such as the self or the primal substance,[157] the view that they are manifestation of a nature or cosmic sound,[158] and the view that the mind of Īśvara or another being precedes creation, respectively, there are the four aspects of cause, origin, production, and condition.

As antidotes for the view that there is no liberation; the view of thinking that Brahma, Viṣṇu, and so forth are freed from suffering; the view of the bliss of dhyāna as sublime; and the view that liberation is not forever since one regresses repeatedly from the path, respectively, there are the four aspects of cessation, peace, sublime, and emancipation.

As antidotes for the view that there is no path, the view that the path of realizing selflessness is inferior, the view that thinks that meditating on the self is the path, and the view that thinks, "This path is once again impermanent," respectively, there are the four aspects of path, reasoning, accomplishing, and deliverance. As it says in the *Commentary*:

> Projecting onto the four truths
> The sixteen unreal aspects of
> Being stable, pleasurable, me,
> And mine, and so forth, one has craving.[159]

The essences of each of the four truths will appear below and should be known from their respective appearances in the text.

The selflessness of phenomena is known by way of the three characteristics. What are the three? you ask. The characteristic of dependence, the characteristic of the imaginary, and the characteristic of the absolute.

The characteristic of dependence is any awareness assembled by seeds in the ground consciousness, incorrect misconceptions. What are those? you ask. The awareness of body and that which has a body; the awareness of the consumer;[160] the awareness of what that enjoys; the awareness of what in that enjoys; the awarenesses of time, number, object, and designations; and the awarenesses of self, other, higher realms, lower realms, death and migration, and birth.[161]

There are three types of imprints in the ground consciousness: conceptual imprints, imprints of viewing the self, and imprints of the elements of existence. Conceptual imprints are the seeds stained by thoughts that have the aspect of the names of all phenomena from form to omniscience[162] and are the causes for various conventions to arise. The second type is the seeds stained by the afflicted mind that in the future will produce cognitions that have the aspect of self or mine. The third type is the seeds stained by the virtue and nonvirtue of the six consciousnesses that in the future will produce the fully ripened portion of the ground consciousness. These are also called karmic imprints or the imprints of full ripening.

The awarenesses of body, that which has the body, the consumer, what that enjoys, what in that enjoys, time, number, object, and conventions arise from conceptual imprints. The awarenesses of self and other arise from the imprints of viewing the self. The awarenesses of the high realms, low realms, death and migration, and birth arise from the imprints of the elements of existence.

Awarenesses of body and that which has a body are the six inner elements of the eye and so forth.[163] Awarenesses of consumer and enjoying are the six inner elements of the eye consciousness and so forth.[164] Awarenesses of what they enjoy are known as the six outer elements of form and so forth.[165] The remaining awarenesses are classifications of these awarenesses.

The characteristic of the imaginary is the apprehended portion of the dependent that is projected as being a self or phenomena by thought. Conventionally, this exists as the sphere of ordinary individuals' cognition, but it cannot withstand analysis and thus cannot be established as even the slightest substantial nature.

In what aspect does which thinker imagine what object of thought? you ask. The mental consciousness imagines, because the other consciousnesses do not have thought. The mental consciousness arises from its own conceptual imprints as well as from the seeds of the conceptual imprints of all other awarenesses. Thus it is the subject of infinite faculties, objects, consciousnesses, and so forth. Congruently with its own aspects, it projects a self, the essence of phenomena, and various features, and then labels them as being so with conventions. For that reason, the thoughts in the mental consciousness themselves imagine.

The dependent nature is the basis for its imagination, because the awarenesses of body, that which has the body, and consumer are the basis imagined to be the self. This is because it holds the internal aggregates, elements, and sense bases to be a self, and the internal aggregates are nothing more than those three awarenesses. The awarenesses of what that enjoys and what in that enjoys are the basis imagined to be phenomena, because childish ordinary individuals fixate upon the appearances of object and subject as apprehended and apprehender, and the appearances of object and subject are nothing more than those two awarenesses. Until those mere dependent appearances are transformed, they are apprehended as the attributes of the essence of self and phenomena. They are fixated upon as such and conventionally labeled. Projecting that they exist as such-and-such even though they are not established as such is the aspect of how the thinking mental consciousness imagines the dependent about which it thinks.

The characteristic of the absolute is the emptiness of those same dependent incorrect misconceptions never having been established as the essence of the above-described imaginary. It is the essence of the phenomenal selflessness that is the sphere of thought-free wisdom. Because that never changes into anything else during any phase, it is suchness. Because it is unmistaken, it is the right end. Because conceptual elaborations have fully subsided, it is the absence of attributes. Because it is the sphere of exalted wisdom, it is the ultimate. Because one achieves the noble qualities by realizing it, it is the cause of the noble qualities, and thus the dharma expanse. As is said in *Differentiating the Middle from Extremes*:

> The synonyms of emptiness
> In brief are suchness, the right end,
> Absence of attributes, the ultimate,
> And the dharma expanse.

> Respectively, the meanings of the synonyms
> Are since it is not other, not wrong,
> Their cessation, the sphere of the nobles,
> And the cause of noble qualities.[166]

There are two types of the absolute: the emptiness of the absence of things and the emptiness of the essence of the absence of things. The first is the nature of the emptiness no-negation[167] that is the dependent devoid of other meanings, the individual and phenomenal self. The second is the nature of the emptiness not-negation[168] of that dependent not being established as the essence of the two selves. It is that which is called the natural essence of dependent awareness, the luminous nature of mind. As is said in *Differentiating the Middle from Extremes*:

The absence of things that are
Individuals or phenomena is emptiness here.
The thing that is their absence exists.
In that, there is another emptiness.[169]

How is incorrect misconception dependent, and why is it called the dependent? you ask. As it arises from the seeds of its imprints, it is dependent upon conditions, and it does not persist longer than an instant after arising. Therefore it is called dependent.

How is that which is projected as being an individual or phenomenon imaginary, and why is it called imaginary? you ask. Because it is the focus of misconceptions in the mental consciousness that have infinite aspects, it is imaginary. Since it cannot be established as its characteristics and is merely observed as a misconception, it is imaginary.

How is emptiness absolute, and why is it called the absolute? you ask. Because it never becomes anything else, it is absolute, and because it is supreme of all dharmas, it is called absolute. This is because it is the focus of the utterly pure, and it is the supreme of all virtuous dharmas.

How many types of the dependent are there? you ask. If you classify them extensively, they are innumerable because all of the classifications of incorrect misconception are its classifications. If combined, there are two: the dependent that is imprints and the dependent that is not established as the essence of either the all-afflicted or the utterly pure. The first is presented in terms of the incorrect misconception appearing dualistically due to the seeds of its imprints. The second is not established categorically as the essence of the all-afflicted as it is naturally pure, but it is not established categorically as the essence of the utterly pure either as it is adventitiously stirred up by the all-afflicted.

How many types of the imaginary are there? you ask. If you classify them extensively, they are innumerable because thoughts are infinite, so there as many as those thoughts imagine. If combined, there are two: the imaginary misconceived as an essence and the imaginary misconceived as features.

How many types of the absolute are there? you ask. Just as with the mandala of space, there is a single flavor to the essence of the dharma expanse, so ultimately there are no classifications at all. However, from the perspective of those who like complication, in terms of the classifications of what is associated with it, there are two types:

the utterly pure path and its focus. The first as well has two, the cause and result.

The first is the naturally present family. This is the seeds of the undefiled in the all-ground that have been passed down from beginningless time and gained by the dharma nature. And what are those? you ask. They are the imprints of listening to True Dharma that have been primordially present because of the dharma nature and that are causally compatible with the dharma expanse,

And what are the imprints of listening? you ask. When someone listens to dharma from the Buddha and so forth, these are the seeds arisen from listening that cause them to realize its meaning. These as well have been present from beginningless time due to the dharma nature. Listening revives them but does not produce them anew.

In *The Compendium of the Mahayana*, Master Asaṅga says:

> The lesser, medium, and greater seeds of the imprints of listening are viewed as the seeds of the dharmakāya. As they are the antidote to the ground consciousness, they are not the essence of the ground consciousness. They are both worldly and causally compatible with the transworldly, thoroughly pure dharma expanse, so they are the seeds of transworldly cognitions.[170]

Thus according to Noble Master Asaṅga, the dharma nature suchness is not the naturally present family, whereas the imprints of listening described above are themselves the naturally present family. This is because the imprints of listening make the distinctions of each separate family in sentient beings' inner six sense bases. For that reason, the so-called "distinctions of the six sense bases" are the naturally present family.

And how is that? you ask. The imprints of listening that are the cause of the mahayana path distinguish the six inner sense bases of someone who has them in their being from the inner sense bases of sentient beings who do not, because they indicate that the sentient beings who have them in their being are in the mahayana family. Similarly, the imprints of listening that are the causes of the paths of the listeners and self-buddhas also indicate that the sentient beings who have them in their beings are in the families of the listeners and self-buddhas and in this way distinguish their six inner sense bases from others'. Therefore other than the six inner sense bases, there is nothing at all that can be called an individual in the families of the three vehicles.

In some parts of the canon, the above-described imprints of listening are described as obscurations that should be discarded. In other parts, they are described as the seeds of the undefiled and in others as distinctions of the six sense bases.

Why are these included in the absolute? you ask. They are not either imaginary or dependent, because they are included among the antidotes to the all-afflicted. *The Compendium of the Mahayana* says:

> Though worldly, those of beginner bodhisattvas should be viewed as included in the dharmakāya and those of listeners and self-buddhas as included in the body of liberation as well.[171]

Second, the path that is their result is the thirty-seven factors of enlightenment, six transcendences, and so forth included in the paths of the three vehicles. Their focus, the three precious baskets of the True Dharma of the three vehicles and so forth, is also included within the absolute. Because they are the cause of the utterly pure, they are not imaginary, and because they do not arise from the seed of the all-afflicted but instead are causally compatible with the realization of the thoroughly pure dharma expanse, they are not dependent.[172]

In this way, the dependent is like the basis for emanating illusions, and the imaginary is like projecting that basis for emanating illusions, which appears variously as men, women and so forth though there are none, as being what it appears to be. Unlike the imaginary, the absolute does not project nothing as being something or something as being nothing, and unlike the dependent, it does not arise in dependence upon other conditions—the seeds of all-afflicted imprints. However, the absolute cannot be described as either the same as or other than the dependent. For that reason, the absolute is indivisible in essence from the dependent and merely mentally labeled as separate, because they are phenomena and the phenomenal nature.[173] As it says in *The Thirty Verses*:

Therefore it said to be neither different
Nor not different from the dependent,
Like impermanence and so forth.[174]

Well then, which of the three characteristics is established merely in the relative, and which as ultimate? you ask. Two, the dependent and imaginary, are established merely in the relative, because they are confusion and confused appearances. The absolute is established to be ultimate, because it is true as the object of exalted transworldly wisdom. As it says in *Differentiating the Middle from Extremes*, "The ultimate is singular."[175] Its commentary also says, among other things, that the dependent characteristic exists conventionally but is not true, because it is confused.[176] Therefore saying that the dependent is truly established in the Yogācāra tradition is merely the laziness of confusing Idealism for the Yogācāra Middle Way.

There are some who assert that saying appearances are mind and accepting the three characteristics are all Mind Only, but that is not the case, because even the Sutra school asserts that appearances are mind, and because in the chapter requested by Maitreya from the prajñāpāramita sutras, all phenomena from form to omniscience are determined and taught by way of the three characteristics. Thus the Sutra school would be Mind Only and that text its tradition.

Therefore the Yogācāra Great Middle Way that follows Noble Asaṅga and his brother determines that the apprehended and apprehender, which obscure suchness, are not established to be two as they appear. It primarily teaches the wisdom that realizes the self-aware, self-knowing mind. Through the great reasonings, Noble Nāgārjuna and his disciples thoroughly analyze clinging to truth, which obscures suchness, and its object, establishing that those have no nature. They primarily teach that the essence of the clear mind resides in emptiness. In teaching the ultimate suchness, there is no distinction at all between the two great traditions, because the clear essence of mind has been emptiness from the very beginning, and that emptiness has abided as the character of clarity from the very beginning.

Therefore, both Master Dignāga and glorious Dharmakīrti came to understanding through the logics of the stainless tradition that descends from Noble Asaṅga and uphold that tradition, so they are proven to be Yogācāra Middle Way. Thus it is reasonable to say that the final intent of their texts including *The Compendium of Validity* and the seven treatises fits within and falls within the textual tradition of the Yogācāra.

ii. The meaning of the text

148ab   Or else the protector
                          Is he who teaches the four noble truths.

It has been explained in terms of the forward order of the *Compendium's* homage how reasons of nature by which one infers later results from earlier causes such as wishing to benefit beings prove the Bhagavan is valid. Or else in reverse order, reasons of result that prove earlier causes from the later results establish the Bhagavan to be valid.

The Bhagavan is the protector of those who wish to fully pacify suffering, because he teaches them unerringly the method to fully pacify the suffering of samsara, the four noble truths. Because non-Buddhists and so forth teach erroneous paths such as animal sacrifice, they are not able to protect from suffering.

b. Explaining the nature of the four truths that he taught. This has four topics: i. What is to be known, the truth of suffering; ii. What is to be abandoned, the truth of the origin; iii. What is to be manifested, the truth of cessation; and iv. What is to be adopted, the truth of the path.

i. What is to be known, the truth of suffering. This has two topics: (1) General discussion, and (2) The meaning of the text.

(1) General discussion

What is the truth of suffering? you ask. It is the five aggregates that are the basis all sentient beings hold to be a self. As it says in *The Commentary*, "Suffering is the samsaric aggregates."[177] In terms of coming to understand the knowable, the external environment of the world is also explained to be suffering. As explained in the abhidharma, "If you ask what the truth of suffering is, it is also known as the births and places of birth of sentient beings." The explanation in this treatise of just the inner aggregates as suffering is from the perspective of practice.

The aggregates are viewed as a self by personality view.[178] This is because, as the Bhagavan said in a sutra:

> Any spiritual person or brahmin who views a self views these
> five aggregates of grasping.[179]

It is also because the yogis meditate on selflessness as the antidote for personality view. As it says in *The Commentary*:

> Therefore all those who wish for freedom should
> Eradicate the personality views
> That arise out of seeds of the same kind
> In a beginningless continuum.[180]

The fearless Master Candrakīrti also said:

> The faults of the afflictions all arise
> From personality view, the mind can see.
> After realizing its object is the self,
> The yogi refutes the self.[181]

In this way, in the fertile field of ignorance that has the characteristic of ego-clinging, the cause of suffering, conscious individuals perform virtuous and unvirtuous acts, planting the seeds of the six migrations. When these are in some way watered with the moisture of craving and grasping, they become the link called becoming that has the power to produce birth. From that, the seedling of birth arises. From that, the trunk of name and form is established. From that spread the limbs and branches of the six sense bases. From those come the flowers of contact and feeling. From those ripens the fruit of aging, which eventually falls onto the field of death.

Until one arrives at the level of nirvana, the great tree of existence exists in this way from beginningless time in a manner similar to how a mechanic hangs buckets from a windlass in a well. Thus the buckets of the twelve links of interdependence are tied with the rope of karma and afflictions, moved furiously by the mechanic who is consciousness, and hung in the deep and broad well of the three realms that reaches from the Peak of Existence to the Incessant Hell. They naturally fall down into the lower realms but must be hauled up to the higher realms with effort. From ignorance to aging and death, there are the all-afflicted three phases of the afflicted, karma, and birth, but no beginning or middle or end can be definitely recognized. One is tormented every single day without interruption by the three sufferings of the suffering of suffering, the suffering of change, and the suffering of formation. In this way, these samsaric aggregates that are suffering are similar to buckets in a well. In brief, that which is the cause of those sufferings has clinging to a self as its root, so those who wish to pacify suffering strive to defeat that clinging to a self.

(2) The meaning of the text. This has three topics: (a) Identifying suffering, (b) Proving that through reasons, and (c) Explaining its aspects.

(a) Identifying suffering

> 148c   Suffering is the samsaric aggregates.

What is the truth of suffering? you ask. It is the five aggregates of grasping that cycle in samsara by force of karma and the afflictions.

(b) Proving that through reasons. This has four topics: (i) Proving suffering through the evidence of habituation, (ii) Proving the aggregates are samsara through the evidence that the mind's aspects would be similar to the body's, (iii) Proving samsara through the evidence that what is not consciousness is not the substantial cause of consciousness, and (iv) The absurd consequence if there were no past lives.

(i) Proving samsara is suffering through the evidence of habituation. This has two topics: A. Actual, and B. Refuting criticism.

A. Actual

It is not logical for samsara to be suffering because there is no samsara where one comes from a previous life to this one and goes from this to a next, you say. To explain:

> 148d   It's seen habituation intensifies

> 149a   Desire and so forth.

It is seen even in this life, that in some people who previously had little desire, intelligence, and so forth, habituation according to circumstances later greatly intensifies desire, intelligence, and so forth. For this reason, immediately after birth, desire, intelligence, and so forth also arise from habituation to desire, intelligence, and so forth in previous lives. From the desire and so forth of this life, the desire and so forth of future births will arise, so samsara is proven. This is according to both Devendrabuddhi and Prajñākaragupta.

B. Refuting criticism. This has three topics: 1. Refuting that desire and so forth arise without cause, 2. Refuting that desire and so forth arise from wind and so forth, and 3. Refuting that desire and so forth arise from the elements.

1. Refuting that desire and so forth arise without cause

Some say that desire and so forth do not arise from habituation because they arise without cause. To explain:

> 149ab   It's not happenstance—
> Arising without cause is contradictory.

Desire and so forth do not arise without a cause by happenstance, because they are seen to arise intermittently from causes, and because arising without cause is contradictory of arising occasionally.

2. Refuting that desire and so forth arise from wind and so forth. This has two topics: a. The actual logic of the refutation, and b. Dismissing the rebuttal.

a. The actual logic of the refutation

Others say that desire, hatred, and delusion actually arise respectively from phlegm, bile, and wind; they do not arise from the power of habituation. To explain:

149cd As that's fallacious, they're not qualities
Of wind and so forth.

They (delusion and so forth) are not resultant qualities that are actually produced by wind, bile, and so forth, as that (the entailment and reverse entailment with the presence of wind and so forth) is fallacious. There are also people with phlegm who have a lot of hatred and little desire.

Others say:

149d If there were no fault

150a Because the nature is mixed,

If you say that in phlegmatic people with great anger, their nature is mixed with bile, the direct cause of hatred, and because of this there is no fault of anger not being entailed by bile, to explain:

150ab then why would not
Its other qualities be seen as well?

Then why would not its (bile's) other qualities than its direct result hatred, such as bad odor, sweat, and bad fortune, be seen in that phlegmatic person as well? They would be seen, because bile, the direct cause of bad odor and so forth, is present.

If you say that desire, hatred, and delusion are all the result of the three—wind, bile, and phlegm—so there is no fault, to explain:

> 150cd   It's not a quality of all because
> All would have equal desire as a consequence.

If desire and so forth each arose out of all of them, wind and so forth, as a consequence there would be the fault that all people would have equal amounts of desire. For that reason, it (desire) is not a quality that is a direct result of all three, wind, bile, and phlegm. Likewise, everyone would also have similar qualities of hatred, delusion, pride, arrogance, jealously, stinginess, intelligence, and so forth, because they have the same causes. This is according to Devendrabuddhi.

Others respond:

> 151ab   "Like bodies and so forth, there is no fault,"
> You say,

If you say that people's bodies are the same in arising from the cause of the elements, but there are dissimilarities in having a good or bad body and so forth, and likewise the causes—wind and so forth—are similarly present, but there is no fault that the results—desire and so forth—must be the same, to explain:

> 151b–d   but without any distinctive karmas
> That would be the dominant for that,
> The criticism here would be the same.

If people's good or bad bodies arose solely from the elements without any distinctive cause, previous karma, that would the dominant condition for them, then the same criticism would apply here as well: It follows that all people, the subject, would have equally good or bad figures because the causes—the elements—are equally present. This is according to Prajñākaragupta.

b. Dismissing the rebuttal. This has four topics: i. Refuting it because the faults are not proven to be entailed or reverse entailed by wind and so forth, ii. Explaining that refutation at length, iii. The absurd consequence if entailment and reverse entailment were proven, and iv. Rebutting criticism of that.

i. Refuting it because the faults are not proven to be entailed or reverse entailed by wind and so forth

152ab Although there are distinctions in the faults,
There's no distinction.

Desire and so forth would not be the direct result of phlegm and so forth, since though there are distinctions of the faults—phlegm and so forth—increasing, there is no distinction of lust and so forth increasing.

You might say that the reason is not proven, because you do not assert that wind, bile, and so forth are all the causes, but that some of their changes are causes, because when bile increases, the body is tormented by pain, increasing hatred. To explain:

152b–d It is not unproven,
Because a change in all of them will make
A change,

By that alone, it (the reason) is not unproven, because hatred does not arise from a change in all of them (phlegm and wind) but does arise from an increase and change in phlegm and wind that distresses the body with pain.[182] This is according to Prajñākaragupta.

If you say that there is no fault because hatred arises from all of them—wind, bile, and so forth:

152d and they do not arise from all.

Hatred does not arise from all of them, wind and so forth, because of the fault previously explained:

It's not a quality of all because
All would have equal desire as a consequence.

ii. Explaining that refutation at length. This has three points: (1) If the cause increases, it is not tenable for the result to decrease, (2) It is not tenable for pain to impede desire, (3) Refuting the response.

(1) If the cause increases, it is not tenable for the result to decrease

153a–c   If causes increase, it's illogical
          For the results to decrease, as with heat
          And so forth.

As explained, if the cause phlegm were to increase, it would be illogical for the result (desire) to decrease, because desire is the direct result of phlegm. It is, for example, just as when bile and so forth increase, illnesses of heat and so forth increase. This supports the text "Although there are distinctions in the faults. . ." according to Devendrabuddhi.

If you say that desire arises from a balance of phlegm and bile whereas hatred from an imbalance, so they do arise from phlegm and bile, to explain:

153cd   Changes of desire and so on
               Arise from pleasure and so forth.

The changes of desire from a balance of phlegm and bile and hatred and so on from an imbalance do not arise directly from the causes phlegm and bile. This is because they arise directly from the pleasure that arises in association with the body consciousness that has as its apprehended object particular internal feelings at times when phlegm, bile, and so forth are balanced or from the pain that arises in association with the body consciousness that has as its apprehended object particular internal feelings at times when phlegm, bile, and so forth are imbalanced.[183] This applies to desire and hatred respectively.

(2) It is not tenable for pain to impede desire

Others say:

154ab   And if desire is not produced because
          Of pain that was created by imbalance,

When phlegm and so forth increase but desire and so forth do not, the pain that was created by an imbalance in phlegm, bile, and so forth makes an impediment, so desire is not produced, you might say. Well then, to ask what its cause is:

> 154cd   Do tell whence it arises. "Semen increases
>   From balance, and desire increases from that."

Well then, do tell what is the cause whence it (desire) arises. If you say, "Semen increases from the cause of a balance of the three humors, and desire increases from that increase of semen."

> 155.   It's seen that even some with imbalances
>   Are lustful, whereas some in balance aren't.
>   Some are, though they emit blood, being depleted.
>   Semen's not definite for any one woman,

> 156a   And there might not be strong lust for that one.

It is not logical that desire would be the result of semen arising from balanced humors, because it is seen that there are even some people with imbalances in the humors who are extremely lustful, and because some who naturally have little lust may have balanced humors but are not lustful. Also, some lustful men are seen to still be extremely desirous, even though they emit blood, as their semen has been depleted. And there are some who have large amounts of semen but are seen not to be lustful. Therefore, a balance of the humors and the increase of semen are not the cause of desire, because their presence or absence neither entail nor reverse entail any effect.

Additionally, it is not definite that semen will increase in a lustful man after he observes any one beautiful woman.[184] That man might not have strong lust for that one woman but definitely would for others. Therefore an increase in semen is not the cause of desire. This is according to Devendrabuddhi.

(3) Refuting the response

Others say:

> 156b   If figure and so forth were factors, too,

If you say that since a beautiful figure, courtship, and so forth increase semen, and those were cooperating factors in producing lust for a woman, too, there is no fault, to explain:

> 156cd   Not so—it is not certain for everyone.
> It also is not definite. It would occur

> 157a   For those who do not hold them qualities.

It is not so that a woman's beautiful figure and so forth and an increase in semen are causes that actually produce desire, because among men with similar amounts of semen who focus on a woman, some feel lust and some feel aversion, thus it is not certain for every man that desire will arise. It is also because for some lustful men, it is not definite that they lust for a beautiful woman's body; it is also seen that they also act upon desire for ugly bodies. A beautiful figure and so forth are not the cause of lust.

Additionally, it (lust) would also occur for those men who do not hold women to have the qualities of cleanliness but have the quality of perceiving them to be unclean, because the direct causes—a beautiful figure and semen—would be present.

Others say:

> 157b   If holding them as qualities were a factor,

If you say that holding a woman's beautiful figure to be a quality is a cooperating factor for desire so there is no fault, to explain:

> 157cd   Then all would hold them to be qualities
> Because there's no distinction in the cause.

Then all men who see a woman's beautiful figure would hold that woman's beautiful figure to be a quality. This is because there is no distinction in the causes for holding a woman's beautiful body to be a quality—the body, semen, or others teaching it to be the cause of desire—themselves being comparably present. This is according to Devendrabuddhi.

iii. The absurd consequence if entailment and reverse entailment were proven

158. At times when someone is asserted to
Be lustful, he would not be hostile since
The essences of the two are disparate.
That is not necessarily seen here either.

If desire and so forth were to arise from the nature of phlegm and so forth, at times when the direct cause of desire, phlegm, were continually present, one would have to assert that a person in such a phase would be continually lustful. It would follow that he would not be hostile since the essences of the two—desire and hostility—are disparate and cannot focus on a single object simultaneously. It is not necessarily validly seen here that a phlegmatic person has only desire either, because it is seen that hatred, jealousy, and stinginess also arise periodically. This is according to Devendrabuddhi.

Here Prajñākaragupta states, "Here they are not necessarily seen at the same time."[185]

iv. Rebutting criticism of that

Others might say that the consequence that anger would not occur in a phlegmatic person's being is comparable for us as well. To explain:

159. Such faults are not a consequence
For those to whom desire and such
Engage dependent on distinctions
In imprints that are the same class.

For those of the Buddhist tradition, desire, hatred, and such engage and arise dependent on distinctions in imprints that are of the previous instances' same class, the views of the self and mine. They do not assert that they arise from phlegm and so forth. For that reason, lust and so forth arise from previous instances of similar kind, and such faults as that phlegmatics would not get angry are not a consequence.

3. Refuting that desire and so forth arise from the elements. This has three points: a. Refuting that desire and so forth are supported by the elements, b. The intent in explaining that they are supported by the elements, and c. Refuting the response.

a. Refuting that desire and so forth are supported by the elements

The Cārvākas say that desire and so forth do not arise from phlegm and so forth but do arise from the elements, because desire arises from a predominance of earth and water, hatred from fire and air, and delusion from water and air. To explain:

> 160ab   And this refutes an elemental nature,
> As the support as well has been disproven.

This logic that refutes that desire and so forth arise from the humors also refutes the assertion that the nature of desire and so forth is a result of the elements, because the entailment and reverse entailment with whether or not the sources such as earth are present as a beneficial factor is fallacious. Prajñākaragupta states that this has been refuted in the line, "At times when someone is asserted to / Be lustful. . ." Devendrabuddhi says, "Because the nature of the humors of wind and so forth is the elements."[186] Both Devendrabuddhi and Prajñākaragupta state that this is because "What is and what is not are not supported"[187] and so forth have also disproven that desire and so forth are supported by the elements.

Some might say that just as whiteness and so forth are supported by the elements, so too are desire and so forth. To explain:

> 160cd   Whiteness and so forth are not
> Supported by earth and so forth.

In this way, whiteness and so forth—forms that are derived from the elements—are not supported in the manner of remaining without perishing by the elements of earth and so forth, because they arise out of the elements. This is according to Devendrabuddhi.

Prajñākaragupta states that one would have accepted that form and so forth are separate from the elements, so they are not supporter and supported in nature.[188]

b. The intent in explaining that they are supported by the elements

Some might wonder how the convention "on the basis of the great elements" could be used. To explain:

> 161.   The expression "on the basis of" means cause,
> Or else since they exist inseparably
> From their supports, they are supports.
> It otherwise would not be logical.[189]

The expressions or scriptures that explain that form and so forth that are derived from the elements are on the basis of the elements do not teach that the elements are supports for form and so forth to persist after being created. Instead, they mean causes, or else that they (the elementally derived[190]) exist inseparably from the elements that are their supports and simultaneous with them. For that reason, it is tenable to say that the elementally derived and their support—the elements—are supporter and supported. But it would not be logical to say otherwise that desire and so forth are supporter or supported, unlike the elementally derived.

c. Refuting the response

Others say:

> 162ab   "Just like the potency to intoxicate
> And such, it's separable."

If you say that though beer and the potency to intoxicate are not supporter and supported, heating beer may not destroy the substance of the beer but does destroy its intoxicating potency, so they are separable. Similarly the evidence here is indeterminate, you say. It is not indeterminate. It is thus:

> 162b–d The potency
> Is not an object other than the thing.
> When a thing perishes, if the support

> 163a Remains intact, the supported does not perish.

It is not so that the substance of the beer remains while its potency is destroyed. The potency of beer is not another object than the thing that is beer. When the supported (the potency of the beer) perishes, the support (the thing beer) also perishes, and if the support (the thing beer) remains intact and does not perish, the supported (the potency of the beer) also does not perish. For that reason, they exist indivisibly, unable to be divided. This is according to Prajñākaragupta.

Others say with regard to this:

> 163b If you say this is similar,

If you say that similarly to how beer and its intoxicating potency are inseparable, the elements and mental factors such as desire are also inseparable, to explain:

> 163b–d not so.
> Perceived with separate appearances,
> The elements and mind are separate.

It is not so that similar to beer and its potential to intoxicate, the elements and mind are inseparable, because the elements and mind have separate characteristics and because they are perceived separately by unmistaken cognitions with separate appearances. This is according to Devendrabuddhi.

(ii) Proving the aggregates are samsara through the evidence that the mind's aspects would be similar to the body's

164a–c   Until the body changed, the essence of
The mind would still remain the same, like form,
Et cetera.

If the mind were supported by the body, until the body changed to
another aspect such as moving and so forth, the essence of the mental mind would still remain the same without changing or moving,
because it is directly supported by the physical. As an analogy, it is like
how when someone does not move, their form et cetera do not move.

If you say it is actually supported by the body, but at that time dependent upon other objects and other things, there are differences in mind,
so there is no fault, to explain:

164cd   And how is it that thoughts
Could be dependent on an object

How is it that mental thoughts could change in dependence on an
external object, because they arise from the mere awakening of imprints
independent of the object? This is according to both Devendrabuddhi
and Prajñākaragupta.

If you say the same fault applies to us, to explain:

165.   When independent of the body
Some cognitions have as a cause
The awakening of the imprints of some?
Therefore some arise from some.

When thoughts move toward an object, some consciousnesses that
engage independent of the movement of the support—the body—
move even though the body does not change. This is not contradictory,
because they are consciousnesses that move and engage from the cause
that is the awakening of the imprints of some moving cognitions.

Therefore it is proven that the five aggregates of grasping are samsara,
because there are some consciousnesses that arise from the substantial
cause of some consciousnesses but do not arise from the body. This is
according to Prajñākaragupta.

(iii) Proving samsara through the evidence that what is not consciousness is not the substantial cause of consciousness

> 166ab   Nonconsciousness is not the substantial cause
> Of consciousness, so it is also proven.

The consciousness of a person who has just been born is preceded by an earlier consciousness of the same kind, because it is consciousness with a substantial cause. This is because the body and so forth that are not consciousness are not appropriate to be the substantial cause of consciousness. The word "also" means that if they had the body and so forth as a cause, desire and so forth would consequentially occur simultaneously, so previous and later samsara is also proven. This is according to both Devendrabuddhi and Prajñākaragupta.

Some might say:

> 166cd   If you assert that all things are endowed
> With a capacity for consciousness,

If you say, "All things are endowed with a capacity for consciousness that is present in an unapparent manner. For that reason, we also agree with the explanation that consciousness does not arise from nonconsciousness, so that is trying to prove what has been proven." To explain:

> 167.   Other than a Sāṃkhya ox,
> What modest[191] person would attempt
> To say there were on a blade of grass
> One hundred elephants not seen before?

Are the cognition and elephants asserted to exist as the essence of the capacity for such in the elements and grass that have unapparent cognition and elephants the same as or different from the cognition and elephants during the phase when they are apparent?[192] If it is the latter, since they are other, it is illogical for them to be present. If you say that they are the same as the cognition and elephants during the apparent phase, to say that there exist on a blade of grass the result—

one hundred elephants—as the essence of capacity, though not clearly seen before during the time of the cause, is the immodest assertion of the Sāṃkhyas, who are as stupid as oxen. Other than them, what modest Cārvāka who imagines himself to be the crown jewel of intellectuals would attempt to say that? It is illogical to try. If they existed, their essence would be observed. Therefore:

> 168.   Any essence that appears,
> That essence did not appear before.
> Dissect the cause one hundred times,
> But how could it exist?

Though one might mentally dissect and analyze grass and the elements one hundred times during the causal phase, if any essence of cognition or elephants existed, it would be able to appear, but that essence of a cognition or an elephant did not appear before during the time of the cause. For that reason, how is it that that essence of cognition or an elephant could exist? This is according to both Devendrabuddhi and Prajñākaragupta.

(iv) The absurd consequence if there were no past lives. This has four topics: A. Explaining the actual argument of the refutation, B. Refuting criticism of it, C. The untenability of the analogy, and D. The consequence that desire and so forth would not be occasional.

A. Explaining the actual argument of the refutation

> 169ab   It follows greed and such would be uncertain
> When those who didn't exist before arise.

If there were no next world, then greed and such would arise only from the cause, the bodies of sentient beings who did not exist before. If that were so, it would follow that it would be uncertain whether they would be born with greed and such. Some would also be free of desire from the first. This is according to Prajñākaragupta.

Others respond:

169cd   If all had greed and such because they don't
               Transcend the character of the elements,

If you say that because all sentient beings do not transcend the character of the elements, they would all have greed, hatred, and such, and thus freedom from attachment and so forth are impossible, to explain:

170a   Then all would have identical desire.

Then all sentient beings would have identical degrees of desire, hatred and so forth, because the direct cause—the elements—is identically present. This is according to Prajñākaragupta. Devendrabuddhi states that even were people not to transcend the character of the elements, their color, shape, faculties, and so forth are dissimilar in size.[193]
Some might say:

170b   "Not so, due to distinctions in the elements,"

If you were to say that the different degrees of desire and so forth are due to distinctions in the increase or decrease of the cause, the elements, to explain:[194]

170cd   In terms of living, there's no difference
               In the elements, and yet as the support

171ab   For this distinction grows or else decreases,
               They'd go from having those to lacking them.

It is not logical that different degrees of desire and so forth would come from differences in the elements. In your tradition, there is no difference in the elements in terms of alive, very alive, and extremely alive, but there is a distinction between desirous, very desirous, and extremely desirous. As the elements that are the support for this distinction—the elements that are the substantial cause—grow or else decrease, the resultant desire and so forth would also increase and decrease. According to this assertion, it would be possible that they (sentient beings) would go from having those (desire and so forth) earlier to lacking them later, because desire and so forth would be entailed or reverse entailed by the increase or decrease of the cause and thus eliminable.

B. Refuting criticism of it

Others say:

171cd   If it's not so since although separate,
         The causes of greed and such have the same nature,

172a   Which has not ceased,

If you say that although their increase and decrease of greed and such may be separate, because their causes—the mere universal nature of the elements that are entailed by them all in the same way—have not ceased, it is not so that there could be a person or elements that have exhausted desire and so forth forever, to explain:

172ab   because the causes are like
         In character, all would have like desire.

Well then, because they are all the same in being desirous people born from the cause that is like in the character of the degree of desire—permanent elements—all people would have like degrees of desire.
To give an analogy for this:

172cd   There are not any degrees of distinction
         In the perception of cow, which arises

173ab   From the same nature, or in livingness,
         Et cetera, in earth and so forth here.

As an analogy, the Sāṃkhyas say that when one says "cow," there are not three distinctions of "cow," "very cow," and "extremely cow," because it arises from the nature of the same cause of the perception of a cow, cowness. Or here in the Cārvāka school, there are not any degrees of distinction between living, very living, or extremely living in the elements earth and so forth of living creatures, because they arise from the same cause, the elements, like extreme desire.

C. The untenability of the analogy. This has two points: 1. The reasons it is not the same as the analogy, and 2. The reason it is not the same as the elements and form.

1. The reasons it is not the same as the analogy

Some say:

> 173cd   If you should say, "There are degrees of heat,
> But there's no fire that's without heat. Here, too,

> 174a   It is the same,"

If you should say, "There are degrees of heat in fire—hot, very hot, and extremely hot—but there is no fire that is entirely without heat. Here, too, there are degrees of desire in earth and so forth, but it is impossible for there to be a person who entirely lacks desire and so forth, so it is the same." To explain:

> 174ab   it is not so because
> It's been disproven fire is other than heat.

That analogy is not the same as the meaning. Desire and so forth are a separate substance from the body and can be removed, but here it has been validly disproven that fire is a different, other substance than heat that can be separated from it.

Because the analogy is not similar to the meaning:

> 174cd   When something has qualities that are other
> And that have a distinction in degree,

> 175ab   Some of those—its features—in some cases
> Can be removed, like whiteness and so forth.

When something—a living being, earth, or so forth—has qualities that are other objects which can be removed and that have a distinction of degree of increase or decrease, it is possible that some of those (desire and so forth), which are its features, can be removed and stopped in some cases. For example, it is like the white color of a blanket and so forth. This is according to Prajñākaragupta.

2. The reason it is not the same as the elements and form

Some say that the evidence "It follows greed and such would be uncertain. . ."[195] is indeterminate because form, scent, taste, and so forth are predicates of the elements only, but it is impossible for the elements to always be them. To explain:

175cd   They are not definite like form and such,
        Which are inseparable from the elements.

They (desire and so forth) are not definitely present in living creatures or the elements, unlike form, scent, taste and such being present in the elements. Form and so forth are inseparable from the elements and cannot be removed from them, but desire and so forth are other objects that can be removed from living creatures or the elements.
Some say:

176a   If you say it's the same,

If you say that it is the same as how form, scent, taste, and so forth are inseparable from the elements, desire and so forth are inseparable from living beings or the elements, then to explain:

176ab   it's not, because
        Desire and such would occur at the same time.

That as well is not true, because it would follow that just as form, scent, taste, and so forth all arise at the same time, desire, hatred, jealousy, and such would also all arise at the same time.
If you say that desire and so forth arise in dependence upon the

proximity of the object, so there is no fault that they would arise simultaneously, to explain:

176cd   Because the object is conceptual,
          The object also is not definite.

Desire and so forth are not unheard of for unattractive objects; they take a conceptual projection as their object and arise. Because of this, it is not definite that they will only arise when focused on an attractive object.

D. The consequence that desire and so forth would not be occasional

177.   From the cause of same status being absent,
          Desire and so forth are not definite,
          Or due to the cause always being present,
          All cognitions always would arise.

From the cause of same status—arising from a previous instance of the same kind—being absent, desire and so forth are intermittent and have no definite arising. Or alternatively, were they to arise from the substantial cause of just the elements, all cognitions of desire and so forth would always arise for all objects, in all times, and on all occasions due to the cause for them to arise—the body that is the elements— always being present. For that reason, the reasons explained above such as "It's seen habituation intensifies / Desire and so forth. . ."[196] all prove that the five samsaric aggregates of grasping are suffering. This is according to both Devendrabuddhi and Śākyabuddhi.

(c) Explaining its aspects. This has four points: (i) An explanation of the aspect impermanence, (ii) The aspect suffering, (iii) The aspect emptiness, and (iv) The aspect selflessness.

(i) An explanation of the aspect impermanence

178ab   It is impermanent as it's observed
          Occasionally

As they[197] (the five aggregates of grasping) are observed to arise occasionally, they are impermanent.

(ii) The aspect suffering

178bc   and suffering from being
         A support for faults and controlled by causes, too.

Similarly, because the five aggregates are the support for faults such as desire, because they occur defiled, controlled by and under the power of causes, and because (as the word "too" indicates) they depend on mere habituation, they are suffering, as said in the verse "Others' control is always suffering." This is according to Prajñākaragupta.[198]

(iii) The aspect emptiness and (iv) The aspect selflessness

178d   Not self, nor taken into control either.

179a   Not cause, and not the one who takes control.

The five aggregates of grasping are not a self, because they are impermanent and under another's control. Therefore, they are empty of being an individual's, because they are not something of mine that is taken into the control of a permanent self either. Therefore, the aggregates not being the same as or different from the self in any way is the aspect of emptiness. Not being the same is the aspect of selflessness. Additionally, the self is not the cause of the aggregates, because it is not the one who takes control of the aggregates.

If you say the reasons are not proven, to explain:

179b   How could the permanent be a producer?

The reasons are not unproven. How could a permanent self be the producer of the aggregates, since the permanent can perform no beneficial action, as has been explained at another point? This is according to Devendrabuddhi.

Therefore to teach that it is illogical for a result to arise from a single cause:

179cd   And for that reason, multiple will not
          Arise from one at separate times.

Because a permanent self is not the cause, for that reason, multiple aggregates will not arise from one single, permanent self at separate earlier or later times. If it were otherwise, the aggregates would only arise simultaneously, because the causes would always be present, never incomplete.

An additional logic:

180.   Even if other causes are assembled,
          Results do not arise, and for that reason
          One can infer that there are other causes.
          This is not present in the permanent.

If the causes are not complete, the result does not arise. For example, even when the other causes of an eye consciousness—the eye faculty and attention—are assembled, if the objective condition form is not present, the result—eye consciousness—does not arise. For that reason, one can infer that for an eye consciousness to arise, there is a cause other than the faculty and mind that must also be present, the objective condition form. When the cause is present or not as a beneficial factor, the result is entailed or reverse entailed, and this is not present with permanent causes and the result, the aggregates. This can similarly be applied to the remaining faculties—the ear, nose, tongue, and so forth—and the objects sound and so forth. This is according to Devendrabuddhi.

ii. What is to be abandoned, the truth of the origin. This has two topics: (1) General discussion, and (2) The meaning of the text.

(1) General discussion

What is the truth of origin? you ask. It is craving that has the characteristic of being attached to and fixated on the five aggregates of grasping of the present and future. As it says in *The Commentary*:

Thus craving is the support of existence.[199]

A sutra also states:

> What is the noble truth of the origin of suffering? you ask. It
> is craving that arises again: that which has the desire of lust
> and that which has the nature of truly lusting that or there.
> It is this: the craving of desire, craving existence, and craving
> destruction.

The meaning of the sutra is this: "It is craving that arises again" is the
overview; any craving from which the aggregates of rebirth arise is the
origin. The detailed explanation is "that which has the desire. . ." and
so forth. The craving that is truly attached to the present aggregates is
the craving that has the desire of lust. The craving that truly wants the
future aggregates is the craving which has the nature of truly lusting
that or there.[200] Its classifications are from "It is this. . ." Craving the
mere essence of the aggregates is craving existence, craving the attain-
ment of the aggregate's temporary pleasure is the craving of desire,
and craving the elimination of suffering is craving destruction.

In *The Commentary*:

> The cause is the attachment formed by clinging
> To me and mine[201]

teaches the craving of existence. The lines:

> Acting on wishes to gain happiness
> And cast off suffering is asserted to be
> The craving of desire and of destruction.[202]

teach both the craving of desire and the craving of destruction.

Alternately, the three phrases from "craving that arises again..."
respectively teach craving for the future, present, and past aggregates.
The remainder is as above.

Scholars of the abhidharma assert that craving in the Desire and higher realms are respectively the craving of desire and of existence, and wishing for the aggregates of suffering to cease is craving destruction.

"If both ignorance and karma are also causes of suffering, how is it that only craving is explained as the origin?" you ask. Ignorance and karma are merely the propelling causes of suffering but not the causes that actually create it, so they are not the primary causes. Craving is both, so it is primary. By teaching the primary, the general are implicitly understood. It is with this in mind that the sutras say craving alone is the cause of suffering, and the Master also intends it thus. As he says:

> Although not knowing is a cause of existence,
> It is not mentioned—only craving is taught
> Since that propels the continuum to existence
> And is immediate. Karma is not either. . .[203]

(2) The meaning of the text. This has four topics: (a) An explanation of the aspect cause, (b) The aspect origin, (c) The aspect production, and (d) The aspect condition.

(a) An explanation of the aspect cause

> 181.   It's proven suffering has a cause
>   Because it is occasional.
>   The causeless always or never exists,
>   Since it does not depend upon another.

Because it arises in occasional times and places, it is proven that the truth of suffering explained above has a cause. Otherwise, it would naturally have a fault:

> The causeless always or never exists,
> Since it does not depend upon another.

With regard to this, some say:

> 182.   "Just as the sharpness and so forth
>   Of thorns and so forth have no cause,

In the same way, these have no cause,"
There are some who expound.

"Just as the sharpness, shape, color, roughness, smoothness and so forth of thorns and a lotus stem, petal, stamen, pistil, and so on have no cause, in the same way these sufferings have no cause," expound some Cārvākas.

But this is not so:

183.   If when something exists, something arises
            Or when it changes, that is changed as well,
            It is considered as the cause of that,
            And such exists for those as well.

If when some phenomenon exists as a beneficial factor, some result arises, or a phenomenon which, when it changes, that result is changed as well, it (that phenomenon) is considered by the wise to be the cause of that result. Such a relation between cause and result exists for the sharpness of a thorn and the shape, color, and so forth of a lotus as well, because those are entailed or reverse entailed by the presence or absence of their own seeds.

Others say of this that the tactile would also be the cause of eye consciousness because by force of a tactile object ceasing, eye consciousness also ceases. If that were so, cause and result would be confused, they say. To explain:

184ab   As touch is causative of form, it is
           A cause of seeing.

As touch that is a cause of form is causative of form, it is indirectly a cause that benefits the eye consciousness that sees form. This also implies that the scent and taste that precede the form that is the apprehended object of eye consciousness are also indirect causes of eye consciousness.

Thus refuting that suffering is causeless proves that the origin is the cause of suffering. This is the aspect of cause.

(b) The aspect origin

184b–d   Because permanents
Have been refuted, it's not possible
To be from Īśvara and so forth since

185a   They've no capacity.

Likewise, it is not possible for suffering to arise from Īśvara, the primal substance, the *puruṣa*,[204] and so forth because there is nothing at all that arises from a permanent cause, as has been refuted at other points, and since they (Īśvara and so forth) have no capacity to produce results at all times. This is according to Devendrabuddhi. Prajñākaragupta says it is because they lack the capacity to produce either successively or simultaneously.[205]

Thus refuting that Īśvara and so forth are permanent causes proves that suffering has impermanent reasons, establishing the origin.

(c) The aspect production

185a–d   For that reason,
Wanting existence is the cause because
Humans appropriate a particular place,
Which is done through the intent to obtain that.

Neither causes other than craving nor the body and ignorance are causes of production. For that reason, wanting existence that has the aspect of seeking a future birth is the cause that produces suffering. The reason for this is because wanderers such as humans grasp and appropriate a particular place, a mode of birth such as a womb, and that is done through craving, the intent of wanting to obtain that.

You might say, "The craving that seeks a distinctive place is not the origin because that would contradict what the Bhagavan said in a sutra: 'What is the noble truth of the origin of suffering? you ask. It is craving that arises again: that which has the desire of lust and that which has the nature of truly lusting that or there. It is this: the craving of desire, craving existence, and craving destruction.'"

In response, Devendrabuddhi says, "The craving just mentioned that seeks the place of birth is named 'the craving of existence.'"[206] Master Prajñākaragupta says that there is no contradiction here, because:[207]

186.   This is a wish for existence, because beings
               Acting on wishes to gain happiness
               And cast off suffering is asserted to be
               The craving of desire and of destruction.

Craving for a place, possessions, and so forth is the three types of craving. This is because the craving of living beings seeking places and so forth is the craving of existence, and acting there to gain happiness is the craving of desire. As these are asserted to benefit, there is no contradiction of the scriptures at all.

(d) The aspect condition. This has three points: (i) The explanation of the actual aspect, (ii) Comparing that with citations, and (iii) Refuting criticism of that.

(i) The explanation of the actual aspect

187.   Due to the cause of clinging to a self,
               One enters anywhere, conceiving of
               That which is not pleasure as being pleasure.
               Thus craving is the support of existence.

The craving that arises due to the cause of clinging to a self, the basis for ego-clinging, is the cooperative condition or support for cycling in existence. The reason is from erroneously conceiving of that which is not ultimately pleasure as being pleasure, of the impermanent as permanent, of the lack of a self as a self, and of what is not mine as being mine, one enters anywhere (all places) and acts on possessions and so forth.

Saying it is a support means it is merely a condition and not the substantial cause itself. The substantial cause is the previous mind, and its condition is sometimes craving and sometimes compassion, according to Master Prajñākaragupta.[208]

(ii) Comparing that with citations

> 188ab   The masters have explained this is because
>   Those free of desire are not seen to take birth.

Because those free of desire for the Desire realm and so forth are not seen to take birth in samsara, desire itself is the cause for birth in the samsara, the masters of the past have explained, including Vasubandhu, who said "Those free of craving have no rebirth." Thus here it is explained that "craving is the support of existence."

Some Cārvākas respond:

> 188cd   "Because without a body, desire's not seen,
>   Desire arises from the body as well."

"Just as birth in samsara is not seen without desire, so desire is a cause for rebirth in samsara. Without a body, desire is not seen, and because of that, you must accept that desire arises from the body as well," they say.

To give the response:

> 189ab   Since we assert the reason, we accept,
>   But being substantial cause has been refuted.

Since we assert the reason that desire and so forth arise from the body acting as just a cooperative condition, we accept that the body is merely a condition for desire and so forth and that inappropriate attention itself is the substantial cause. However, we have refuted and disproven that the body is the substantial cause of desire and so forth, so how could there be a fault? To teach that if you were to accept this, it would contradict that there were no previous or future worlds:

> 189cd   If you accept this reasoning, you will
>   Contradict your own positions yourself.

If you follow and accept this reasoning that the combination of inappropriate attention that has been passed down without beginning and the body are the causes and conditions for desire and so forth, you are accepting the proof of previous and future lives. Thus you Cārvākas, your own contradictory earlier and later positions will contradict your assertion that there are no past or future lives and you Cārvākas' analysis has been burnt by the fire of logic. This is according to Prajñākaragupta.

Others say:

190ab   "Desire arises simultaneously
            With birth as it is seen at birth," you say.

If you were to say that since desire and so forth are seen to arise immediately after living beings are born, desire and so forth arise simultaneous with birth, to give the response:

190c   Same status arising proves the previous.

As desire and so forth immediately after birth arise from their same status cause—a previous instance of the same kind—desire from the time of the previous birth is proven.

(iii) Refuting criticism of that

Ignorance, craving, and karma are all three causes of suffering, so some might wonder why it is that only craving that "truly lusts for that" is taught to be the cause of suffering. To give the response:

190d   Although not knowing is a cause of existence,

191.   It is not mentioned—only craving is taught
        Since that propels the continuum to existence[209]
        And is immediate. Karma is not either
        Because though it is there, there's no becoming.

The ignorance that does not know suchness is an indirect cause of the suffering of existence, but there is a reason why it is not mentioned as its cause: ignorance alone is not the immediate condition for the suffering of existence, and it does not actually induce samsara. Only craving is taught to be a cause of taking birth, since that definitely propels the continuum of samsara and since birth is immediately effectuated upon the presence of craving. Without craving, karma is not a cause for rebirth in samsara, because if there is craving, karma does produce samsara, but without craving, even though it (karma) may be there, there is no birth in samsara.

iii. What is to be manifested, the truth of cessation. This has two topics: (1) General discussion, and (2) The meaning of the text.

(1) General discussion

This has already been explained in the discussion of the sugata.[210]

(2) The meaning of the text. This has four topics: (a) The explanation of the aspect cessation, (b) The explanation of the aspect peace, (c) The explanation of the aspect sublime, and (d) The explanation of the aspect emancipation.

(a) The explanation of the aspect cessation. This has two topics: (i) Refuting that cessation is impossible, and (ii) Refuting criticism of that.

(i) Refuting that cessation is impossible

Here the truth of cessation is explained to be the stoppage of suffering, the result, and of the origin through the path. Others say with regard to this that suffering is permanent, so a truth of cessation that stops it is impossible. To explain:

> 192ab That is not eternal, as it is
> Possible to impede the cause and so on.

Here, that (suffering) is not eternal because it has a cause. If you say that is inconclusive, it pervades, as it is possible that impediments might impede things with causes or that the assembly of causes, the favorable conditions, might be incomplete, and so forth.

(ii) Refuting criticism of that. This has six points: A. Refuting the criticism that liberation is impossible, B. Refuting the criticism that remaining in samsara would be impossible, C. Refuting the criticism that the detached would have the view of sentient beings, D. Refuting the consequence that they would have desire, E. Refuting the consequence that one would have anger, and F. Refuting the criticism that there would be no liberation.

A. Refuting the criticism that liberation is impossible

Others say:

> 192c   "Because they cycle, there's no liberation."

Because they (living creatures who have the characteristic of a self) have the property of cycling in samsara, there is no liberation from samsara. For example, since fire has the property of heat, it cannot be liberated from heat, you say. To explain that this is illogical:

> 192d   No, because we agree; it's not established.

That consequence does not apply negatively to Buddhists, because we agree that living beings with the characteristic of a self have no liberation from samsara and because it is not established that they have the property of cycling in samsara.

Here Prajñākaragupta says:

> That which is bound has no liberation because that is its nature. In liberation there is no bondage, because that is always the nature of liberation. However, it is solely that another pure part is produced from distinctions in the assembly of the mental continuum that is impure. Then that later pure part is not established as samsaric. Ultimately, there are no samsaric beings because instants are not samsara and because the continuum does not ultimately exist either. Therefore the reason "because they cycle" is unproven. Nor is there is any liberated person who has liberation.[211]

Some say that people would not strive at the path to free themselves from samsara and achieve liberation because there is not any self at all who cycles in samsaric or is liberated. To explain:

> 193.　　As long as attachment to a self has not
> 　　　　Been conquered, they will be tormented.
> 　　　　That long they will project their suffering,
> 　　　　Not dwelling in the natural state.

A liberated person does not strive at the path for liberation, but as long as attachment to a self has not been conquered, they (people who have ego-clinging) will enter samsara by force of clinging to a self and mine and be tormented by suffering for that long. This is because as long as they cling to a self, they will project the sufferer as being me or mine and not dwell in the natural state of the way objects are.

Clinging to a self is the cause of samsara. Therefore:

> 194ab　　Though there is no one who is liberated,
> 　　　　Strive to conquer false projections.

For learned individuals, even though actually there is no self who is liberated, it is logical to strive at the path, because one must strive to conquer the cause of samsara, falsely projecting a self.

B. Refuting the criticism that remaining in samsara would be impossible

Some might say that those who are free of attachment to a self would never enter into samsara, because they have abandoned the cause of samsara, clinging to a self, and thus would not view it as being of any benefit at all to themselves. To explain:

> 194cd　　Remaining while free of desire
> 　　　　Is from compassion or else karma,

> 195a　　As they do not wish to block the propulsion.

The reason is indeterminate: Those who remain in samsara while free of desire do not remain because of clinging to a self. They stay from great compassion or to help others, not for their own happiness or from attachment to sentient beings. Or else alternatively, the detached[212] listeners and self-buddhas who remain in samsara do not remain from attachment to a self but because the continuum of the aggregates propelled by previously committed karma naturally engages on its own and remains, because there is no wish to block the continuum of the aggregates propelled by karma naturally engaging on its own. Instead, they remain equanimous. As it is said:

> Do not take joy in death;
> Do not take joy in life.
> As if paying rent,
> I will stay for a time.[213]

This is according to Devendrabuddhi.

Some might say that if those free of desire remain because of karma, that karma would also link rebirth to a later existence. To explain:

> 195b–d   For those who have transcended craving existence,
> Their other actions have no power to propel,
> Since cooperating factors have been exhausted.

There is no such fault. For those arhats who have the nature of transcending craving, the cause of existence, their other actions that would link rebirth in later existences do not have the craving that has the power to propel future existence. This is since the cooperating causes that link rebirth in a later existence, erroneous craving and the craving for existence, have both been exhausted.

C. Refuting the criticism that the detached would have the view of sentient beings

Others say that compassion focuses on sentient beings in order to protect them from suffering. If that is so, those free of desire would not have abandoned the view of sentient beings.[214] To explain:

196.   Those who know suffering have no enmity.
         Continuing the previous conceptions,
         The actual quality compassion arises,
         But not in relation to a sentient being.

Those who know the aspects of the truth of suffering—imperma-nent, suffering, empty, and selfless—have no enmity that would be con-tradictory of compassion, because they continue previous conceptions from cultivating compassion for sentient beings. For such a detached person in whom the actual quality of natural great love and compas-sion has arisen, it is not related to a view of the self or of a sentient being.

D. Refuting the consequence that they would have desire

Some might say, "Well then, there is no difference between desire and compassion, because desire itself is compassion." To explain:

197.   Desire is from projecting another self
         Onto phenomena that aren't that self.
         Compassion arises out of mere awareness
         Of the continuum of suffering.

There is an enormous distinction between desire and compassion, because their causes are separate and their objects are separate. It is thus: desire arises from focusing on its object of focus, the aggregates—phenomena that are not that self-nature of being a self, mine, perma-nent, or blissful—and projecting onto them another self-nature than that character of being free of self, free of mine, impermanent, and suf-fering, projecting them as a self, mine, permanent, and blissful. Great compassion arises out of mere awareness of its object of focus, the con-tinuum of suffering, without projecting a self, mine, permanence, or bliss onto the aggregates. This is according to Devendrabuddhi.

E. Refuting the consequence that one would have anger

Others say that it is true that love will not transform into the essence of desire, but it might become the nature of aversion. To explain:

198.   Delusion is the root of faults, and that
        Is to perceive as beings. Lacking this,
        There is no anger from the cause of faults.
        Thus we assert compassion to be faultless.

Delusion is the root of all the faults of desire, hatred, and so forth, and that is the delusion that perceives the aggregates as sentient beings. Because they lack this delusion that perceives the aggregates as sentient beings, those who are free of desire have no anger for sentient beings, which would come from the cause of faults, delusion, because there is no perception of the aggregates as a sentient being. Thus we assert that loving great compassion has no faults such as hatred and so forth. This is according to Prajñākaragupta.

F. Refuting the criticism that there would be no liberation

Others say those who are free of desire are under the control of the karma propelled by previous acts, so that is not liberation from samsara. To explain:

199.   They're not unliberated—prior formations
        Have been exhausted; they take no other birth.
        Those who remain without having exhausted
        The power of formations have no faults.

Arhats do remain through the power of the propulsion of previous actions, but they are not unliberated from samsara, because the power of karma, prior formations, has been exhausted and they will not take birth in another existence. Those bodhisattvas who, without having exhausted the power of the formations of virtuous karma, remain in samsara by power of compassion have no faults because they are not stained by faults of samsara. This is according to both Devendrabuddhi and Prajñākaragupta.

You might say that if they remain in samsara by force of compassion, since compassion never ceases, they would remain continuously in samsara. To explain:

200.   Since their compassion is inferior too,
         They do not make great efforts to remain,
         While those who are greatly compassionate
         Remain in the perceptions of others.

Since their (noble listener and self-buddha arhats') compassion is inferior and their karma of formation is being exhausted, too, they do not make great efforts to remain a long time in samsara for the sake of sentient beings. However, those buddhas and bodhisattvas who are greatly compassionate and supremely kind and gentle to sentient beings and who have previously aroused bodhichitta remain in samsara in the perceptions of others, students. This is according to both Devendrabuddhi and Prajñākaragupta.

(b) The explanation of the aspect peace. This has two points: (i) A brief overview, and (ii) Detailed explanation.

(i) A brief overview

Others say:

201ab   "Since they are free of personality view,
          There would be no rebirth on the first path."

You might say that the explanation "Delusion is the root of faults, and that / Is to perceive as beings..." is illogical because there would be no rebirth for noble stream-enterers who dwell on the first of the three undefiled paths—the path of seeing—since they are free of personality view.[215] They have abandoned personality view, doubt, and overesteeming discipline and austerity and thus become stream-enterers. Therefore the other paths would be pointless. To explain:

201cd   It's from not having abandoned the instinctive.
          If that's abandoned, how is there existence?

Noble stream-enterers have not abandoned all personality views, because they have abandoned just the imaginary perception of a self but not the instinctive personality view. If that instinctive personality view is abandoned, how could there be rebirth in existence?

Therefore there are two personality views, the imaginary and the instinctive. The imaginary is holding there to be a permanent self and so forth as projected by inferior philosophical schools. The instinctive is the perception of me that all sentient beings have from beginningless time.

(ii) Detailed explanation

202. And when one thirsts, "May I be happy"
    Or else "May I not suffer,"
    The mind that conceives "I" is the
    Instinctive view of beings.

As just explained, noble stream-enterers have not abandoned instinctive personality view because the mind that conceives "I" with the aspect of wishing, "May I be happy" or else "May I not suffer" and that arises by force of beginningless imprints is present. That is the instinctive personality view that views sentient beings.

To establish this position:

203. Anyone who does not see a me
    Has no attachment to a self,
    And lacking any clinging to a self,
    They don't rush off, wanting happiness.

If noble stream-enterers had abandoned the instinctive view of the self, they would have no view of the self that sees a so-called me. For that reason, they would have no attachment to a self at all. And lacking any clinging to or craving for a self, they would not rush off to rebirth, wanting happiness for themselves. For that reason, they have not abandoned instinctive view of the self.

This teaches that the view of sentient beings is samsaric. For that reason, once all views of sentient beings have been discarded, one will be liberated without a doubt, so this is the aspect peace. This is according to both Devendrabuddhi and Prajñākaragupta.

(c) The explanation of the aspect sublime. This has two points: (i) Refuting that a permanent self is the sublime, and (ii) Refuting that an ineffable self is the sublime.

(i) Refuting that a permanent self is the sublime

Others say that there would be no bondage in samsara and no liberation from that, because there is no permanent self who is bound or liberated. For example, it is like Devadatta being bound in iron chains. Therefore there is a permanent self that is the basis for bondage and liberation, because there is liberation from bondage. For example, it is like Devadatta being released from the iron chains.

> 204.   The causation for suffering to arise
> Is bondage. How could permanents have that?
> The causation for suffering not to arise
> Is freedom. How could permanents have that?

The causation for the suffering of samsara to arise is itself what binds one to samsara. How could a permanent self have that bondage? It follows it does not, because it is not a cause that produces suffering, since it does not entail or reverse entail that. Similarly, the causation for suffering not to arise is freedom. How could a permanent self have that liberation? It follows it does not, because it is not the cause for suffering not to arise.

(ii) Refuting that an ineffable self is the sublime

Some say that it is true that a permanent self has neither bondage nor liberation, but they assert that a self that cannot be described as permanent or impermanent is bound or liberated. To explain:

> 205.   What cannot be described as impermanent
> Is not the cause of anything at all.
> It is not logical—how could there be bondage
> Or liberation for the ineffable?

Is that self momentary or not? If you say it is not, it follows that the self which cannot be described as impermanent is not a cause that produces any result at all. Therefore, how could there be either bondage or liberation for a self that is ineffable? There is not.[216]

If you say there is no fault because the self cannot be described as permanent, to explain:

> 206.   The wise say that is permanent
> Whose nature never perishes.
> Therefore abandon this embarrassing view
> And say that it is permanent.[217]

It would be logical to say a self whose nature remained without perishing is permanent, because the wise call permanent that which remains whose own nature never perishes. Therefore this view is a projection of an individual self that cannot be asserted to be either permanent or impermanent, so abandon this view which is embarrassing in the company of the wise or which is a projection of a self, and say that it, the self of the individual, is impermanent. "What use is there," says Devendrabuddhi, "to focusing on ambiguous words that are like the thoughts from a child's game?"[218]

Master Prajñākaragupta presents the opponent's position saying, "If it does not become something else, it has the natures of both."[219] Then he says:

> The wise say that is permanent
> Whose nature never perishes.
> Therefore abandon this embarrassing view
> And say that it's impermanent.[220]

> To say it perishes and yet is permanent is contradictory. The reason is that what does not perish is permanent. . .[221]

Saying this refutes that the individual self is either permanent or impermanent. Therefore, abandon this embarrassing view that says that the individual self is both permanent and impermanent, and admit that it would be permanent.

(d) The explanation of the aspect emancipation

This will be explained in connection with the truth of the path.[222] From *The Ornament of Validity:*

> Because the aspect of cessation emancipation is taught in connection with the path, now to explain "From cultivating the path that was taught. . ."[223]

iv. What is to be adopted, the truth of the path. This has two topics: (1) General discussion, and (2) The meaning of the text.

(1) General discussion

What is the truth of the path? you ask. It is the wisdom that, from the total perfection of meditation, blocks forever the predilections of the afflictions in the meditator's mind stream. *The Commentary* says:

> From cultivating the path that was taught,
> The basis is transformed.[224]

What is that wisdom? you ask. It is the intelligence that realizes the lack of a self, because that is the antidote for clinging to a self, and because that clinging to a self is the cause of everything afflicted. Thus if that is abandoned, the afflicted will be eliminated. As *The Commentary* says:

> The cause is the attachment formed by clinging
> To me and mine whose sphere of experience
> Is the composite. What opposes that
> Is seeing selflessness, exclusive of it.[225]

There are two types of selflessness, the selflessness of the individual and of phenomena. The listeners and self-buddhas meditate on just the selflessness of the individual and of the apprehended as antidotes for the afflictive obscurations, because that is enough to accomplish their desired aim, nirvana. Bodhisattvas meditate primarily on the selflessness of phenomena as the antidote for the cognitive obscurations, because one cannot achieve omniscience without abandoning the cognitive obscurations and without achieving that, one will not be able to accomplish the deeds of a buddha and turn the Wheel of Dharma in accordance with students' capacities. Therefore meditating properly as previously described on the two types of selflessness by way of the four truths and three characteristics respectively, abandons entirely the views of an individual and phenomena as well as the afflictive and cognitive obscurations those cause.

What are the stages of the path of meditating on the two selflessnesses? As explained in the abhidharma:

> With conduct, listening, contemplation,
> Completely train in meditation.[226]

An individual who has renunciation from samsara and dwells in discipline first listens to the scriptures that teach the nature of truths and the three characteristics in order to become knowledgeable about them. Following that, they properly analyze with logic the meaning of what they have heard and contemplate. Following that, they meditate by familiarizing themselves one-pointedly on the meaning they contemplated. When they come to the culmination of their meditation, the meditator's mind stream becomes the antidote, the nature of wisdom, and all the impediments to that, karma and the afflicted, entirely cease. When those cease, the birth they cause ceases. In this way, the progression of the twelve links of interdependence ceases, and they achieve the state of liberation.

Others say it is not tenable for the antidote to eliminate the discards, because the past and present afflictions and clinging to the truth have already arisen, so they cannot be eliminated, whereas the future ones have not arisen so there is no need to eliminate them. For that reason, there is no liberation that is eliminating the discards with the antidote, they say.

That is not the case. For each aspect to be discarded, there are four paths: the path of joining, the path of no obstacles, the path of liberation, and the distinctive path. The first suppresses the discard and actually leads to the path of no obstacles. The second makes the discards cease at the same time as it arises. The third is the single instant of the path that immediately follows that. The fourth is all the paths that arise after that. The first weakens the discard, the second uproots it, the third manifests liberation, and the fourth distances one from the discard.

There are two types of discard, manifest and seeds. The first is not abandoned, because the past have ceased and the present cannot engage simultaneously with the path. As the future have not arisen, they cannot produce faults, so discarding them is unnecessary. Therefore it is the seeds that are discarded. Among the seeds, it is the future that are discarded, not the past or present, because those that have arisen cannot be discarded. *The Commentary* states:

> And if the cause should not be incomplete,
> What would prevent it having a result?[227]

The future seeds can be abandoned by way of the antidote blocking the gateway through which arising seeds arise. *The Commentary* states:

> Since it eliminates the fault of wanting
> To be reborn, that which prevents the faults
> Has power over the actions they produce,
> But how could what's been done be eliminated?[228]

If future seeds are not prevented from arising, afflictions will arise from them, and various faults will arise from the afflictions. Thus they must be abandoned. Abandoning them also abandons future manifest discards, because when the cause is blocked, the result is also blocked. Therefore it is unnecessary to meditate on an antidote for the manifest separately from the antidote for the seeds. As it says in *The Commentary*:

> Even if one strives to exhaust them both,
> Tiring oneself to exhaust karma is pointless.[229]

The sutras say to meditate on repulsiveness as the antidote for desire, loving-kindness as the antidote for hatred, and interdependence as the antidote for delusion. Those are intended as antidotes for the arising of manifest afflictions, but they are not able to discard the seeds, because as *The Commentary* explains:

> Since they are not exclusive of delusion,
> Loving-kindness and so forth do not
> Destroy the faults completely.[230]

You might say that just as the antidote can overcome desire and so forth habituated from beginningless time, it is also possible that the antidote, the wisdom of selflessness, could be overcome by desire and so forth as well, so the liberation of lasting freedom is pointless.

That is not the case, because desire and so forth stray from the nature of the object through the condition of their own confusion, so their nature is weak. It is also because they are caused by the errors of purity, bliss, permanence, and so forth, but those errors are merely conceptual projections, so they are adventitious. Since they do not engage the actual state, they have little strength.

The transformed wisdom is naturally powerful because it is the subject that perceives impermanence, emptiness, selflessness, and so forth—the nature. The nature of things cannot be made into anything else, so it is naturally powerful. Therefore when the mind stream has become the antidote wisdom, there is no chance for greed to arise, just as there is no chance for darkness to arise in an object near powerful illumination. From *The Commentary*:

> The nature of the mind is luminous;
> The stains are adventitious.[231]

It also says:

> That which is mistaken about the nature
> Of nonhostility and the true meaning
> Does not interfere, though it might make an effort,
> Because the mind is inclined in that direction.[232]

(2) The meaning of the text. This has three topics: (a) It is logical that realizing selflessness is liberation, (b) It is not logical for those who cling to a self to be liberated, and (c) Refuting citations that say that those who have ego-clinging may be liberated.[233]

(a) It is logical that realizing selflessness is liberation. The first has two topics: (i) The direct cause of liberation, and (ii) Rebutting criticism.

(i) The direct cause of liberation

> 207ab From cultivating the path that was taught,
> The basis is transformed.

From cultivating the path that was previously taught during the discussion of the teacher in the lines "From a long time of cultivation / In many ways with many methods. . ."[234] and so forth, one perfects the meditation of the path of seeing selflessness. At that time, the mind that has faults becomes a phenomenon that will not arise at all and becomes the transformed wisdom that is the nature of the antidote.[235] This is according to Devendrabuddhi.

Prajñākaragupta says:

> Cultivating the truth of the previously explained path purifies the basis, the continuum of mind or all-ground. When that becomes in character the selflessness that is incompatible with clinging to a self or mine, it becomes free of all the faults.[236]

(ii) Rebutting criticism. This has two topics: A. The criticism, and B. The response.

A. The criticism

Others say:

> 207bc "Though it transforms,
> The faults arise, just like the path," you say.

"Though it (the mind) may temporarily transform into the nature of the antidote, just as the path arises in a mind that has faults, the faults—wrongs—will once again arise and occur in a mind stream that has the path. For that reason, there is no lasting emancipation and liberation from samsara," you say.

B. The response. This has three topics: 1. It is not tenable that faults arise even though there has been transformation, 2. It is not tenable for loving-kindness and so forth to be the antidote for delusion, and 3. Proving that the view of emptiness is the antidote for delusion.

1. It is not tenable that faults arise even though there has been transformation. This has three topics: a. The faults have no capacity, b. Though the faults may make efforts, they cannot block the path, and c. Attachment and aversion are not antidotes for each other.

a. The faults have no capacity. This has two topics: i. The lack of capacity to produce faults, and ii. Even when there is capacity, it does not last long.

i. The lack of capacity to produce faults. This has two points: (1) The nature of the object and subject, and (2) The distinction between what is the nature and what is not.

(1) The nature of the object and subject

> 207d   Not so, since they have no capacity.

Desire and other such faults do not rearise in a mind stream habituated to the path, because the faults have been overcome by the antidote and they have no capacity to rearise. This is because qualities of the mind such as the intelligence that realizes the lack of a self are the nature of the mind and because the faults are the opposite of that.[237]

How is that? you ask. To explain:

> 208.   The quality of consciousness—apprehending
> An object—apprehends it as is.
> The character of what is present
> Is also what produces it.

209a   Such is the nature.

In this way, qualities are the nature of the mind and faults are not. The nature or quality of consciousness is to apprehend an object. It apprehends it (that object) just as it is in its actual condition. The nature of the object—the character of what is present just as it is—is also what produces and what is realized by its conscious subject, the consciousness, by way of directing that toward itself. Therefore the nature of the object is the sixteen aspects of impermanence, selflessness, and so forth, and realizing that is the nature of the wisdom that realizes the selflessness of phenomena. Such is the nature of object and subject.

(2) The distinction between what is the nature and what is not

209a–d   But because of reasons
           That differ from that, it can deviate.
           Reversing that depends upon conditions,
           So that's unstable, like cognizing a snake.

For that reason, the view of selflessness is the nature of the mind. But because of reasons that differ from that, adventitious confusion that holds that to be permanent, a self, and so forth, it can deviate into viewing a self. Reversing and eliminating those confusions depends upon the condition of cultivating the antidote, the valid cognition that refutes that. So for that reason, that is by nature baseless and unstable, like, for example, a cognition that confuses a mottled rope for a snake. This is according to Prajñākaragupta. For that reason:

210.   The nature of the mind is luminous;
           The stains are adventitious. For that reason,
           They have no power either earlier
           Or later when that becomes the character.

The nature or basic state of the mind that realizes selflessness is luminosity free of the darkness of permanence, projections, and so forth, because it sees the sixteen aspects of the four truths such as impermanence, selflessness, and so forth just as they are. The stains of attachment to a self and so forth are not the nature of the mind, since they appear adventitiously in the mind due to confusion. Because the stains such as desire and so forth are not the nature of the mind and are adventitious, they have no power to harm either earlier during the time of establishing that the aggregates are selfless through hearing and contemplating or later when the mind stream has become transformed into the character of that, the path of realizing selflessness.

ii. Even when there is capacity, it does not last long

Others say, "Isn't it explained that arhats whose faith and so on is weak regress? Therefore how is it that the faults do not rearise?" To explain:

211.   Even when there is power, they lack the power
       To remain a long time in the entity
       That has the essence to produce what will
       Counteract them, like a fire on wet ground.

Even when there is some slight power for the faults to arise, they (the faults such as desire) lack the power to remain a long time in the entity that is the mind of some noble stream enterers and so forth, because that is the supreme essence to produce the antidote, the realization of selflessness that will counteract them (the faults). It is, for example, just as how fire can arise on wet ground saturated with water but does not remain for long. This is according to Prajñākaragupta.

b. Though the faults may make efforts, they cannot block the path

Others say, "The path arises in those who dwell in the character of the faults, so why do the faults not arise in people who dwell in the character of the path, because both of them are exclusive of each other?" To explain:

212.   That which is mistaken about the nature
       Of nonhostility and the true meaning
       Does not interfere, though it might make an effort,
       Because the mind is inclined in that direction.

Because they hold it to be permanent and a self, minds that are mistaken about the wisdom of realization—the wisdom that has none of the hostility of the incompatibilities and that is the subject of the nature of the true meaning, the sixteen aspects such as impermanence and so forth—might make an effort, but that does not interfere. The reason is because the mind is inclined in the direction of the antidote—the wisdom that realizes selflessness—and makes efforts and because there are no faults, so they are blocked. This is according to Devendrabuddhi.

c. Attachment and aversion are not antidotes for each other

Others say that the above explanation "From cultivating the path that was taught, / The basis is transformed. . ."[238] is inconclusive about this, because seeing selflessness is not logically the antidote that eliminates attachment to a self. For example, desire and hatred have mutually exclusive manners of perception, but strong habituation to one does not thoroughly weaken the other, they say. To explain:

> 213.   Since they have the same cause, which is self-clinging,
>   And are entities that are cause and result,
>   Desire and anger do not counteract
>   Each other, even though they're separate.

Since they (desire and anger) both arise from the same cause (clinging to a self), and since it is possible to prove that desire is the entity that is the cause and anger the result, desire and anger do not counteract each other in a way that is able to uproot each other's seeds, even though they have separate, mutually exclusive manners of apprehension.

2. It is not tenable for loving-kindness and so forth to be the antidote for delusion. This has two points: a. Actual, and b. Rebutting criticism.

a. Actual

Others say, "Loving-kindness is the antidote for hatred, repulsiveness the antidote for desire, compassion the antidote for hostility, sympathetic joy the antidote for jealousy, and equanimity the antidote for everything, so why aren't loving-kindness and so forth the antidotes for the faults?" To explain:

214.　　　Since they are not exclusive of delusion,
　　　　　Loving-kindness and so forth do not
　　　　　Destroy the faults completely. It's the root
　　　　　Of all the faults: it is personality view.

Since meditation on loving-kindness focused on sentient beings and so forth is not exclusive of the root of faults, afflicted delusion, it does not completely destroy from their root the faults of desire and so forth. The pervasion is not indeterminate, because all the faults of desire and so forth are results that have it (afflicted delusion) as their root, and it (afflicted delusion) is personality view.

b. Rebutting criticism

Some Buddhist schools say, "Ignorance is an unclear nature that lacks discrimination, but isn't personality view considering[239] by nature? How is it that ignorance is personality view itself?"[240] To explain:

215.　　　Since it is the antithesis of knowing,
　　　　　Since it has a focus, being a mental factor,
　　　　　Since wrongly focusing was said to be
　　　　　Ignorance, others aren't tenable.

It is not logical that the ignorance just explained would be an object other than personality view characterized by self and mine, since it is the actual opposite and antithesis of wisdom, knowing the realization of selflessness. And it is since it is not a mere cessation of knowing but has a focus, being a mental factor, it is concurrent with mind through the fivefold concurrence of support, focus, substance, aspect, and time. Also it is since the Bhagavan said in the sutras that focusing wrongly with a focus and aspects other than the wisdom that realizes selflessness is ignorance.

As it is said in the *Noble Samādhi of the Lamp of the Moon*, "What is being free of ignorance? It is being free of any extraneous projections onto phenomena as they are."

It is also said in the *Sutra of the Ten Levels*:

> When viewing the arising and destruction of the world, they think this: "All the bonds that arise in the world arise out of fixation on a self. If one is free from fixation on a self, there is no becoming in this world either." They think this: "Those with childish intelligence who are fixated on a self, obscured by the cataracts of fixation and unknowing, and fascinated by existence and nonexistence, engage in wrong paths that arise out of inappropriate attention and follow the incorrect. They accumulate meritorious, unmeritorious, and unmoving formations. The seeds of that mind stained by those formations, with the defilements and grasping, in the future go to establish and arise in a rebirth whose nature is birth and aging and death."[241]

Others say that clinging to a self is view, and that is concurrent with ignorance. Thus it should be known that this is said to be ignorance in terms of the view, and personality view is not ignorance. If ignorance itself were personality view, it would be meaningless for the sutras to speak of ignorance concurrent with view, because view is not concurrent with ignorance. To explain:

216a   To explain here what seems contradictory:

I will explain here how the apparent contradiction between some of the Bhagavan's words where he spoke of ignorance and personality view as concurrent and this context of explaining afflicted ignorance to be personality view is not actually a contradiction.

When it speaks in the sutras of "ignorance that is concurrent with view," that does not mean a separate substance with the fivefold concurrence. Instead, "Ignorance that has view" indicates a nominal concurrence of separate whole and parts, so there is no contradiction in the scripture. For example, it is like saying "A forest that has *palasha* trees"[242] or "a body that has a hand." Therefore ignorance is proven to be the general and personality view to be a particular or feature, according to both Devendrabuddhi and Prajñākaragupta.

3. Proving that the view of emptiness is the antidote for delusion

216b–d   Because the view of emptiness is exclusive
Of that, it's proven to be exclusive of
The faults that have that as their nature.

Because the view of emptiness that directly realizes selflessness is actually exclusive of that view and the self's manner of apprehension, it is proven to be exclusive of coexistence with the whole that is the nature of self view and its features, all the faults such as desire and so forth born of the view of the self. It is, for example, just as fire exclusive of the feature cold touch is also exclusive of the natures of features of cold such as the touch of hoarfrost and results of cold such as getting goose bumps. This is according to Devendrabuddhi.

Prajñākaragupta says, "This explains the aspect emancipation of the truth of cessation."[243]

Others say:

217ab   If they are not exhausted, being the nature
Of living beings, like form and such,

If you say that cultivating the antidote may block the afflictions, but they are not exhausted and nonarising phenomena, because the afflictions are the nature of living beings, just like, for example, the form of the elements, the heat of fire, and such, to explain:

217b–d   not so.
That is not proven. When connected to
The antidote, they're seen to be relinquished.

It is not so that since afflictions are the nature of living beings, they cannot be extinguished forever, because they are not proven to be the nature of living beings and because they have been shown to be adventitious. If you say that what merely arises from living creatures is their nature, the reason is indeterminate, because just like the perception of a rope as a snake, that which arises intermittently from something is not appropriate as its nature. It is also because when connected to the antidote, the direct realization of selflessness, they (desire and so forth) are seen to be relinquished and lessened. For example, the connection to a cold touch reverses the touch of a hot rock and so forth.

Others say that desire and so forth might be eliminated once by the antidote, but they will arise again. For example, when gold is melted, it becomes liquid in character but will return to being solid in character. To explain:

218.   Unlike solidity, they don't arise
         Again, because prevention of the faults
         Is not removable, since it's the nature,
         And since it's inconclusive, as with ash.

In a mind stream where the antidote of seeing selflessness has overcome and prevented the faults such as desire, it is not like molten gold which becomes solid when fire is absent. When the antidotes are absent, they (desire and so forth) do not arise again, because the antidote is not removable, as it is the nature of that mind. And just as when fire has reduced wood to ash, the ash does not revert to wood even though the antidote may be absent, it is inconclusive that desire and so forth would rearise, since the cause of the faults—clinging to a self—has been abandoned. This is according to Devendrabuddhi.

(b) It is not logical for those who cling to a self to be liberated. This has two topics: (i) It is not logical to achieve liberation by cultivating a self, and (ii) Rebutting that freedom from clinging to mine brings liberation.

(i) It is not logical to achieve liberation by cultivating a self

Others say that meditating on a self also brings liberation because there are scriptures that say, "Contemplate the self." Therefore why bother with the view of selflessness? To explain:

219.   Those who see a self, saying "me"
         Will cling to it as if eternal.

From clinging, they'll crave happiness,
And craving will conceal the faults.

220.   Seeing qualities, they'll lust for them
And grasp at means to get the mine.
Therefore as long as one is attached
To a self, one is in samsara.

Among sentient beings, there is no liberation from samsara for those who fixate on and see a self. They will cling to the lack of a me, calling it "me" as if it were eternal. From clinging thus, craving for their own happiness arises, and craving will conceal the faults of the self and mine. As those are concealed, they will see the self and mine as qualities and lust for them. As that is so, you who are free of desire for the Desire realm[244] will grasp at the means to get the mine, the self's. Therefore as long as one has fixation on and attachment to a self, one will cycle in the destinations of samsara.

To establish this position:

221.   If there's a self, then one conceives of others.
From the division into self and other,
There's clinging and aversion. All the faults
That are connected to those two arise.

Any person who has a conception of a self has the conception of other, which depends on that. If they have that, then from the division into self and other there are respectively fixated clinging and aversion, and all the faults—jealousy, stinginess, and so forth—that are connected to those two (clinging to self and aversion for others) arise. This is according to both Devendrabuddhi and Prajñākaragupta.

(ii) Rebutting that freedom from clinging to mine brings liberation.
This has six topics: A. Rebutting that they have abandoned clinging to mine, B. Rebutting that they have abandoned clinging to a self, C. Rebutting the proof of abandoning clinging to a self, D. Summary, E. The absurd consequence of having abandoned mine, and F. Advice to therefore abandon personality view.

A. Rebutting that they have abandoned clinging to mine

Some say, "Our liberated individuals do have attachment to a self, but because they are free of attachment to 'mine,' they do not cycle in samsara." To explain:

> 222ab   Necessarily those who cling to a self
>   Are not free of desire for mine.

Those individuals who are attached to and cling to a self necessarily are not liberated from samsara, because those who have attachment to a self also possess and are not free of desire for mine. This is according to Prajñākaragupta.

B. Rebutting that they have abandoned clinging to a self.

This has three points: 1. The actual logic of the rebuttal, 2. Rebutting that attachment is abandoned because it is faulty, and 3. Attachment is not even proven to be faulty.

1. The actual logic of the rebuttal

Others say that there is no faultless self; the self has been abandoned. To explain:

> 222cd   There is no cause for freedom from
>   Attachment to a faultless self.

The person you assert to have achieved liberation is not a faultless self free of suffering and solely free of hostility. For this reason, it is no cause for freedom from attachment to self.

2. Rebutting that attachment is abandoned because it is faulty

Others say:

> 223a   If you say clinging is what's faulty,

If you say, "The self has no faults, but clinging to a self is faulty, so it is something the wise discard, like a finger that has been bitten by a snake," to explain:

> 223b–d   What comes of that? "It is abandoned."
> Unless its object is disproved,
> One is unable to abandon that.

We ask what comes of seeing that attachment to a self is faulty. If you reply "From seeing it in this way, it (attachment to a self) is abandoned," unless its (clinging to a self's) object is disproved and shown to not exist by way of seeing it as having faults, the person you assert as having achieved liberation is unable to abandon that clinging produced by seeing the self as faultless.

To establish this position:

> 224.   Desire, aversion, and so forth, which follow
> From qualities and faults, are eliminated
> By not perceiving those within the object,
> Not in the way external things would be.

The reason is not indeterminate. Desire and aversion, which respectively follow from seeing qualities and faults, and so forth including jealousy are eliminated by not perceiving those (qualities and faults, the causes) within the object. Mental faults cannot be discarded in the way that external things would be discarded, such as by pulling out a thorn. This is according to Devendrabuddhi.

Therefore it is not that we cling to a self through seeing attachment to a self as faulty. Instead, attachment arises from seeing the qualities of the self, so one must abandon seeing qualities in the self. To explain:

> 225.   Clinging is not from qualities of clinging;
> It is from seeing the object's qualities.
> And if the cause should not be incomplete,
> What would prevent it having a result?

Seeing clinging to a self as faulty cannot abandon ego-clinging, because it is not exclusively the cause of ego-clinging. This is because clinging to a self does not arise from merely seeing clinging to a self as having qualities. Instead, it is from seeing the qualities of the object, the self. For that reason, for a person asserted to be liberated, the subject, what would prevent them having the result, ego-clinging? It follows that the result cannot be prevented, because the cause for clinging to a self is present and not incomplete.

The *Ornament* explains, "This is a verse in summary."[245]

3. Attachment is not even proven to be faulty

226a   And what is the faultiness you see in clinging?

We ask, what is the faultiness you see in clinging to a self so that such clinging to a self is discarded?

Others respond:

226b   If it is the support for suffering,

If you say, "It is from clinging to a self that one grasps at samsara that is suffering conjoined with craving for happiness; it is the support. For that reason clinging to a self is faulty, like a finger that has been bitten by a snake." To explain:

226cd   Even so, this is not freedom from desire
           Because it's seen as mine, just like the self.

Clinging to a self does support suffering, yet even so, this is not freedom from desire for that self-clinging, because it is seen as mine and fixated on. For example, it is like the self, for which one is not free of desire even though it supports suffering. This is according to Devendrabuddhi.

The *Ornament* says:

From the very first, the support for suffering is the self. If there is a self, fixation later causes suffering, but if there is no self, who suffers?[246]

Others say:

> 227ab   If without those, the self were not the cause
>   Of suffering,

If you think, "The self that supports suffering is assembled together with fixation on a self, dharma and non-dharma, and formations. Without those being assembled, the self alone is not the cause or support of suffering." To explain:

> 227b–d   it would be similar.
>   The both of them would thus be free of fault,
>   And therefore neither is free of desire.

Well then, it (clinging to a self) would also be faultless, because similarly to the self, it does not produce suffering if the assembly is incomplete. Both of them (the self and self-clinging) would thus individually be free of the fault of causing suffering. And therefore neither the self nor clinging to a self would be free of desire. This is according to Prajñākaragupta.

C. Rebutting the proof of abandoning clinging to a self. This has eight topics: 1. The reason that meditating on suffering does not abandon attachment, 2. Even knowing ego-clinging to be suffering does not prevent attachment, 3. It would be untenable for a faultless self to have suffering, 4. Knowing it to be suffering is not exclusive of the cause of attachment, 5. Refuting the detachment of the Kāpilas, 6. Disgust with suffering is not detachment, 7. Explaining detachment itself, and 8. Rebutting that this is contradictory of the instruction to meditate on suffering.

1. The reason that meditating on suffering does not abandon attachment. This has four topics: a. The analogies for discarding attachment are not comparable, b. It is not logical to assert the self exists, c. If there is attachment to a self, one is unable to abandon attachment to mine, and d. The absurd consequence if one were free of attachment to a self.

a. The analogies for discarding attachment are not comparable. This has three points: i. Teaching that eliminating the thought "mine" causes detachment, ii. Refuting what others assert to be the cause of detachment, and iii. Rebutting the response.

i. Teaching that eliminating the thought "mine" causes detachment

Others say:

> 228ab   If like a snake-bitten limb, it were discarded
>   By meditating upon suffering,

If you say that for example, one discards a limb that has been bitten by a snake by meditating on it as suffering, likewise one discards it (attachment to a self) by meditating upon it as suffering. Therefore the reason of being free of fault is not proven.[247] To explain:

> 228cd   Eliminating the concept of mine
>   Abandons this; the opposite does not.

The snake-bitten limb is forsaken by eliminating the concept of the snake-bitten limb being mine. Unlike eliminating the concept of mine, the opposite of that—merely meditating on it as suffering—does not get one to relinquish the bitten limb.

Therefore, to teach that the analogy is not a good comparison for you either:

> 229.   In maintaining that the faculties
>   And so forth are the supports for enjoyment,
>   What will prevent the thought of them as mine?
>   For them, how could there be detachment?

In maintaining that the eye faculty, body faculty, and so forth are the supports for enjoyment even while seeing them as suffering, what will prevent your individual free of desire for Desire who sees the faculties of the eye and so forth as suffering from thinking of them as mine? For that reason, how could there be detachment for them through meditating on the faculty of eye as suffering? There is not.

To teach an analogy for this:

230. It's obvious to everyone
That feelings of disgust arise
For hair and such shed from the body
While clinging occurs for the other.

For example, since there is no thought of them as mine, feelings of disgust and non-attachment arise for hair, nails, spit, and such that are shed from the body while feelings of clinging occur for the other, hair and such that has not been shed. This is obvious to everyone, all people. For that reason, seeing suffering is not a cause of detachment, whereas eliminating the thought of mine is the cause of detachment. This is according to both Devendrabuddhi and Prajñākaragupta.

ii. Refuting what others assert to be the cause of detachment

According to the Vaiśeṣikas:

231ab If the conception "mine" arose out of
Relations of inherence and so forth,

Desire and so forth are abandoned by meditating on them as suffering, but the conception of "mine" that arises with regard to hair and so forth that have not been shed from the body arises out of relations of inherence between that and the self, the body as the support of enjoyment, the faculties as the means to get enjoyments, and so forth. For that reason, they are not free of desire, they say.

To explain:

231cd Since those relations would remain the same,
Even if faults were seen, they'd not be abandoned.

If that were so, for the person you assert to be free of desire, the cause that definitely produces clinging to me and mine and so forth, the self and those relations of inherence and so forth, would remain exactly the same in later periods as they were in the previous period when they were not free of desire. For that reason, it would follow that even if the faults of clinging to me and mine were seen, clinging would not be abandoned.

The Sāṃkhyas say that attachment does not arise from relations of inherence to self or mine. As long as there is a conception that ascertains the primal substance to be the same as the *puruṣa*, faculties, and so forth, there is samsara. When one knows that the primal substance is different from the puruṣa, faculties, and so forth, then because one knows the distinction between the primal substance and the puruṣa, one is liberated, they say.

To explain:

> 232ab   Even without inherence and so forth,
>   There is the benefit for everything.

Even without inherence and so forth, the mind that holds the primal substance to be the same as the puruṣa, faculties, and so forth is not the cause of attachment, because even without holding external enjoyments such as food, clothing, and so forth to be the same as the puruṣa, they are seen to be beneficial, and there is clinging to everything as mine.

iii. Rebutting the response

Others say:

> 232cd   If there were no idea of them as mine
>   Since they, like a finger, produce suffering,

Since they are causes that produce suffering, there would occur no idea of them (the body faculty and so forth) as mine. It is like, for example, a finger bitten by a snake: since there is no conception of it as mine, it is abandoned. Therefore, the reason is not proven, they say.

To explain:

> 233a   They are not solely suffering.

They (the body, faculties, and so forth) are not solely the causes of suffering because it is also possible that they might produce pleasure in some instances.

Others say:

233b "They mostly are, like poisoned food."

"They (the body, faculties, and so forth) mostly are the cause of suffering. For that reason there is freedom from attachment, as with poisoned food," you say. To explain:

233cd Because of lusting for superior pleasures,
One is detached from what's exclusive of that.

234ab Because of craving a superior pleasure,
One would forsake some minor satisfaction.

People who have found food that does not endanger their lives lust for food and enjoyments that cause the superior pleasures such as increasing physical strength without endangering their lives. Because of that, they will become detached from that poisoned food that endangers their lives, which is exclusive of that food which does not endanger their lives. The pervasion is not indeterminate, because when people find food and enjoyments that cause the superior pleasures such as increasing physical strength without endangering their lives, they crave those, because of which they would forsake poisoned food that causes some minor satisfaction by merely tasting good and being filling.

To establish these positions:

234cd Unthinkingly, from clinging to a self,
One acts upon whatever one obtains.

235ab It's just as men who cannot get a woman
Are seen to perform carnal acts with beasts.

Even if you obtain superior food and do not eat poisoned food, that alone does not make you detached. Because they do not actually find superior food and so forth that cause pleasure, from coming under the power of clinging to a self, some unthinking fools act upon and cling to whatever poisoned food or so forth they obtain. For example, it is just as some lustful men who cannot get a woman are seen to perform carnal acts with female animal beasts. This is according to Devendrabuddhi.

b. It is not logical to assert the self exists

Some say that the self at the time of liberation is not the support for the experience of pleasure and pain, so there is no fixation on "my" pleasure, and therefore one does not seek mine. To explain:

> 235cd How could someone who loves the self
> So dearly wish it be destroyed?

> 236. How could fixation wish the basis
> Of all experience, conventions,
> And qualities would cease to be?
> The nature of fixation is not so.

How could a person said to be liberated who asserts[248] the self exists wish that it (that self) be destroyed and not exist as a support for experience and so forth? Because the wish that the self—the basis of all experiences of pleasure, pain, and so forth, of all conventions, and of all qualities such as intelligence—would cease to be is contradictory of the assertion that the self truly exists as they are fixated upon it. Therefore if the self is not accepted to cease, the nature of fixation is not, and is not established as being, such fixation on the cessation of the self, the support of experience. This is according to Devendrabuddhi.

c. If there is attachment to a self, one is unable to abandon attachment to mine

> 237. Apprehending a self will reinforce
> In every way the clinging to a self.
> That is the seed of fixating on mine.
> In such a situation, that remains.

In this manner, apprehending a self reinforces in every way the clinging to the self, and that clinging to a self is the seed of fixating on "mine." For that reason, as long as the person you assert to be liberated is in such a situation of clinging to a self, that fixation on mine will remain. Therefore those who possess the cause—clinging to a self— also possess the result—clinging to mine—just as, for example, those who have the cause of illness have the illness.

To establish these positions:

238.   Despite their efforts, behavior based upon
                The portions that are qualities prevents
                Freedom from attachment to a mine,
                And that conceals its faults as well.

Despite the efforts the people you assert to be liberated may make to abandon clinging to mine, if they are attached to a self, they see the portions of mine that are qualities. Based upon that, according to circumstances, clinging to me arises and they act. This is because not abandoning clinging to a self prevents freedom from attachment to mine and because that conceals the faults of mine from being seen as well. This is according to Devendrabuddhi.

d. The absurd consequence if one were free of attachment to a self

Others say:

239a   If also free of clinging to the self,

At the time of liberation, just as they are free of mine, they are also free of clinging to the self. Therefore, all the explanations of personality view in terms of clinging to a self are unfounded, they say.

The faults of this have already explained in the verses "There is no cause for freedom from / Attachment to a faultless self."[249] Additionally:

239b–d   In that case, there is no one free of clinging.
                 The self has in this manner been discarded;
                 Meditating on suffering would be pointless.

In that case, it follows that at the time of liberation, there is no self that is to be free of clinging to a self, because they are free of clinging to a self. Additionally, it follows that it would be pointless for a person who is trying to abandon clinging to mine to meditate on suffering in order to become free of attachment to mine in this manner, because the self has been discarded by way of becoming free of attachment to it, so it is proven that they are free of attachment to mine.

2. Even knowing ego-clinging to be suffering does not prevent attachment

240.   By meditating on suffering as well,
         Suffering would be distinctly known itself,
         But that was evident earlier as well,
         And likewise they would not become detached.

By meditating on mine as suffering as well, the yogis that you assert to be detached would distinctly know that directly to be suffering itself. However, because they cling to a self, even though they know it to be suffering, they would likewise not be free of attachment to mine. For example, earlier as well—during the period of being an ordinary individual before meditating on suffering—that was directly evident and seen, but they were not detached to a self.

Others say, "It is seen that some people are freed of desire by seeing the faults of the object of attachment. Therefore your reason is not proven or is indeterminate." To explain:

241.   And if perchance because of something's faults,
         Their thoughts are displaced from it for a moment,
         They are not free of desire for that thing,
         As with a lustful man and other women.

If perchance for some people who have self-clinging, when they see some faults in something that is the object of desire, their (the desirous people's) thoughts of desire might be displaced from it for the moment of seeing the faults, but they are not completely free of desire for that thing which is the object of desire, because they have not abandoned desire for all objects. This is because it is possible that desire will once again arise from seeing the qualities of the object of desire. For example, some lustful men see faults in some women and thus are free of desire for them, but they are not free of desire for other women.

To establish this position:

242. If there's a difference between what to shun
    And what to appropriate, the attachment that
    Arises for the one becomes the seed
    Of all desires when they arise in order.

If there are various differences between what to shun (such as the women some men do not want) and what to appropriate (such as the women they want), the attachment that arises for the one object that is desired to be appropriated becomes the seed of all desires when they arise through a variety[250] of causes and conditions. For that reason, the person asserted to be free of desire may be temporarily free of attachment to some objects, but the attachment they have for other objects is indirectly the seed for attachment to arise for that for which they are temporarily free of attachment. This is according to Devendrabuddhi.

3. It would be untenable for a faultless self to have suffering

243. Objects would have no faults, nor would attachment,
    And the means to attain would have none either.[251]
    If beings were just that, then in that case
    What would they be freed from attachment for?

If the self were faultless, attachment to the faultless self would then be faultless, because it is interest that is the conscious subject of a faultless self, like interest in liberation. Similarly, the mine that is faculties and so forth, which are the means to attain the enjoyments of the faultless self, also would be faultless and freed from the fetters of samsara. Therefore, if beings as well were just that self, attachment to the self, and the mine that is the faculties, objects, and so forth, then in that case, those persons, attachment to mine, and mine would all three be something to meditate on as being freed from attachment, because the self, attachment to self, and mine would be faultless. The word "and" indicates a distinction.[252]

Others reply:

> 244a   If that for it had faults as well,

That (attachment) for it (the self) is not a faultless subject of the self, but has faults as well because it is the support for suffering, you say. To explain that this is similar for you as well:

> 244a–d   that also
> Would be the same for the self. It would not
> Be free of attachment for its faults, so then
> What would they be freed from attachment for?

For the person you assert to be liberated, that (functioning as a support of suffering) would be the same for the self also. For that reason, the self would have faults. It (the self) would not be free of attachment for its faults, the support for its suffering, so then what attachment to a self and support for suffering would they be freed from attachment for by seeing the faults of those? It follows it would not be, because they are not freed of attachment to a self by seeing that it has the fault of supporting suffering. This is according to Devendrabuddhi.

4. Knowing it to be suffering is not exclusive of the cause of attachment. This has two points: a. Seeing faults is not the cause of detachment, and b. Seeing qualities is not the cause of attachment.

a. Seeing faults is not the cause of detachment

> 245.   Fixation born of seeing qualities
> Would be neutralized by seeing faults,
> But it's not so for faculties and so on
> Since it is seen in children and so forth,[253]

> 246.   Since it occurs for what has faults as well,
> Since it does not occur for others even

If they have qualities, and since there's none
For the mine of the past, et cetera.

Meditating on mine, the faculties, and so forth as faulty is not exclusive of the cause of attachment to the faculties and so forth. For that reason, it is not the antidote for attachment to the faculties and so forth. If there were fixation that was born of seeing an object as having qualities, it would be neutralized by seeing that object's faults, but it is not so that the attachment to the faculties and so on as mine arises from seeing the qualities of the faculties and so forth. This is because it is seen that children, cattle, and so forth lack any analysis as to whether there are qualities and faults, but they are attached to the faculties such as the eye; because it (attachment) occurs for the faculties and so forth that have faults such as cataracts, blindness, being crippled, being ugly, and so forth as well; because it does not occur for other beings' faculties even if the faculties have qualities; and since there is no attachment as mine for one's own appendages of the past that have perished or those limbs or appendages that have fallen from the body, et cetera, even if they have qualities.

b. Seeing qualities is not the cause of attachment

Others say that the thought "mine" arises from seeing qualities. Therefore meditating on them as suffering interrupts the continuum of the perception of qualities that causes the thought of mine. Due to that, one becomes free of attachment to mine, so therefore the reason is not proven, they say.

To explain:

247.   Thus for that reason, seeing qualities
        Is also not the cause of thinking "mine,"
        And therefore it is not eliminated
        By seeing that does not have qualities.

Thus for those reasons such as "Since it is seen in children and so forth. . ." and so on, seeing qualities in the mine is also not the cause that produces the thought "mine." And because seeing qualities in

mine does not produce clinging to mine, therefore the seeds of it—
the mind that clings to mine—are not eliminated by seeing that mine
does not have any qualities. Therefore, as long as one is not free of
attachment to the self, one will have the thought "mine" and as long
as one has that, one will have attachment to mine. This is according to
Devendrabuddhi.

To describe additional faults:

248.   Projections of nonexistent qualities
        Because of clinging are seen there as well.
        Therefore, how can accomplishing that which
        Does not prevent the causes prevent it?

There are these additional faults: the person you assert to be free of
attachment does not become detached by seeing the faults of mine and
then meditating on it as suffering. This is because they project nonexistent qualities as being existent and cling to a self, the qualities of the
mine are seen there as well, and there is absolutely no opportunity to
see faults. That attachment to mine does not arise from seeing qualities;
the cause it arises from is clinging to mine. Therefore, because it does
not prevent the cause of attachment to mine, how can accomplishing
rituals of meditating for the sake of liberation on mine—the faculties
and so forth—as suffering prevent it (attachment to mine)? It could
only not prevent it. This is a summary.

5. Refuting the detachment of the Kāpilas

The Kāpilas say, "We do not say that attachment is from seeing qualities. If you wonder what it is like, holding the primal substance, the
puruṣa, and the mind to be the same causes attachment to arise. Understanding the primal substance and the puruṣa to be different discards
the thought of oneself, and thus one becomes free of desire." To explain:

249.   Because they seek another that is better
        And since they know arising and perishing,
        These individuals understand the self
        Is separate from the faculties and so forth.

250.   Thus clinging is not due to seeing sameness.
    And for that reason those who cling to a self
    Will naturally become attached to the
    Perceptual internal body parts.

It follows that these childish ordinary individuals are free of desire because they understand that the self is separate from the faculties and so forth. How do they know they are separate? you ask. It is because when the eye faculty and so forth in their continuums lack qualities, they seek another that is better, thinking, "May mine be better than other eye faculties or so forth," and because they don't think, "May my self become something else." It is also since they see themselves to remain while having the understanding that knows that faculties, hair, nails, limbs, and so forth arise and perish.

Knowing that the nature and the individual are separate is not the cause of freedom from desire, and thus seeing the nature and individual as the same is not the cause for desire to arise, because clinging arises even without seeing those two as the same. And for that reason, clinging to a self is the cause of clinging to a mine, because attachment to the five faculties of eye and so forth—the internal body parts that make a cognition perceive an object such as form—as mine will inherently or naturally arise.

6. Disgust with suffering is not detachment

Others say, "Doesn't one become detached by seeing the suffering of others, living beings? How is it that one does not becomes detached by meditating on suffering?" To explain:

251.   Weariness felt for present suffering
    Is aversion—such is not freedom from desire.
    At that time, there is clinging and so forth,
    As one will seek another situation.

The revulsion such as that felt by a person who meditates on seeing the faults of being afflicted by present suffering is not freedom from desire. It is despondence concurrent with aversion from the mental displeasure of seeing suffering. Thus it is like the explanation from the noble Theravāda school that all mental displeasure is concurrent with aversion. Such weariness that is concurrent with aversion is not detachment because the two of them—this and detachment—have the different characteristics of being unvirtuous and virtuous. The Bhagavan said that although such mental displeasure is solely nonvirtue, it can produce virtuous qualities, and therefore it is taught. Additionally, at that time that weariness arises because of displeasure with suffering, there is clinging to mine, as one will want and seek another situation than that of suffering, happiness.

Others say of this that a permanent arising of hatred is not detachment. To explain:

252. Because aversion's source is suffering,
It only stays as long as there is that.
When that has ceased, they once again
Return to their own nature.

Because aversion arises from the presence of suffering as a cause or source, it does not continually occur even if there is no suffering. Therefore it (aversion) only stays as long as there is that suffering. When that suffering has ceased and is not present, aversion also ceases and is not present. Thus they once again return to their own nature itself.[254]

7. Explaining detachment itself

Others ask, "Well if weariness with suffering is aversion and not detachment, then what is it that is called 'freedom from attachment?'" To explain:

253. As they've abandoned shunning and adopting,
Those who are equanimous toward all
And for whom sandalwood and axes are
The same are said to be free of desire.

Noble arhats who are are free of desire for the three realms are said to be free of desire because they have abandoned any fixation on the "entity" of the self—the necessary assemblies of the aggregates of grasping—as something to adopt as "this is me and this is mine" or faults as something to shun. It is also because they have the equanimity of equally feeling neither attachment nor aversion toward all objects, pleasant or unpleasant, and because they do not feel attachment when someone with a faithful mind massages them from one side with sandalwood, nor do they fixate on it as something to reject when another person chops their limbs with an axe out of anger; for them those are the same. "Instead, they dwell in the equanimity that has the characteristic of being free of attachment or aversion for either,"[255] according to Devendrabuddhi.

From the *Ornament*:

> Our position is that by seeing the mere dharma nature, they achieve equanimity for sentient beings. Because they are free of attachment. . ., yogis are detached. It is not otherwise.[256]

8. Rebutting that this is contradictory of the instruction to meditate on suffering.

Others ask, "Why then did the Bhagavan say to meditate on suffering?" To explain:

254.   Thinking of the suffering of formations,
          He said to meditate on suffering.
          Ours as well arises from conditions,
          And that supports the view of selflessness.

The Bhagavan did not merely intend the suffering of suffering when he said to meditate on suffering: When the pleasures of desire abate for them, those who are desirous have the suffering of formation by way of falling to an extreme or losing something. Thinking of meditation on this aspect, he said to meditate on suffering. It is also because our object of meditation—the pervasive suffering of formation—as well is just the dependent momentariness that arises from causes and conditions, and we meditate on that merely as the support for the view of selflessness.

If meditating on the suffering of formation is the support for the view of realizing emptiness, what good is it to realize that view? you ask. To explain:

255ab   The view of emptiness will liberate;
          Remaining meditations are for that sake.

From meditating on the suffering on formation, the ultimate emptiness of all composites being free of me or mine will be realized, and viewing emptiness will liberate one from the bonds of samsara. Therefore, remaining meditations on impermanence, suffering, and so forth are practiced for the sake of realizing that emptiness, but meditating on them is not able to completely liberate one.

To establish the text:

255cd   Thus from impermanence is suffering;
          From suffering is selflessness, he stated.

Meditating on impermanence and suffering is a method of seeing emptiness but is not a direct cause for liberation. Thus for that reason, from the method of meditating on impermanence, one knows suffering. From the cause of knowing suffering, the realization of selflessness will arise, it was stated. As the Bhagavan said in a sutra:

"Bhikshus, is form permanent or impermanent?"
    "Venerable, it is impermanent."
    "Is that which is impermanent suffering or pleasant?"
    "Venerable, it is suffering. That which is impermanent is suffering, a changeable phenomenon."
    "Is it logical to view that as 'This is mine' or 'This is my self'?"
    "Venerable, it is not."[257]

For that reason, the Bhagavan's teachings lead to emptiness. This is according to both Devendrabuddhi and Prajñākaragupta.

D. Summary

256.   Those who have craving and aren't free of attachment,
        Dependent upon every undertaking,
        Not liberated from actions and afflictions—
        Such beings as these are called samsaric.

Therefore, such beings as these, those you assert to be free from desire, are called samsaric beings because they are not free of attachment to a self and mine, because they have the craving of wishing to achieve pleasure and cast off suffering, because they are dependent on every undertaking to engage in taking up pleasure and giving up suffering, and because due to their attachment, craving, and engagement in efforts, they are not liberated from the afflictions and the virtuous or unvirtuous actions those motivate, like, for example, an ordinary individual.

E. The absurd consequence of having abandoned mine

Others say:

257a   And if one were not to accept the mine,

At the time of liberation, mine has been abandoned and it is not accepted, they say. To explain:

257b–d   Then its consumer, too, would not exist.
           Its self, whose characteristics are action
           And experience, would also not exist.

Then for the self you assert to be freed from samsara, the subject, it follows that the mine that is the consumer's mine, too, would not exist, because there is no mine to consume or experience. As this is accepted, when its characteristics of performing actions and so forth and experiencing ripening are not accepted, at that time its self would also not exist.

F. Advice to therefore abandon personality view

258.   Therefore all those who wish for freedom should
         Eradicate the personality views
         That arise out of seeds of the same kind
         In a beginningless continuum.

Because seeing egolessness is the path for reaching the city of nirvana whereas meditating on something else such as suffering is not
the path, therefore you who wish for freedom from pointless samsara
should with great effort eradicate from their roots and destroy personality views by cultivating selflessness. What are those personality
views like? you ask. They have beginningless causes:[258] because of the
seeds or previous instances of the same kind, later instances arise. "The
meaning is that they have engaged since beginningless time," says
Devendrabuddhi.[259]

**(c) Refuting citations that say that those who have ego-clinging may
be liberated.** This has five topics: (i) The actual refutation, (ii) Rebutting
criticism of that, (iii) Refuting that destroying unseen karma liberates, (iv)
Refuting that the power of a self would apply, and (v) Refuting that samsara
is impossible.

(i) The actual refutation

Some say that the self is existent and its liberation is proven in the
scriptures.[260] Such liberation is solely the nature of bliss, and it never
becomes nonexistent. Since samsaric pleasure has an end, it never produces complete satisfaction. Because this is established through rites
such as empowerments, all the prior arguments are pointless.[261] As it
is said:

> The words of the sages who have seen
> With their own eyes the entity
> That transcends the senses and cannot be touched
> Cannot be disproven by inference.

It is the same with words that are not of human origin, they claim.[262]
To explain that this is illogical:

259.   For those who have not seen the reasoning
           For why the scriptures have such reality,
           Stating that scriptures alone bring liberation
           Is not completely satisfying.

For those discerning people who want liberation, the scriptures that
state that the scriptures empowered by Īśvara alone bring liberation
are not scriptures that are completely satisfying to the discerning,
because they have not validly seen the reasoning for why the meaning
expressed in the scriptures would have such reality.

Others say of this that it is seen that through rituals that empower
seeds and so forth, the sprout becomes a non-arising phenomenon, and
this is the same. To explain:

260.   Rites that affect a seed or so forth lack
           The power to make a human not be born
           Since it would follow that anointing oil
           And burning and so forth would liberate.

It is not the same: Rites that affect a seed or so forth, making it unable
to produce a seedling, lack the power to make a human not be born in a
later birth. If you say the reason is not proven, well then, it follows that
anointing a person with sesame oil, burning them with fire, grinding
them into flour, cooking them, crushing them, and so forth would liberate them because smearing seeds with sesame oil and so forth makes
them not produce seedlings.

Others say:

261a   "Since heavier before and lighter after,"

A person's misdeeds are exhausted when a guru takes him and
performs a fire offering, since when he is weighed on a scale before
and after, it is seen that he is heavier before and lighter after, they say.
To explain:

261b–d   But that does not eliminate misdeeds.
          Their weight may cease to be, but misdeeds are
          Not physical and thus do not have weight.

But that, merely seeing that a person who has performed a fire offering weighs more before and less after, is not able to prove that eliminates misdeeds, because through tormenting the person with fire in the fire offering, a slight amount of the weight of their body—water, earth, and so forth only—may cease to be, but misdeeds of the mind are not physical and thus do not have heavy or light weight that can be measured on a scale.

(ii) Rebutting criticism of that

Some say, "If empowerments of Īśvara and so forth are not the path, then your selflessness is not the path, either." To explain:

262.   Due to the volitions of misconception
           And of the craving that is born of that,
           There's birth in the inferior destinations.
           Thus if that's severed, there is no migration.

263ab   Those two themselves have power over birth
           Since it will occur merely due to them.

Volitions concurrent with the misconception that erroneously holds suffering to be pleasure and with the craving of seeking samsara that is born of that are the causes of birth in samsara. Due to them, one will go to and be born in the inferior destinations such as the womb and so forth. Thus because mistaken craving is the cause of samsara, if the wisdom that realizes egolessness severs and eliminates that mistaken craving, there is no migration into samsara. Since it (samsara) occurs merely due to those mistaken cravings, those mistaken cravings themselves have the power over birth in samsara to produce samsaric birth.

Others say, "Previously committed actions are also causes of birth in samsara, so how is it that samsara has the nature of arising just from those mistaken cravings?" To explain:

263cd Because those two intentions are themselves
     Actions, the cause for birth is not destroyed.

Past actions that are not those two intentions are not the cause of samsara, because those two are themselves the actions that cause samsara. Therefore empowerments of Īśvara are not the path to liberation because they can never destroy the cause for birth in samsara, mistaken craving.

(iii) Refuting that destroying unseen karma liberates. This has two points: A. The actual logic of the refutation, and B. Refuting an assembly with the qualities of the self.[263]

A. The actual logic of the refutation

Others say:

264.   "The agents are supports for going and
     For realization. They're from the unseen.
     When the unseen is destroyed, there's no migration.
     So therefore it is formation, not volition."

"The faculties of the eye and so forth are supports or causes for going from one place to another and for the realization of objects such as form. These agents occur from either the dharmic or the undharmic karma, which are both unseen. Thus when the ritual of empowerment destroys the unseen karma, there is no migration to inferior places for the faculties that have been empowered. So therefore it (the unseen karma) is the formation that can be produced by engagement in the twenty virtues and nonvirtues,[264] and it is not the volition concurrent with mistaken craving that you assert," they say.

To explain:

265.   Since it is consequent to the presence or
     The absence, mind's capacity to produce
     The agent is perceived, but not the other's.
     If that is present, why would they not go?

Since it is consequent to the presence or prevented by the absence of cognition that is concurrent with misconceptions and craving, the capacity of the mind of mistaken craving to produce the agents—the six faculties—is perceived. They are not produced by the other, formations that are consequent to the unseen karma of the twenty virtues and nonvirtues. Therefore, though one might receive an empowerment, because that mistaken craving is present, why would they (the agents or faculties) not go into samsara? They would go. This is according to Devendrabuddhi.

B. Refuting an assembly with the qualities of the self

Others say:

> 266a   If they had no capacity,

The cause of samsara is the assembly of mistaken craving and the qualities of the self. If those are destroyed by empowerment, they have no capacity to produce, you say. To explain:

> 266a–d   right after
> Initiation and so forth, there'd be
> No apprehension, engagement, disturbance,
> Or cessation under the power of volition.

If that were so, right after people received an initiation or means for liberation such as a mantra or so forth, for those people there would be no apprehension of objects, turning away from engaging an object at one's pleasure, engagement in a desired object, disturbance of engaging unevenly, or the perishing of cessation under the power of volition concurrent with mistaken craving. This is because immediately after initiation, the power of the assembly of mistaken craving and the qualities of the self would have been eliminated, so the mind would be impaired. This is according to Prajñākaragupta.

Devendrabuddhi explains:

It says, "There'd be / No apprehension, engagement, disturbance, / Or cessation under the power of volition." Without
anything to prevent the engagement of its own object, *apprehension. Engagement* causes engagement in the object. *Disturbance* is producing a change in the mind from a blow or so
forth. *Cessation* is the cessation of disturbance even when it
conforms with the mind.[265]

Others say:

267ab   "What if, because at that time there's no mind,
         They would not.

"What if immediately after an initiation, there are distraction, cessation, and so forth, but because at that time (the time of death), there
is no mind of mistaken craving and so forth, they (the agents of the
faculties and so forth) would not be propelled," they say.
    We ask why there would be no mind to propel the faculties and so
forth. The opponents reply:

267bc   It's the stains that make the mind
         Link rebirth, but they lack capacity."

It is the stains of the afflictions such as misconceptions, clinging to
a self, and so forth that make the mind or those faculties and so forth
at the time of not having been empowered link rebirth in an existence.
But if an initiation has been performed, they (the faculties) would lack
the capacity to link rebirth due to the stains, they say.

267d   Then living, they'd be powerless as well.

Then while the person who received the initiation were living, they
(the stains such as mistaken craving) would be powerless to link to
the next faculties as well, because the initiation would have eliminated
the power of mistaken craving while they remained alive. "Therefore
one would be liberated immediately upon initiation,"[266] according to
Prajñākaragupta.

To teach that one cannot agree:

> 268.   Since when the antidote or their own side
> Increases, they will decrease or increase,
> The faults' continuum, with its own seeds,
> Is not averted by initiation.

Since when the antidote—the wisdom that realizes selflessness—or mistaken craving's own side—inappropriate attention—increase, they will decrease or increase respectively, the faults' continuum of inappropriate attentions, which arises from its own seeds (previous instances of the same kind), is not averted by initiation without eliminating those seeds. This is according to both Devendrabuddhi and Prajñākaragupta.

(iv) Refuting that the power of a self would apply. This has two points: A. The self cannot logically be a cause, and B. Refuting criticism of selflessness.

A. The self cannot logically be a cause

Some say that the self produces mistaken craving and so forth. To explain:

> 269.   Because the permanent is not dependent,
> It's contradictory for it to produce
> Sequentially and to have a like nature
> Of acting when it's acting and not acting.

> 270a   Cause and result would be the same as well.

Because a permanent self would be a permanent that is not dependent upon causes and conditions, it would be contradictory for it to produce results sequentially. Additionally, because the self that is acting to make a result and the permanent self that is not acting to make a result would always have a like nature of not depending on conditions, it follows that would be contradictory for it to act to make a result during times when it was not making a result. This has already been explained in detail in the context of:

Just as that entity is the cause,
In the same way, then, at the times
It's not the cause, why do you assert
It is the cause, not not a cause?[267]

The self during the phase of the cause and the self during the phase of enjoying the result would be the same, because the two are the same permanent self.

If you say the reason is not proven, to explain:

270b–d   If that were to be separate from those,
The actor and consumer would be lost,
And the capacity would not be proven.

If those[268] (the selves of those who accumulate karma and of those who experience its ripening) were to be separate from and unrelated to the accumulators of karma and the experiencers of its ripening, being the actor who does an act and the consumer of the ripening would be lost. Not only that, it would follows that the permanent self, the subject, does not produce a result because its capacity to produce a result would not be validly proven.

B. Refuting criticism of selflessness

Others say that if some self did not exist, then another would remember, something done by one would be experienced by another, one would not remember what they had experienced, one would be certain of what another had doubted, one would recognize what another had seen, and so forth.

To explain:

271.   The consequence that another would remember,
Experience, and so on does not refute,
As there's no memory of anyone's.
Thus memory is from experience.

The consequence that because there is no self, another would remember what someone else had done, that another would experience the acts of someone else, that one would not remember what he had experienced, and so on do not refute us, as there is no later memory of anyone's—any permanent self's—earlier experience, and we answer that we agree. Thus although there is no permanent self, what one has experienced is not remembered by another continuum, because later memory arises from one's own previous experience.

(v) Refuting that samsara is impossible. This has three topics: A. The actual refutation, B. Refuting criticism of that, and C. Refuting liberation through austerity.

A. The actual refutation

Others say that since there is no self, there would be no entry into samsara, because if there were no self there would also be no personality view. Therefore samsara itself would not exist.

To explain:

> 272.   Projecting onto the four truths
>   The sixteen unreal aspects of
>   Being stable, pleasurable, me,
>   And mine, and so forth, one has craving.

Because the cause of samsara exists, samsara is not non-existent. It is like this: among the sixteen aspects of the four noble truths, by projecting being permanent and stable on the aspect impermanence of the truth of suffering, and likewise being pleasurable on suffering, being me on selflessness, being mine on emptiness, and so forth including projecting not being the cause, not being the origin, not being production, and not being a condition on the truth of origin; projecting not being cessation, not being peace, not being sublime, and not being emancipation on the truth of cessation; projecting not being the path, not being reasoning, not being accomplishing, and not being deliverance on the truth of path—the sixteen unreal, fallacious aspects—craving for the permanent, pleasurable, and so forth arises. Thus the two types of mistaken craving are the causes of samsara. This is according to Devendrabuddhi.

Master Prajñākaragupta says:

> Samsara is unreal projection, and ultimately samsara does not exist. Those with craving for the nature of the projections of the sixteen unreal aspects imagine that they are in samsara due to karma, but samsara is not otherwise possible.[269]

To teach that the path is the antidote itself:

273.   Meditating thoroughly on those
         With realization of the aspects of thatness—
         The meaning that is contrary to those—
         Right view eliminates craving and its suite.

Meditating thoroughly on those (the four noble truths), the wisdom that realizes selflessness with realization of the sixteen aspects of those four noble truths—impermanence, suffering, and so forth—that are the meaning that is contrary to those—permanence, bliss, and so forth— the right view that properly sees selflessness directly is the antidote that discards samsara, because by way of actually eliminating ignorance, craving and its suite—stinginess, envy, and so forth that are causes of suffering—are eliminated. This is according to Devendrabuddhi.

The *Ornament* states:

> The object nirvana, whose characteristic is the cessation of all ignorance, becomes visible. Therefore seeing suchness and stopping craving is liberation.[270]

B. Refuting criticism of that

Others ask how abandoning craving could be liberation since one has karma and a body.[271] To explain:

274.　　　Though karma and the body still remain,
　　　　　It is impossible for that which has
　　　　　Three causes to be born since one is absent,
　　　　　Just as no sprout will grow without a seed.

It is thus: for a person who has abandoned the primary cause of samsara (craving), though karma and the body still remain, since craving (one of the three causes karma, the body, and craving) is absent, it is impossible to once again be born in samsara, just as, for example, no sprout will grow without a seed even if there are moisture, manure, and so forth.

Others say, "If one is liberated by abandoning craving among the three causes, since karma and the body are also causes, it is logical to say that one can be liberated by exhausting them." To explain:

275.　　　Not by discarding karma and the body,
　　　　　Because an antidote does not exist
　　　　　Since there is no ability because
　　　　　If there is craving, they will reoccur.

People who want liberation and have realization do not make efforts at antidotes to discard karma and the body for the sake of liberation. This is because antidotes able to eradicate karma and the body without eliminating craving are not validly realized to exist, and since there is no ability to abandon karma and the body from their root if craving has not been abandoned. Additionally, if craving, not having been abandoned, is present, one might abandon karma and the body once, but they will reoccur. This is according to Devendrabuddhi. Prajñā-karagupta says, "There is no other antidote for karma and the body than blocking craving."[272]

Others say:

276a　　Even if one strives to exhaust them both,

One might say that one should strive to exhaust them both, karma and the body. To explain:

276b   Tiring oneself to exhaust karma is pointless.

Tiring and fatiguing oneself to exhaust karma with antidotes other than the antidotes that exhaust craving is pointless, because without abandoning craving, karma cannot be abandoned and will reoccur and if craving has been abandoned it is unnecessary to abandon karma.

C. Refuting liberation through austerity. This has three points: 1. Refuting that a single austerity could exhaust all karma, 2. Refuting that the power of actions is mixed, and 3. Refuting criticism.

1. Refuting that a single austerity could exhaust all karma
Some sky-clad Jain ascetics say that tormenting the body exhausts the results of previously committed actions by means of experience, and one is liberated as long as one does not commit new future actions. With regard to this, some say that if experiencing the unwanted from undergoing torments through austerities were not the result of karma, the experience of that action and its result would not exhaust it because one engages in it voluntarily. Though they say this, if it were so, a kingship that a man achieved through his actions would also not be the result of karma. Therefore, anything whatsoever—whether desired or not—is the result of actions. As it says in the scriptures of the noble elders:

> Whether the higher or the lower realms,
> The unwanted that arises from volition
> And has the five sense bases as conditions
> Is asserted to be the result of evil acts.[273]

Therefore a single torment through austerities cannot exhaust the various results of various actions. To teach this:

276cd   Since various results are seen, the powers
        Of actions are inferred to be distinct.

277ab   Therefore a single entity inflicting
        Austerity cannot extinguish them.

Since various results of karma—great and little wealth, illness and good health, complete or incomplete limbs and appendages, and so forth—appear and are seen to arise, it can be inferred that the actions in a person's continuum have distinct powers to produce multiple results. The various results of those actions that have the power to produce various results are experienced, so therefore it is not logical that a single entity of the infliction of austerity could extinguish all karmas by way of experiencing all their results; it cannot extinguish them. For example, destroying the power to produce a millet seedling does not destroy the power to produce barley or *sālu* seedlings.

The pervasion is also not indeterminate:

> 277cd   In some ways, the results that are produced
> Are lessened, but not those of different kinds.

In some ways—such as by tormenting the body through austerities like pulling out hair—the results of unvirtuous actions that produce such suffering can be merely lessened, but those results of virtuous actions different in kind from nonvirtues are not extinguished. This is according to Devendrabuddhi.

The *Ornament* cites the root as:

> In some ways, the results that are produced
> Are lessened. By experiencing results
> Of conditions of a different kind. . .[274]

It then says:

> Any action produces results only of its own class. Because a portion of that is experienced, the result produced by that action is lessened, but results incompatible with it are not diminished.[275]

Master Jina's commentary explains:

> The actions done that are extremely hard to transcend
> Might be palliated by abusing oneself,

But self-laceration and bondage
Do not eradicate them lastingly. . .[276]

He thus explains that some manners of abusing oneself—lacerating oneself—can exhaust small or temporary acts, but not those of a different class.

2. Refuting that the power of actions is mixed

Others say:

278ab   "What if the power of austerity
          Were to extinguish powers that are mixed?"

"But what if the power of austerity mixed all the power of actions into the power to produce one result, and that one result were extinguished by physical self-mortification such as pulling out one's hair and so forth?"

First of all, there would be this fault from the proposition that the powers were mixed:

278c   A tiny bit of affliction would discard,

It would be pointless for people practicing austerity to strive at severe self-mortification of their body by pulling out their hair and so forth, because a tiny bit of the affliction of mortification through austerities such as pulling out a single body hair would also discard them. That is because that austerity would mix the powers of all actions into the power to produce that size result.

There are also faults in the proposition that coarse power can be exhausted. We ask whether the mortification of the body is suffering that is the result of bad actions or not. Others reply:

279ad   If one asserted that austerity were
          Affliction that is other than affliction,

If one were to assert that the mortification of the body from austerity is a virtue that is other than the affliction that results from bad actions, to explain:

278d   Or all would be abandoned *sans* affliction.

Once a person who practices austerity has exhausted the coarse power of actions through the physical mortification from austerity, it would be pointless to strive in severe physical mortification such as pulling out the hair to eliminate the slight remainders of actions, because all the results of karma would be abandoned through austerity *sans* the affliction of suffering of pulling out hair and so forth. The word *affliction* designates just the misery from pain, not desire and so forth.

If you say that the austerity is an affliction of suffering resulting from bad actions, to explain:

279cd   Because it is the result of an action,
            It would not mix the powers or so forth.

Because it (the austerity from engaging in physical mortification such as pulling out one's hair) is suffering that is the result of an unvirtuous action or else the fully ripened result of an action, it is not a path that would mix the powers of karma, extinguish them, or so forth.

3. Refuting criticism

Others say, "But you assert that realizing selflessness is itself a method to extinguish karma, and that contradicts your position that methods to exhaust karma are not the path." To explain:

280.   Since it eliminates the fault of wanting
            To be reborn, that which prevents the faults
            Has power over the actions they produce,
            But how could what's been done be eliminated?

Because they eliminate the seeds of desire and so forth—the fault of wanting karma to arise in the future—the paths of realizing selflessness that prevent the faults of desire and so forth have power over eliminating the actions they (those afflictions such as desire) produce. Therefore it has power to discard actions that have not previously been done, but how could the actions that have been done in the past be eliminated and extinguished? They could only not be.

Devendrabuddhi says:

> If that were said based upon past actions, it would be unproven, but it is proven based on future actions, so this proves it.[277]

Prajñākaragupta says:

> That which is without a doubt the power to produce a result will solely without a doubt produce a result. One does not train in austerities for its sake, because that comes from its power.[278]

Others say that just as actions occur if there is craving, craving also arises from actions. Therefore an arhat would once again take birth in samsara. To explain:

281ab   Faults aren't from actions. Those with faults
                 Will act. Not from the opposite.

The faults of desire and so forth will not rearise from the actions of an arhat, a person who has extinguished the faults. This is because those with the fault of mistaken craving will accumulate new actions, but those arhats who have turned away[279] from the faults of mistaken craving will not accumulate new karma ever again. This is according to both Devendrabuddhi and Prajñākaragupta.

Others say that virtuous and unvirtuous actions are the causes from which pleasurable and painful feelings, the results, arise respectively, and desire and hatred are seen to arise from those. Therefore afflictions arise from karma as well, they say. To explain:

281cd   Without mistaken thoughts, desire
                 Will not arise, even from pleasure.

Arhats free from attachment for the three realms have no mistaken thoughts, the inappropriate attention of thinking "me" and "mine." For that reason, desire will not arise even from sensations of pleasure. This is according to both Devendrabuddhi and Prajñākaragupta.

2. Establishing from that the perfect benefit for self, the sugata

> 282.   From the protector, his distinctive knowing
> Of suchness, stable and complete, is proven.
> *Gata's* the meaning realized. Thus he surpasses
> Non-Buddhists as well as learners and nonlearners.

Because he teaches the four noble truths, he is the protector, and from (or because of) that, the Bhagavan is the sugata. What is that? you ask. Sugatahood is the wisdom of the distinctive knowing of knowing suchness excellently, of knowing irreversibly and stably, and of knowing all aspects completely. Possessing those three qualities proves him to be the sugata. Previously sugata was explained in terms of abandonment, but here it is explained as the meaning that is realized. Because he has these three meanings, the Bhagavan is the sugata who is the perfection of abandonment and realization. Thus by knowing suchness, he surpasses and is superior to the outsiders; by knowing stably, the learners; and by knowing all aspects without exception he surpasses the noble listener and self-buddha nonlearners.

3. Establishing from that the perfect training, the teacher

> 283ab   And for that reason, he who trains in knowing
> The benefit of others is the teacher.

And for that reason that he knows the three meanings, the cause—the teacher who is perfect training—is established from the result, the sugata. This is because during the causal stage, he cultivated training in the path of meditating on selflessness in order to know the benefit of others. In this way, cultivating the path during the causal stage is designated as the teacher.

4. Establishing from that the perfect intent, the wish to benefit others

283cd   Love is from that: compelled by others' needs,
             He never abandons bringing benefit.

From that, the teacher who cultivated the path himself for others' sake, the love that wishes to help others is proven, because from the perspective[280] of others—disciples—he trained and accomplished the path of realizing the meaning of the nature of the four truths in his own being, and that as well arises from the great love and compassion that never abandons wanderers. As an analogy, proving a shoot proves a seed.[281]

5. Thus establishing he is valid

284.   He taught the excellent from his compassion;
             From wisdom, truth and the means to establish.
             He was intent on teaching them as well,
             And for those reasons, he is therefore valid.

Beginning with the intent, the great compassion that wishes to eliminate others' suffering, he then practiced by training in the path of the truly excellent that realizes the nature of the four truths, and thus became the teacher for others who needed to be tamed. Because of those two causes, the perfect intent and training, he accomplished sugatahood that is the perfection of abandonment and wisdom, the two kāyas of the svābhāvikakāya and the dharmakāya. From that sugatahood, he accomplished the protector, the sambhogakāya and nirmaṇakāya who teach without mistake what to do and what not to do and the four truths appropriately for the perceptions in disciples' minds. Thus the result (the two perfect benefits) has the cause, the means to accomplish that (perfect intent and training).

For those reasons, the Bhagavan, the subject, is therefore proven to be valid, because he teaches the perfect cause and result that he himself has manifested to other disciples as well, and because he is intent on that and can bring them to those states.

C. Explaining the reason for praising the Bhagavan as being valid

Well then, if the Bhagavan has limitless qualities, what is the necessity or cause for praising him only in terms of validity? To explain:

> 285a–c   Praising the teaching of such entities
> Is to establish the reality
> Of validity from his own teachings.

The necessity for Master Dignāga to praise the Bhagavan in terms of teaching that the Bhagavan is such a valid entity is to establish that Dignāga explained the reality of perceptual validity, inferential validity, and so forth—the topic of the treatise *The Compendium of Validity*—just as the Bhagavan taught it in the scriptures of his own teachings and that Dignāga did not fabricate anything himself. The way that perception and so forth are taught in the sutras are taught can be known in the context of each of the texts.

Others say it is true that perception is taught in the sutras, but inferential validity is not taught at all. To explain:

> 285d   And inference as well is not refuted,

> 286.   Because one sees such syllogisms as
> "Everything with the slightest nature of
> Arising is a phenomenon that ceases,"
> Et cetera, in many various ways.

It is thus: inferential validity was not refuted or negated by the Bhagavan, so therefore he considered it valid. If he had not accepted it as valid, he would have refuted it, just as, for example, he refuted verbal validity when he said, "All the outsiders have said up to now is false: I alone have taught thatness." Additionally, it is because one sees that he has explained in many various ways the cause of inferential validity, reasons of such syllogisms with correct reasons of nature as "Everything with the slightest nature of arising is a phenomenon that ceases," et cetera.

To explain that if he accepted syllogisms with reasons, it is logical that he also accepted the inferential validity based on them:

287.　　　The basis of inference is reasons that
　　　　　Are characterized by not arising if absent.
　　　　　He explained these clearly, too, because he taught
　　　　　Through propositions with reasons and pervasion.

Reasons that have been explained are characterized by the reason that this will not arise if that is absent, as explained, are the basis of inferential validity. He (the Bhagavan) explained this clearly too, because he taught reasons fulfilling the three modes with entailing and reverse pervasions of the predicate of the proposition and with the propositional property.

Second, the pledge to compose the *Compendium*.

　　　　　I will, to prove validity,
　　　　　Compile from all my works and here
　　　　　Make what was scattered into one.

Once Master Dignāga has thus praised the Bhagavan, what will he do? you ask. He will write. What? This *Compendium of Validity*. What is the necessity? To prove that the Bhagavan, the actual validity, and his teachings—the validity that arises from scriptures—are authentic validity. In what manner? By compiling all the points on the topic from his, Master Dignāga's, own works that teach the proof of validity such as *The Gateway to Logic*. You might say that there is no need to compile here what was taught in other texts, but that is not the case. It is difficult for those with lesser intelligence and diligence to explain, listen to, read, and realize the various words of his texts that are long and scattered in different works. Seeing this, compassion for those people causes him to make here in this *Compendium* one work that teaches the vast meaning of the topic, expressing it with few words. Thus there is the necessity that it be easy to explain, listen to, read, and realize.

In explaining it thus, the phrases "all my works" and "scattered" are not redundant, and "compile from all" and "here make. . . into one" are also not redundant. As it says in the autocommentary:

> Having prostrated, in order to prove validity, I will compile my own analyses from *The Gateway to Logic* and so forth and compose *The Compendium of Validity*.[282]

Here the author of the *Commentary* did not explain the pledge to compose. The thought is that it is easy to understand. As is said in Devendrabuddhi's commentary:

> The latter half of the first verse of the treatise is easy to understand, so now that the explanation of the first half has been completed. . .[283]

From the extensive commentary on *The Compendium of Validity* entitled *The Ocean of Literature on Logic, Which Collects the Rivers of Fine Explanations of Validity*, this was the first chapter of the explanation of the *Compendium*, called "Establishing that the Bhagavan is a Valid Being."

May the blaze of auspiciousness, the teachings of the Karma Kagyu, flourish in the ten directions as an ornament of the world. *Sarva maṅgalaṃ.*

PART 2

Establishing Validity

The First Chapter of *The Commentary in Verse on Validity*

by Ācārya Dharmakīrti

In the Indian language: *Pramāṇavārttikakārikā*
In Tibetan: *tshad ma rnam 'grel gyi tshig le'ur byas pa*
In English: *The Commentary in Verse on Validity*

I prostrate to the noble youthful Manjushri.

1.   He's cleared away the net of thought
And has the profound and vast bodies.
I bow to him who shines the light
Of the All-Good over all.

2.   Attached to the vulgar and lacking strong intelligence,
most people
Not only take no interest in the fine explanations,
The stains of jealousy goad them to ire.
Therefore I have no thought that this will be of help
to others,
But from long training of my mind in the fine explanations,
To rouse enthusiasm, I feel joy for this.

3.   The valid is an undeceiving mind.
To dwell in the ability to function
Is undeceiving. Verbal is as well,
Because it indicates intention.

4.   The validity of a verbal expression
Is that the object of the speaker's action—
The meaning—appears to the intellect,
Not consequent to the suchness of the meaning.

5.   It grasps the apprehended, so we don't
Accept the relative. The mind is valid,
Since it is the main factor in engaging
The things to be accepted and rejected,

6. Since due to separate aspects of the objects,
    The mental realizations are thus separate,
    Because if there is that, there must be this.
    Its own essence is known from itself.

7. Validity is from conventions, and
    Treatises are to eliminate delusion.
    Or that which clarifies the unknown meaning.
    "Following realization of its essence,

8. Consciousness of the universal is gained."
    Cognition that knows the unknown specific
    Characteristics is intended, since
    One analyzes specific characteristics.

9. The Bhagavan endowed with those is valid.
    It says "became" in order to refute
    That he did not arise. Thus based on the means
    To achieve that, it's logical he is valid.

10. There is no permanent validity.
    Validity is knowing existing things.
    Knowables are impermanent and thus
    That is unstable. It is illogical

11. That what arises sequentially be born
    Out of the permanent. Dependence is
    Untenable. He has no effect at all.
    Even impermanent, there's no validity.

12. "At rest until engaged, distinctive shape,
    Performs a function, and so forth." These prove
    Our own position, the analogy
    Is not established, or else they breed doubt.

13. The way a shape or so forth is conforms
    To whether or not there's someone in control,

And any inference that one might draw
From that is proven to be logical.

14. "It's proven for a different thing because
The word's the same; there is no difference."
The inference is not logical; it's like
Inferring a fire from a light-colored substance.

15. Otherwise, since the vases and so forth
A potter makes are alterations to
The shape of clay, it also would be proven
That termite mounds were made by him as well.

16. We assert a similar effect is claiming
A fault of being separate, since in proving
The effect through the general (as it entails
The thesis), the related is separate.

17. Seeing that a verbal universal
Is established in an instance of a type
Is not a logical proof. It's as if speech
And so forth would be horned because they're "cow."

18. Since words depend on the intended meaning,
There's nothing to which they may not refer.
If their mere presence could establish the object,
Everyone would accomplish everything.

19. This also analyzes the Kāpilas
And so forth: "Since impermanent and so forth,
It has no mind, et cetera. If its bark
Is peeled it dies, and thus it has a mind."

20. If the thing's essence has not been established,
When the logic is proven, though that is not proven,
It does not interfere with particulars,
Like sound's that is supported upon space.

21.   Although not proven verbally, if the thing
      Is proven, it's established, for example,
      As Buddhists explain to the Aulūkyas
      That the material and such are proof.

22.   And if that is mistaken or so forth,
      Even if the word is not mistaken,
      It should be known to be a faulty proof
      Because a thing is proven by a thing.

23.   In proofs like "Since it goes, it's horned" or else
      "It has a hand, so it's an elephant,"
      The meaning of the terms is common parlance,
      But it is not the meaning that's intended.

24.   Just as that entity is the cause,
      In the same way, then, at the times
      It's not the cause, why do you assert
      It is the cause, not not a cause?

25.   If Caitra's wound is related to a weapon,
      His healing to medicinal herbs and such,
      Why would you not think that something unrelated
      Such as a tree trunk were itself the cause?

26.   Unless there is a difference in nature,
      It also is illogical to function.
      Since permanents have no reverse entailment,
      The power, too, is difficult to detect.

27.   If you should think that something other than
      Those which when they are present, it occurs
      Would be its causes, then for everything
      Causes would be an infinite regress.

27.   If the nature of the soil and so forth
      Transforms in the production of a shoot,

They are the cause. This is because if they
Are properly done, the difference is seen.

28.   "As objects and the faculties assembled
Aren't different, but are the cause of mind,
This is like that," you say. It is not so,
Because there is a difference there as well.

29.   If those, which lacked capacity when separate,
Do not have a distinctive nature, then
Assembled they would lack capacity, too.
So therefore the distinctiveness is proven.

30.   Therefore what lacks capacity on its own
In combination may have qualities.
Those are the causes. Īśvara and so forth
Are not, because there is no difference.

31.   There are those who state, "Validity
Is knowing hidden objects, but because
There is not any method to achieve that,
There is not anyone who would make efforts."

32.   People who have suspicions of being confused
By those who, without knowledge, act as teachers
Will look for someone who possesses knowledge
In order to act upon their explanations.

33.   And for that purpose, they examine
The wisdom that they need to achieve.
We have no use at all for whether
He knows how many bugs there are.

34.   We assert that making known the suchness of
What should be taken up, what given up
Along with the methods is validity.
It is not making everything known.

35. Whether or not they do see far away,
     They should see the suchness that is desired.
     If seeing far away is validity,
     Come here and let us worship vultures!

36. The means is compassion. That's from cultivation.
     They say, "The mind's supported by the body
     So it is not achieved through cultivation."
     Not so, since the support has been refuted.

37. When one takes birth, the inhalation and
     The exhalation, faculties, and mind
     Do not arise from just the physical
     Without depending upon their own kind,

38. For that would be absurd. What else is there
     Than the capacity to make a link
     That has been seen? There is not anything.
     And due to what would it no longer link?

39. There is not any portion at all of earth
     And so forth in which living beings may not
     Be born from warmth and moisture and so forth.
     Therefore all by nature is a seed.

40. Therefore, if faculties and so forth were
     To arise without depending on their kind,
     Then just as one becomes, so too would all,
     Because there is not any difference.

41. If individual faculties
     Are harmed, there is not any harm
     To mental mind. But if that changes,
     Those are seen to change as well.

42. So therefore the support for mind to abide
     And some that are supported by the mind

Are the causes of the faculties, and thus
The faculties are from the mental mind.

43.   If there has been a propeller such as this,
Later as well there will be such as that.
Because its consciousness can benefit,
The body is explained to support the mind.

44.   "In that case, without faculties the mind
Does not." And nor do those without it either.
Accordingly they are each other's cause,
So therefore they are mutual results.

45.   Sequential is not from the non-sequential.
Not different and not dependent either.
If mind were in a sequence from the body,
Then that would indicate its sequence, too.

46.   Earlier moments are the causes
Of later moments, which had not
Existed previously, and thus
It's always seen that they are causes.

47.   How would it be contradictory
For the last mind to link to another mind?
And why is it that you admit
The mind of an arhat will not link?

48.   Why would you follow a philosophy
That has not been established validly?
And if you say, "Because it lacks the causes,"
Why did you not say just that here?

49.   Since it would apprehend like consciousness,
The mental's not from one with faculties.
Since their capacity to produce knowing
Is separate, not from all together either.

50.   As those have no awareness, not from others.
        As these have the same cause, they coexist,
        Just like the faculties, like form and flavor.
        It is affected by way of the object.

51.   That which by being present benefits
        Since that is always consequent to it
        Is a cause. Therefore he used the locative
        And said "because this has arisen."

52.   There are, of course, some instances where it
        May benefit the mind's continuum,
        But like a jug and such with fire and so forth,
        Just that alone does not cause mind to cease.

53.   There would be the consequence that if
        The body remained, the mind would not cease either.
        There if it's there and under its control,
        So breathing is from it, not it from that.

54.   Without exertion where would inhalation
        And exhalation of the breath be from?
        From them diminishing or increasing,
        It also would diminish or increase.

55.   The consequence is the same for them as well.
        It is not similar if the mind's the cause,
        Because it is asserted other factors
        That propel remaining are the cause.

56.   "Like wicks and so forth, it has been degraded
        By humors, so the body is not the cause."
        When death has brought the humors into balance,
        It once again would be brought back to life.

57.   "But even though a fire might be reversed,
        The changes to the wood are not turned back,

And likewise that cannot be brought back either."
Not so, since remedies can be applied.

58.   There are some instances where changes made
    To certain things make them not rearise.
    For other things, they are reversible,
    Like fire with wood or gold as an example.

59.   The first, even small, is not reversible.
    But as with the solidity of gold,
    That to which the alterations made
    Are reversible will once again arise.

60.   It's said some illnesses are totally
    Incurable since cures are to find
    Or life has been used up, but if it is
    Solely the humors, none is incurable.

61.   If the causes of deterioration are
    Removed by halting poison and so forth
    In the dead, or cutting out the bite as well,
    Why would they not come back to life?

62.   Without a change in the substantial cause,
    It is not possible to make a change
    In what is caused, for instance like a basin
    And so forth without changes to the clay.

63.   It would not be logical for a thing
    That is not changed to be the substantial cause
    Of something else that does get changed,
    Like gaur and oxen and so forth.

64.   The mind and body are like that, too.
    Results that arise from its cause
    Cooperating coexist,
    Just as with fire and molten copper.

65.   What is and what is not are not supported.
           If that's not so and the support is the cause
           For it to persist, it has no support
           Since that's not other than that which persists.

66.   If other, it is just the cause of that.
           What is the entity that it has made?
           Consequentially, it would never perish.
           "That's from a cause of perishing," you assert,

67.   But there as well, the consequence is the same,
           And what would the cause of persistence do?
           "That makes it persist till it meets the cause
           Of perishing." The nature of things is

68.   To perish. There is nothing to prevent this,
           So what would the cause of persistence do?
           "For instance, like a support for water and
           So forth," you say. It is the same for this,

69.   As when things perish each and every instant,
           A thing's continuum is thus the cause
           Of it arising, hence that is the support.
           Otherwise it would not be logical.

70.   Because it prevents movement, it is thus
           A support for water and so forth. But why
           Would qualities, universals, or else actions
           That do not move need a support?

71.   This disallows inherence and
           Causes that would have inherence
           As well as that a kind would dwell,
           Because there is not any support.

72.   If something else were to make a thing perish,
           Then what would its cause of persistence do?

If that still perishes without another,
The causes of persistence have no power.

73. Everything with support would have persistence,
     And all that arises would have a support.
     Thus for that reason, no thing ever
     At any time would perish.

74. And if their character is that they perish
     By their own nature, what else makes them stay?
     But if their character is not to perish
     By their own nature, what else makes them stay?

75. Without an increase or decrease of body,
     There can be an increase or a decrease
     In intelligence, et cetera, due to
     Distinctions in the action of the mind.

76. Things that have support, such as the light
     Of a lamp, et cetera, do not have this.
     "From that as well, there are distinctions in this."
     Not so, since that does not affect the mind.

77. Increases of desire and such from thriving
     And such are sometimes born from pleasure or pain.
     They're from the presence of internal objects—
     The balance of the elements and so forth.

78. And this explains how loss of memory
     And such arise from fever and so forth,
     Because the mind born from distinctions of
     Internal objects makes the alteration.

79. As an analogy, it is just as
     How certain types of individuals
     On hearing or else seeing tigers or
     Blood and such are stupefied and so forth.

80.   Therefore it won't arise without
    The mind to whose formations it
    Is definitely consequent.
    Thus it's supported by the mind.

81.   Just as formations of listening and such,
    Formed in the mind, at times are evident
    In mind, these qualities would also be
    In the body, as it is not separate.

82.   Those who have attachment to a self
    Are not led by another sentient being.
    They embrace inferior places from the wish
    To obtain happiness and avoid suffering.

83.   Craving and the cognition that
    Misconstrues suffering are the bonds
    That cause rebirth. Whoever lacks them
    Is someone who will not be born.

84.   If going and coming are not seen, it is
    Because the faculties are not acute
    That they cannot be seen, as for example
    Those with poor vision don't see wisps of smoke.

85.   Although they are corporeal, they are subtle.
    Thus some are not obstructive to some things,
    Like water or like mercury with gold.
    It does not not exist from not being seen.

86.   If the arm or so forth were to move, then all
    Would move. Thus contradictory actions are
    Illogical in a single entity,
    So they'd be proven separate, au contraire.

87.   If one were covered, all would then be covered,
    Or if not covered, all would be visible.

If one changed color, all would change or else
It would be realized that it did not change.

88.   Therefore conglomerations are not single.
You say, "It's multiple. Because there's no
Distinction from before, because of atoms
It therefore is not realized." It's not proven

89.   There's no distinction, because the distinguished
Are objects of the faculties; atoms aren't.
And this disproves as well that they
Would not obscure, et cetera.

90.   How could a mix of gold and mercury
Or so forth or hot rocks or such appear?
How would the faculties and such, which lack
Capacity individually, perceive?

91.   If from conjunction, here the consequence
Is the same. And if you say that the conjunction
Of gold and mercury appears, without
A visible support, how is it realized?

92.   Conjunctions of form, flavor, and so forth
Are contradictory. If you assert
It's attribution, there'd be separate minds.
How could one say a row is long?

93.   The essences of number, conjunction, action,
Et cetera, do not appear to mind
Separate from the essence of that which
Possesses them or separate from expressions.

94.   Objects of words and of cognitions are
Projected by thoughts that follow separate things,
Like qualities and so forth for example,
Or like the perished and unborn.

95.   If you propose that here it's nominal,
        Why would you not assert, then, that the reason
        Because of which you posit that would be
        The cause of those for every entity?

96.   "They are not nominal in every case.
        The separate features are called principal.
        If that from which it's separate should be absent,
        The separate would not have an object," you say.

97.   Though not an object with another reason,
        Expressions for white and such, number and such,
        As well as conjunction aren't synonymous.
        If those were to have other objects, too,

98.   There'd be no distinction between qualities
        And substance. They'd be separate through distinctions
        In isolates, though they're not other objects,
        As in the phrases "not action" and "not substance."

99.   Also expressions signifying things
        That indicate the number and so forth
        As separate from that which possesses them
        Make a distinction from the other features.

100.   In certain cases, one might say to those
        Who want to know just that, without implying
        Anything else, "that which a finger possesses"
        As if it were a separate predicate.

101.   "The finger that is possessed" designates
        The selfsame object but it implies all,
        So it is called a phrase that signifies
        The subject. In this way the sign is made.

102.   By eliminating distinctions of the power
        Of form and so forth, the word *jug* refers

To the exclusion of that which is not
A cause of a comparable result.

103.   For that reason, "the jug is form" is not
An expression with a single referent.
Therefore this is the difference between
Signification of kind and of collection.

104.   Saying "the form and so forth of a jug"
Makes its universal into a part
And indicates distinctions in its power.
This proposition also describes others.

105.   If the entirety should be the cause,
Then not when even one part is removed.
If each one had capacity as well,
Then many would occur at the same time.

106.   As they are the same in being multiple,
The out- and in-breaths aren't determinant.
Even if single, many would manifest,
Because their causes always would be present.

107.   If you say they are not the cause of many,
Since there's no difference, not successive either.
Since multiple objects can be apprehended
During one breath, no certainty from that.

108.   If one mind were to cognize multiple,
That would be simultaneous because
There's nothing contrary. It would not be
Successive either, since there's no distinction.

109.   If you should think that many instants
Of respiration that are at times
That aren't of their own kind should be
The causes of suchlike cognitions,

110.   How could they be sequential if
They lack a cause to be sequential?
If the cause is the previous instance of
Its own kind, then the first would not occur

111.   Because a similar cause does not exist.
If so, they'd certainly be multiple
Because the breaths have separate locations.
Thus minds would simultaneously arise.

112.   And if though multiple, those were the causes
Of a single cognition at one time,
If even one were absent, it would not
Arise, as when the breathing is weak and so forth.

113.   Supposing they were causes as they are,
There'd be a distinction in cognition, too.
It is not a result of that if it
Does not differ from differences in that.

114.   The power of consciousness is ascertained,
So one is the cause of one. Consciousness lacks
The ability to cling to other objects,
Because it does not grasp another object.

115.   And if the mind were to arise one time
From the body and afterward to definitely
Arise from its own kind, why is it that
The body's capability would cease?

116.   If you should say, "It is not the support,
And for that reason when the body ceases
The mind alone persists," if it is from
Acquiring the state of being a cause of that,

117.   The cause for the continuum of mind
To stay does not become an element.

The five sense bases of this lifetime are
The causes that produce another body.

118.   In denying that things are its elements
Or its causation, that they are not observed
Does not bring certitude, as was explained,
And faculties and such are inconclusive.

119.   It has been seen that earlier faculties
Have the capacity for their own kind.
Since change is seen, it is established that
The subsequent ones will arise as well.

120.   If they were to arise from the body,
The consequence would be as before.
If from the mind, another body
Would also arise from this same.

121.   Thus it cannot be not so that since the cause
Is absent, all final cognitions do not link,
And for that reason we assert
That proofs like that are inconclusive.

122.   If you should say, "Though there may be
Distinctions due to cultivation,
It cannot transcend its own nature,
Like jumping or else heating water,"

123.   Once done, if doing it again depends
On effort or if the support's not stable,
Then the distinctions will not multiply.
If that is so, their natures aren't like that

124.   Because the abilities to benefit those
Do not have the capacity to effect
Later distinctions, because the support
Does not persist in perpetuity,

125.   And since though they might increase, the distinctions
        Are not the nature. Whereas once they're made,
        If they do not depend on further effort,
        Other efforts will create distinctions.

126.   Like fire and such with wood, like mercury,
        Like gold and such, compassion in the mind
        And so forth that arise from cultivation
        Naturally engage upon their own.

127.   Therefore the quality that's born
        Of those arises as its nature,
        Thus subsequent and subsequent
        Efforts produce distinctions.

128.   Because those minds of compassion and so forth
        Multiply out of the preceding seeds
        Of instances of a homogeneous kind,
        If cultivated, where would they stay still?

129.   But jumping does not come in that same way
        From jumping—strength and exertion are its causes.
        As there's a limit to their capacity,
        Jumping is inherently limited.

130.   At first they do not jump as later since
        The body has contrary qualities.
        Once effort gradually eliminates
        Contrarieties, they stay within their strength.

131.   Compassion rises out of its own seeds.
        If not impeded by contrary factors
        Originating from seeds of their own,
        The mind will become that in character.

132.   And thus the previous cultivation is
        The root of the acuity of further

Qualities of mind such as compassion,
Detachment, intelligence, et cetera.

133. A compassionate nature is from cultivation
As with detachment, desire, and disgust.
To drive away suffering, the compassionate
Apply themselves to training in the methods.

134. If what is born from method and its cause
Are hidden, it is difficult to explain it.
They investigate through scripture and through logic
And analyze the cause of suffering,

135. Its nature of impermanence and so forth
By way of the attributes of suffering,
Because they see that if the cause remains,
There's no elimination of the result.

136. In order to eliminate its cause,
They examine what is contrary to it.
From realizing the essence of the cause,
Its contrary is recognized as well.

137. The cause is the attachment formed by clinging
To me and mine whose sphere of experience
Is the composite. What opposes that
Is seeing selflessness, exclusive of it.

138. From a long time of cultivation
In many ways with many methods,
The faults and qualities in them
Have become evident, and thus

139. Because their minds are clear, they have abandoned
The cause's imprints. This is the distinction
Between great sages, who work for others' weal,
And the rhinoceroses and so forth.

140.   Because it has that purpose, cultivating
The means itself is said to be the teacher.
They happen first, before accomplishment,
And so the two are described as the cause.

141.   Three qualities of abandoning the cause
Are sugatahood. As it is not a support
For suffering, it is excellent. It comes
From seeing selflessness and from the training.

142.   Reversibility is said to be
The rearising of the faults and birth.
He has abandoned the seeds of the self view,
And thus he has gone irreversibly

143.   Since that and truth have separate characters.
Though free of the afflictions and disease,
Unskillfulness of body, speech, and mind
And unclarity in teaching the path remain.

144.   All are abandoned through the cultivation.
Some say he has not exhausted all the faults
Because he speaks and so forth. This sows doubt
About the restriction and is thus mistaken.

145.   They think the faults are inexhaustible
Because they're permanent or else because
There are no methods or else it may be
Because he has no knowledge of the methods.

146.   They have a cause. The cultivation of
The cause's antidote extinguishes them.
His understanding the nature of the cause
Establishes that he knows that as well.

147.   The protector teaches the path he has seen.
He tells no falsehoods as that would be fruitless.

Because he is compassionate, all the efforts
He undertakes are for the sake of others.

148. Thus he is valid. Or else the protector
Is he who teaches the four noble truths.
Suffering is the samsaric aggregates.
It's seen habituation intensifies

149. Desire and so forth. It's not happenstance—
Arising without cause is contradictory.
As that's fallacious, they're not qualities
Of wind and so forth. If there were no fault

150. Because the nature is mixed, then why would not
Its other qualities be seen as well?
It's not a quality of all because
All would have equal desire as a consequence.

151. "Like bodies and so forth, there is no fault,"
You say, but without any distinctive karmas
That would be the dominant for that,
The criticism here would be the same.

152. Although there are distinctions in the faults,
There's no distinction. It is not unproven,
Because a change in all of them will make
A change, and they do not arise from all.

153. If causes increase, it's illogical
For the results to decrease, as with heat
And so forth. Changes of desire and so on
Arise from pleasure and so forth.

154. And if desire is not produced because
Of pain that was created by imbalance,
Do tell whence it arises. "Semen increases
From balance, and desire increases from that."

155.   It's seen that even some with imbalances
Are lustful, whereas some in balance aren't.
Some are, though they emit blood, being depleted.
Semen's not definite for any one woman,

156.   And there might not be strong lust for that one.
If figure and so forth were factors, too,
Not so—it is not certain for everyone.
It also is not definite. It would occur

157.   For those who do not hold them qualities.
If holding them as qualities were a factor,
Then all would hold them to be qualities
Because there's no distinction in the cause.

158.   At times when someone is asserted to
Be lustful, he would not be hostile since
The essences of the two are disparate.
That is not necessarily seen here either.

159.   Such faults are not a consequence
For those to whom desire and such
Engage dependent on distinctions
In imprints that are the same class.

160.   And this refutes an elemental nature,
As the support as well has been disproven.
Whiteness and so forth are not
Supported by earth and so forth.

161.   The expression "on the basis of" means cause,
Or else since they exist inseparably
From their supports, they are supports.
It otherwise would not be logical.

162.   "Just like the potency to intoxicate
And such, it's separable." The potency

Is not an object other than the thing.
When a thing perishes, if the support

163. Remains intact, the supported does not perish.
If you say this is similar, not so.
Perceived with separate appearances,
The elements and mind are separate.

164. Until the body changed, the essence of
The mind would still remain the same, like form,
Et cetera. And how is it that thoughts
Could be dependent on an object

165. When independent of the body
Some cognitions have as a cause
The awakening of the imprints of some?
Therefore some arise from some.

166. Nonconsciousness is not the substantial cause
Of consciousness, so it is also proven.
If you assert that all things are endowed
With a capacity for consciousness,

167. Other than a Sāṃkhya ox,
What modest person would attempt
To say there were on a blade of grass
One hundred elephants not seen before?

168. Any essence that appears,
That essence did not appear before.
Dissect the cause one hundred times,
But how could it exist?

169. It follows greed and such would be uncertain
When those who didn't exist before arise.
If all had greed and such because they don't
Transcend the character of the elements,

170.   Then all would have identical desire.
         "Not so, due to distinctions in the elements,"
         In terms of living, there's no difference
         In the elements, and yet as the support

171.   For this distinction grows or else decreases,
         They'd go from having them to lacking them.
         If it's not so since although separate,
         The causes of greed and such have the same nature,

172.   Which has not ceased, because the causes are like
         In character, all would have like desire.
         There are not any degrees of distinction
         In the perception of cow, which arises

173.   From the same nature, or in livingness,
         Et cetera, in earth and so forth here.
         If you should say, "There are degrees of heat,
         But there's no fire that's without heat. Here, too,

174.   It is the same," it is not so because
         It's been disproven fire is other than heat.
         When something has qualities that are other
         And that have a distinction in degree,

175.   Some of those—its features—in some cases
         Can be removed, like whiteness and so forth.
         They are not definite like form and such,
         Which are inseparable from the elements.

176.   If you say it's the same, it's not, because
         Desire and such would occur at the same time.
         Because the object is conceptual,
         The object also is not definite.

177.   From the cause of same status being absent,
         Desire and so forth are not definite,

Or due to the cause always being present,
All cognitions always would arise.

178.   It is impermanent as it's observed
Occasionally and suffering from being
A support for faults and controlled by causes, too.
Not self, nor taken into control either.

179.   Not cause, and not the one who takes control.
How could the permanent be a producer?
And for that reason, multiple will not
Arise from one at separate times.

180.   Even if other causes are assembled,
Results do not arise, and for that reason
One can infer that there are other causes.
This is not present in the permanent.

181.   It's proven suffering has a cause
Because it is occasional.
The causeless always or never exists,
Since it does not depend upon another.

182.   "Just as the sharpness and so forth
Of thorns and so forth have no cause,
In the same way, these have no cause,"
There are some who expound.

183.   If when something exists, something arises
Or when it changes, that is changed as well,
It is considered as the cause of that,
And such exists for those as well.

184.   As touch is causative of form, it is
A cause of seeing. Because permanents
Have been refuted, it's not possible
To be from Īśvara and so forth since

185. They've no capacity. For that reason,
   Wanting existence is the cause because
   Humans appropriate a particular place,
   Which is done through the intent to obtain that.

186. This is a wish for existence, because beings
   Acting on wishes to gain happiness
   And cast off suffering is asserted to be
   The craving of desire and of destruction.

187. Due to the cause of clinging to a self,
   One enters anywhere, conceiving of
   That which is not pleasure as being pleasure.
   Thus craving is the support of existence.

188. The masters have explained this is because
   Those free of desire are not seen to take birth.
   "Because without a body, desire's not seen,
   Desire arises from the body as well."

189. Since we assert the reason, we accept,
   But being substantial cause has been refuted.
   If you accept this reasoning, you will
   Contradict your own positions yourself.

190. "Desire arises simultaneously
   With birth as it is seen at birth," you say.
   Same status arising proves the previous.
   Although not knowing is a cause of existence,

191. It is not mentioned—only craving is taught
   Since that propels the continuum to existence
   And is immediate. Karma is not either
   Because though it is there, there's no becoming.

192. That is not eternal, as it is
   Possible to impede the cause and so on.

"Because they cycle, there's no liberation."
No, because we agree; it's not established.

193.   As long as attachment to a self has not
Been conquered, they will be tormented.
That long they will project their suffering,
Not dwelling in the natural state.

194.   Though there is no one who is liberated,
Strive to conquer false projections.
Remaining while free of desire
Is from compassion or else karma,

195.   As they do not wish to block the propulsion.
For those who have transcended craving existence,
Their other actions have no power to propel,
Since cooperating factors have been exhausted.

196.   Those who know suffering have no enmity.
Continuing the previous conceptions,
The actual quality compassion arises,
But not in relation to a sentient being.

197.   Desire is from projecting another self
Onto phenomena that aren't that self.
Compassion arises out of mere awareness
Of the continuum of suffering.

198.   Delusion is the root of faults, and that
Is to perceive as beings. Lacking this,
There is no anger from the cause of faults.
Thus we assert compassion to be faultless.

199.   They're not unliberated—prior formations
Have been exhausted; they take no other birth.
Those who remain without having exhausted
The power of formations have no faults.

200.   Since their compassion is inferior too,
         They do not make great efforts to remain,
         While those who are greatly compassionate
         Remain in the perceptions of others.

201.   "Since they are free of personality view,
         There would be no rebirth on the first path."
         It's from not having abandoned the instinctive.
         If that's abandoned, how is there existence?

202.   And when one thirsts, "May I be happy"
         Or else "May I not suffer,"
         The mind that conceives "I" is the
         Instinctive view of beings.

203.   Anyone who does not see a me
         Has no attachment to a self,
         And lacking any clinging to a self,
         They don't rush off, wanting happiness.

204.   The causation for suffering to arise
         Is bondage. How could permanents have that?
         The causation for suffering not to arise
         Is freedom. How could permanents have that?

205.   What cannot be described as impermanent
         Is not the cause of anything at all.
         It is not logical—how could there be bondage
         Or liberation for the ineffable?

206.   The wise say that is permanent
         Whose nature never perishes.
         Therefore abandon this embarrassing view
         And say that it is permanent.

207.   From cultivating the path that was taught,
         The basis is transformed. "Though it transforms,

The faults arise, just like the path," you say.
Not so, since they have no capacity.

208. The quality of consciousness—apprehending
An object—apprehends it as is.
The character of what is present
Is also what produces it.

209. Such is the nature. But because of reasons
That differ from that, it can deviate.
Reversing that depends upon conditions,
So that's unstable, like cognizing a snake.

210. The nature of the mind is luminous;
The stains are adventitious. For that reason,
They have no power either earlier
Or later when that becomes the character.

211. Even when there is power, they lack the power
To remain a long time in the entity
That has the essence to produce what will
Counteract them, like a fire on wet ground.

212. That which is mistaken about the nature
Of nonhostility and the true meaning
Does not interfere, though it might make an effort,
Because the mind is inclined in that direction.

213. Since they have the same cause, which is self-clinging,
And are entities that are cause and result,
Desire and anger do not counteract
Each other, even though they're separate.

214. Since they are not exclusive of delusion,
Loving-kindness and so forth do not
Destroy the faults completely. It's the root
Of all the faults: it is personality view.

215.   Since it is the antithesis of knowing,
         Since it has a focus, being a mental factor,
         Since wrongly focusing was said to be
         Ignorance, others aren't tenable.

216.   To explain here what seems contradictory:
         Because the view of emptiness is exclusive
         Of that, it's proven to be exclusive of
         The faults that have that as their nature.

217.   If they are not exhausted, being the nature
         Of living beings, like form and such, not so.
         That is not proven. When connected to
         The antidote, they're seen to be relinquished.

218.   Unlike solidity, they don't arise
         Again, since the prevention of the faults
         Is not removable, since it's the nature,
         And since it's inconclusive, as with ash.

219.   Those who see a self, saying "me"
         Will cling to it as if eternal.
         From clinging, they'll crave happiness,
         And craving will conceal the faults.

220.   Seeing qualities, they'll lust for them
         And grasp at means to get the mine.
         Therefore as long as one is attached
         To a self, one is in samsara.

221.   If there's a self, then one conceives of others.
         From the division into self and other,
         There's clinging and aversion. All the faults
         That are connected to those two arise.

222.   Necessarily those who cling to a self
         Are not free of desire for mine.

There is no cause for freedom from
Attachment to a faultless self.

223.   If you say clinging is what's faulty,
What comes of that? "It is abandoned."
Unless its object is disproved,
One is unable to abandon that.

224.   Desire, aversion, and so forth, which follow
From qualities and faults, are eliminated
By not perceiving those within the object,
Not in the way external things would be.

225.   Clinging is not from qualities of clinging;
It is from seeing the object's qualities.
And if the cause should not be incomplete,
What would prevent it having a result?

226,   And what is the faultiness you see in clinging?
If it is the support for suffering,
Even so, this is not freedom from desire
Because it's seen as mine, just like the self.

227.   If without those, the self were not the cause
Of suffering, it would be similar.
The both of them would thus be free of fault,
And therefore neither is free of desire.

228.   If like a snake-bitten limb, it were discarded
By meditating upon suffering,
Eliminating the concept of mine
Abandons this; the opposite does not.

229.   In maintaining that the faculties
And so forth are the supports for enjoyment,
What will prevent the thought of them as mine?
For them, how could there be detachment?

230.   It's obvious to everyone
          That feelings of disgust arise
          For hair and such shed from the body
          While clinging occurs for the other.

231.   If the conception "mine" arose out of
          Relations of inherence and so forth,
          Since those relations would remain the same,
          Even if faults were seen, they'd not be abandoned.

232.   Even without inherence and so forth,
          There is the benefit for everything.
          If there were no idea of them as mine
          Since they, like a finger, produce suffering,

233.   They are not solely suffering.
          "They mostly are, like poisoned food."
          Because of lusting for superior pleasures,
          One is detached from what's exclusive of that.

234.   Because of craving a superior pleasure,
          One would forsake some minor satisfaction.
          Unthinkingly, from clinging to a self,
          One acts upon whatever one obtains.

235.   It's just as men who cannot get a woman
          Are seen to perform carnal acts with beasts.
          How could someone who loves the self
          So dearly wish it be destroyed?

236.   How could fixation wish the basis
          Of all experience, conventions,
          And qualities would cease to be?
          The nature of fixation is not so.

237.   Apprehending a self will reinforce
          In every way the clinging to a self.

That is the seed of fixating on mine.
In such a situation, that remains.

238. Despite their efforts, behavior based upon
The portions that are qualities prevents
Freedom from attachment to a mine,
And that conceals its faults as well.

239. If also free of clinging to the self,
In that case, there is no one free of clinging.
The self has in this manner been discarded;
Meditating on suffering would be pointless.

240. By meditating on suffering as well,
Suffering would be distinctly known itself,
But that was evident earlier as well,
And likewise they would not become detached.

241. And if perchance because of something's faults,
Their thoughts are displaced from it for a moment,
They are not free of desire for that thing,
As with a lustful man and other women.

242. If there's a difference between what to shun
And what to appropriate, the attachment that
Arises for the one becomes the seed
Of all desires when they arise in order.

243. Objects would have no faults, nor would attachment,
And the means to attain would have none either.
If beings were just that, then in that case
What would they be freed from attachment for?

244. If that for it had faults as well, that also
Would be the same for the self. It would not
Be free of attachment for its faults, so then
What would they be freed from attachment for?

245.   Fixation born of seeing qualities
           Would be neutralized by seeing faults,
           But it's not so for faculties and so on
           Since it is seen in children and so forth,

246.   Since it occurs for what has faults as well,
           Since it does not occur for others even
           If they have qualities, and since there's none
           For the mine of the past, et cetera.

247.   Thus for that reason, seeing qualities
           Is also not the cause of thinking "mine,"
           And therefore it is not eliminated
           By seeing that does not have qualities.

248.   Projections of nonexistent qualities
           Because of clinging are seen there as well.
           Therefore, how can accomplishing that which
           Does not prevent the causes prevent it?

249.   Because they seek another that is better
           And since they know arising and perishing,
           These individuals understand the self
           Is separate from the faculties and so forth.

250.   Thus clinging is not due to seeing sameness.
           And for that reason those who cling to a self
           Will naturally become attached to the
           Perceptual internal body parts.

251.   Weariness felt for present suffering
           Is aversion—such is not freedom from desire.
           At that time, there is clinging and so forth,
           As one will seek another situation.

252.   Because aversion's source is suffering,
           It only stays as long as there is that.

When that has ceased, they once again
Return to their own nature.

253. As they've abandoned shunning and adopting,
Those who are equanimous toward all
And for whom sandalwood and axes are
The same are said to be free of desire.

254. Thinking of the suffering of formations,
He said to meditate on suffering.
Ours as well arises from conditions,
And that supports the view of selflessness.

255. The view of emptiness will liberate;
Remaining meditations are for that sake.
Thus from impermanence is suffering;
From suffering is selflessness, he stated.

256. Those who have craving and aren't free of attachment,
Dependent upon every undertaking,
Not liberated from actions and afflictions—
Such beings as these are called samsaric.

257. And if one were not to accept the mine,
Then its consumer, too, would not exist.
Its self, whose characteristics are action
And experience, would also not exist.

258. Therefore all those who wish for freedom should
Eradicate the personality views
That arise out of seeds of the same kind
In a beginningless continuum.

259. For those who have not seen the reasoning
For why the scriptures have such reality,
Stating that scriptures alone bring liberation
Is not completely satisfying.

260.   Rites that affect a seed or so forth lack
The power to make a human not be born
Since it would follow that anointing oil
And burning and so forth would liberate.

261.   "Since heavier before and lighter after,"
But that does not eliminate misdeeds.
Their weight may cease to be, but misdeeds are
Not physical and thus do not have weight.

262.   Due to the volitions of misconception
And of the craving that is born of that,
There's birth in the inferior destinations.
Thus if that's severed, there is no migration.

263.   Those two themselves have power over birth
Since it will occur merely due to them.
Because those two intentions are themselves
Actions, the cause for birth is not destroyed.

264.   "The agents are supports for going and
For realization. They're from the unseen.
When the unseen is destroyed, there's no migration.
So therefore it is formation, not volition."

265.   Since it is consequent to the presence or
The absence, mind's capacity to produce
The agent is perceived, but not the other's.
If that is present, why would they not go?

266.   If they had no capacity, right after
Initiation and so forth, there'd be
No apprehension, engagement, disturbance,
Or cessation under the power of volition.

267.   "What if, because at that time there's no mind,
They would not. It's the stains that make the mind

Link rebirth, but they lack capacity."
Then living, they'd be powerless as well.

268.   Since when the antidote or their own side
    Increases, they will decrease or increase,
    The faults' continuum, with its own seeds,
    . Is not averted by initiation.

269.   Because the permanent is not dependent,
    It's contradictory for it to produce
    Sequentially and to have a like nature
    Of acting when it's acting and not acting.

270.   Cause and result would be the same as well.
    If that were to be separate from those,
    The actor and consumer would be lost,
    And the capacity would not be proven.

271.   The consequence that another would remember,
    Experience, and so on does not refute,
    As there's no memory of anyone's.
    Thus memory is from experience.

272.   Projecting onto the four truths
    The sixteen unreal aspects of
    Being stable, pleasurable, me,
    And mine, and so forth, one has craving.

273.   Meditating thoroughly on those
    With realization of the aspects of suchness—
    The meaning that is contrary to those—
    Right view eliminates craving and its suite.

274.   Though karma and the body still remain,
    It is impossible for that which has
    Three causes to be born since one is absent,
    Just as no sprout will grow without a seed.

275.   Not by discarding karma and the body,
         Because an antidote does not exist
         Since there is no ability because
         If there is craving, they will reoccur.

276.   Even if one strives to exhaust them both,
         Tiring oneself to exhaust karma is pointless.
         Since various results are seen, the powers
         Of actions are inferred to be distinct.

277.   Therefore a single entity inflicting
         Austerity cannot extinguish them.
         In some ways, the results that are produced
         Are lessened, but not those of different kinds.

278.   "What if the power of austerity
         Were to extinguish powers that are mixed?"
         A tiny bit of affliction would discard,
         Or all would be abandoned *sans* affliction.

279.   If one asserted that austerity were
         Affliction that is other than affliction,
         Because it is the result of an action,
         It would not mix the powers or so forth.

280.   Since it eliminates the fault of wanting
         To be reborn, that which prevents the faults
         Has power over the actions they produce,
         But how could what's been done be eliminated?

281.   Faults aren't from actions. Those with faults
         Will act. Not from the opposite.
         Without mistaken thoughts, desire
         Will not arise, even from pleasure.

282.   From the Protector, his distinctive knowing
         Of suchness, stable and complete, is proven.

Gata's the meaning realized. Thus he surpasses
Non-Buddhists as well as learners and nonlearners.

283. And for that reason, he who trains in knowing
The benefit of others is the teacher.
Love is from that: compelled by others' needs,
He never abandons bringing benefit.

284. He taught the excellent from his compassion;
From wisdom, truth and the means to establish.
He was intent on teaching them as well,
And for those reasons, he is therefore valid.

285. Praising the teaching of such entities
Is to establish the reality
Of validity from his own teachings.
And inference as well is not refuted,

286. Because one sees such syllogisms as
"Everything with the slightest nature of
Arising is a phenomenon that ceases,"
Et cetera, in many various ways.

287. The basis of inference is reasons that
Are characterized by not arising if absent.
He explained these clearly, too, because he taught
Through propositions with reasons and pervasion.

Appendix 1

The Outline of "Establishing Validity" According to *The Ocean of Literature on Logic*

First, the necessity for composing the texts on logic and their commentaries
Second, the actual explanation of the texts and commentaries that have that
    purpose

I. The branches composed by the translators to begin the translation
    A. The title of the treatise
        1. The translation of the title
        2. Explaining the meaning of the title
    B. The translators' prostration
II. The nature of the treatise that was translated
    A. Virtue in the beginning: the homage and pledge to compose
        1. The homage (v. 1)
            a. A summary
            b. The purpose
            c. The meaning of the text
                i. Explaining it in terms of the four kāyas
                ii. Explaining it in terms of the three kāyas
                iii. Explaining it in terms of the *Compendium's* homage, where the
                     meaning lies
        2. The pledge to compose (v. 2)
    B. Virtue in the middle: the meaning of the text
        1. The links between the chapters
        2. Explaining the text of each chapter

The explanation of the *Compendium's* introductory sections, the homage and
    pledge to compose
First, the homage
I. Presenting the passage from the *Commentary* to be explained[1]
II. The detailed explanation from the *Commentary* of the *Compendium's* meaning

A. Explaining the meaning of the *Compendium's* homage in order
   1. Overview
      a. A brief teaching of the result, validity
         i. The characteristics of validity
            (1) General discussion
               (a) A general presentation of characteristics, the characterized, and the basis for characterization
               (b) Explaining the characteristics of validity in particular
            (2) The meaning of the text
               (a) Explaining the characteristic of validity in accord with common consensus
                   (i) The actual characteristic (v. 3a–c)
                   (ii) Refuting that it would have the three faults
                       A. *Rebutting the fault of non-pervasion (v. 3c–4)*
                       B. *Rebutting the fault of over-pervasion (v. 5ab)*
                       C. *Rebutting the fault of impossibility (v. 5b–6c)*
                   (iii) Therefore, there is a purpose to the treatises on validity
                       A. *General discussion*
                       B. *The meaning of the text (v. 6d–7b)*
               (b) Explaining the characteristic of validity in accord with its etymology (v. 7c–8)
         ii. Establishing that the Bhagavan, who has those characteristics, is valid. (v. 9a)
      b. Explaining how that result arises from a cause
         i. Actual (v. 9b–d)
         ii. Refuting the proposition that a permanent Īśvara could be valid
             (1) General discussion
                (a) Presenting the opponent's views
                   (i) The characteristics of Īśvara
                   (ii) The positions of the Vaiśeṣikas, who assert his scriptures
                   (iii) Presenting the positions of the Naiyāyikas
                (b) Refuting them
                   (i) Refuting the Vaiśeṣikas
                   (ii) Refuting the Naiyāyikas
              (2) The meaning of the text
                (a) A general refutation of permanent validity (v. 10–11)
                (b) Refuting that Īśvara created the world after previously thinking of it
                   (i) Overview (v. 12)
                   (ii) Detailed explanation
                       A. *Refuting by examining shape and so forth (v. 13–14)*
                       B. *Refuting through an absurd consequence (v. 15)*

(2) The actual explanation of the teacher, which arises from compassion

    (a) The manner of meditating on the four truths (v. 134cd–137)

    (b) The manner in which clear appearances arise from cultivation of that (v. 138–39)

(3) The explanation of why this is called the "teacher" (v. 140)

b. The detailed explanation of the perfect result

  i. The explanation of the perfect benefit for oneself, the sugata

    (1) General discussion

      (a) What the sugata has abandoned

      (b) Tangentially, what the listener and self-buddha arhats have abandoned

    (2) The meaning of the text

      (a) The actual sugata

        (i) Overview (v. 141ab)

        (ii) Detailed explanation

          A. *Excellently gone (v. 141b–d)*

          B. *Irreversibly gone (v. 142–43a)*

          C. *Completely gone (v. 143b–144a)*

      (b) Refuting criticism

        (i) The criticism (v. 144bc)

        (ii) The response (v. 144c–146)

  ii. The explanation of the perfect benefit for others, the protector (v. 147–148a)

B. Explaining the homage in reverse order

  1. Explaining the perfect benefit for others, the protector

    a. Teaching that he is the protector because he teaches the four truths

      i. General discussion

      ii. The meaning of the text (v. 148ab)

    b. Explaining the nature of the four truths that he taught

      i. What is to be known, the truth of suffering

        (1) General discussion

        (2) The meaning of the text

          (a) Identifying suffering (v. 148c)

          (b) Proving that through reasons

            (i) Proving samsara is suffering through the evidence of habituation

              A. *Actual (v. 148d–149a)*

              B. *Refuting criticism*

                1. *Refuting that desire and so forth arise without cause (v. 149ab)*

(iii) The aspect emptiness and (iv) The aspect selflessness
(v. 178d–180)
ii. What is to be abandoned, the truth of the origin
(1) General discussion
(2) The meaning of the text
(a) An explanation of the aspect cause (v. 181–84ab)
(b) The aspect origin (v. 184b–185a)
(c) The aspect production (v. 185a–186)
(d) The aspect condition
(i) The explanation of the actual aspect (v. 187)
(ii) Comparing that with citations (v. 188–90c)
(iii) Refuting criticism of that (v. 190d–191)
iii. What is to be manifested, the truth of cessation
(1) General discussion
(2) The meaning of the text
(a) The explanation of the aspect cessation
(i) Refuting that cessation is impossible (v. 192ab)
(ii) Refuting criticism of that
A. *Refuting the criticism that liberation is impossible (v. 192c–194ab)*
B. *Refuting the criticism that remaining in samsara would be impossible (v. 194c–195)*
C. *Refuting the criticism that the detached would have the view of sentient beings (v. 196)*
D. *Refuting the consequence that they would have desire (v. 197)*
E. *Refuting the consequence that one would have anger (v. 198)*
F. *Refuting the criticism that there would be no liberation (v. 199–200)*
(b) The explanation of the aspect peace
(i) A brief overview (v. 201)
(ii) Detailed explanation (v. 202–3)
(c) The explanation of the aspect sublime
(i) Refuting that a permanent self is the sublime (v. 204)
(ii) Refuting that an ineffable self is the sublime (v. 205–6)
(d) The explanation of the aspect emancipation
iv. What is to be adopted, the truth of the path
(1) General discussion
(2) The meaning of the text
(a) It is logical that realizing selflessness is liberation
(i) The direct cause of liberation (v. 207ab)
(ii) Rebutting criticism

A. *The criticism (v. 207bc)*

B. *The response*

  1. *It is not tenable that faults arise even though there has been transformation*

    a. *The faults have no capacity*

      i. *The lack of capacity to produce faults*

        (1) *The nature of the object and subject (v. 207d–209a)*

        (2) *The distinction between what is the nature and what is not (v. 209a–210)*

      ii. *Even when there is capacity, it does not last long (v. 211)*

    b. *Though the faults may make efforts, they cannot block the path (v. 212)*

    c. *Attachment and aversion are not antidotes for each other (v. 213)*

  2. *It is not tenable for loving-kindness and so forth to be the antidote for delusion*

    a. *Actual (v. 214)*

    b. *Rebutting criticism (v. 215–16a)*

  3. *Proving that the view of emptiness is the antidote for delusion (v. 216b–218)*

(b) It is not logical for those who cling to a self to be liberated

  (i) It is not logical to achieve liberation by cultivating a self (v. 219–21)

  (ii) Rebutting that freedom from clinging to mine brings liberation

    A. *Rebutting that they have abandoned clinging to mine (v. 222ab)*

    B. *Rebutting that they have abandoned clinging to a self*

      1. *The actual logic of the rebuttal (v. 222cd)*

      2. *Rebutting that attachment is abandoned because it is faulty (v. 223–25)*

      3. *Attachment is not even proven to be faulty (v. 226–27)*

    C. *Rebutting the proof of abandoning clinging to a self*

      1. *The reason that meditating on suffering does not abandon attachment*

        a. *The analogies for discarding attachment are not comparable*

          i. *Teaching that eliminating the thought "mine" causes detachment (v. 228–30)*

Second, the pledge to compose the *Compendium*.

APPENDIX 2

WORKS IN THE TENGYUR ATTRIBUTED TO DIGNĀGA AND DHARMAKĪRTI

DIGNĀGA

Works on validity:

The Compendium of Validity (Pramāṇasamuccaya nāma prakaraṇa, tshad ma kun las btus pa zhes bya ba'i rab tu byed pa). DT Tshad ma ce, 1–13a.

The Commentary on the Compendium of Validity (Pramāṇasamucchaya vṛddhi, tshad ma kun las btus pa'i 'grel pa). DT Tshad ma ce, 14a–85b.

Examining the Focus (Ālambana parākṣi, dmigs pa brtag pa). DT Tshad ma ce, 86a.

A Commentary on Examining the Focus (Ālambana parākṣi vṛtti, dmigs pa brtag pa'i 'grel pa). DT Tshad ma ce, 86a–87b.

Examining the Three Times (Trikāla parīkṣa nāma, dus gsum brtag pa zhes bya ba). DT Tshad ma ce, 87b–93a.

Comprehending the Wheel of Reasons (Hetu cakrahamārtha, gtan tshigs kyi 'khor lo gtan la dbab pa). DT Tshad ma ce, 93a.

Works in other genres:

The Alternating Praise (Miśraka stotra nāma, spel mar bstod pa zhes bya ba). DT bsTod tshogs ka, 181a–193b.

A Commentary on the Praise of Infinite Qualities (Guṇa aparyanta stotra ṭīkā, yon tan mtha' yas par bstod pa'i 'grel ba). DT bsTod tshogs ka, 200b–203a.

A Praise of Noble Manjuśrī (Ārya mañjughoṣastotra, 'phags pa 'jam pa'i dbyangs kyi bstod pa). DT rGyud sde nu, 79a–79b.

Verses Summarizing the Noble Prajñāpāramitā (Ārya prajñāpāramitā saṃgraha kārikā, 'phags pa shes rab kyi pha rol tu phyin ma bsdus pa'i tshig le'ur byas pa). DT Shes phyin pha, 292b–294b.

A Summary of the Meaning of The Aspiration for Excellent Conduct (Samantabhadra-carya praṇidhānartha saṃgraha kriti dikanāgapādena, kun du bzang po'i spyod pa'i smon lam gyi don kun bsdus te). DT mDo 'grel nyi, 182a–201a.

A Lamp on the Main Points: A Commentary on Abhdidharma (Abhidharma marma pradīpa nāma vṛitti, chos mngon pa'i 'grel pa gnad kyi sgron ma zhes bya ba). DT mNgon pa nyu, 95b–214a.

Dharmakīrti

Works on validity:

The Commentary in Verse on Validity (Pramāṇavārttikakārikā, tshad ma rnam 'grel gyi tshig le'ur byas pa). DT Tshad ma ce, 94a–151a.

Ascertainment of Validity (Pramāṇaviniścaya, tshad ma rnam par nges pa). DT Tshad ma ce, 152b–230a.

Drop of Reasoning (Nyāyabindu nāma prakaraṇa, rigs pa'i thigs pa zhes bya ba'i rab tu byed pa). DT Tshad ma ce, 231a–238a.

The Drop of Proofs (Hetubindu nāma prakaraṇa, gtan tshigs kyi thigs pa zhes bya ba'i rab tu byed pa). DT Tshad ma ce, 238a–255a.

Examination of Relations (Saṃbandhaparīkṣi prakaraṇa, 'brel pa brtag pa'i rab tu byed pa). DT Tshad ma ce, 255a–256a.

Commentary on the Examination of Relations (Saṃbandhaparīkṣi vṛtti, 'brel pa brtag pa'i 'grel pa). DT Tshad ma ce, 256a–261a.

Auto-commentary on the Commentary on Validity (Pramanavārtttikavṛtti, tshad ma rnam 'grel gyi 'grel pa). DT Tshad ma ce, 261a–365a.

The Logic of Debate (Vādanyaya nāma prakaraṇa, rtsod pa'i rigs pa zhes bya ba'i rab tu byed pa). DT Tshad ma che, 326b–355b.

Establishing Other Continua (Santanānyatarasiddhi nāma prakaraṇa, rgyud gzhan grub pa zhes bya ba'i rab tu byed pa). DT Tshad ma che, 355b–359a.

Works in other genres:

In Praise of the Buddha's Nirvana (Buddhasya nirvāṇa stotraṃ, sangs rgyas yongs su mya ngan las 'das pa la bstod pa). DT bsTod tshogs ka, 203b–204a.

A Praise of the Glorious Vajra Ḍaka in Daṇḍaka (Śrī vajra ḍākasya stotra daṇḍaka nāma, dpal rdo rje mkha' 'gro'i bstod pa rgyun chags zhes bya ba). DT rGyud sde wa, 242a–243b.

Opening the Eyes: A Commentary on the Great King of Tantras, Hevajra (Śrī Hevajra tantra mahārājasya pañcikānetra vibhaṅga nāma, rgyud kyi rgyal po chen po dpal dgyes pa'i rdo rje'i dka'i 'grel spyan 'byed ces bya ba). DT rGyud sde nga, 236b–321r.

A Ritual for Mandala Grids (dkyil 'khor gyi thig gi cho ga). DT rGyud sde ri, 215b–216a.

A Commentary on the Jataka Mala (Jātaka mālā ṭīka, skyes pa'i rabs kyi rgya cher bshad pa). DT mDo 'grel hu, 135b–340a.

SOURCES AND ABBREVIATIONS

ABBREVIATIONS

AK   Vasubandhu. *Verses on the Treasury of Abhidharma* (*Abhidharmakośakā-rikā, chos mngon pa mdzod kyi tshig le'ur byas pa*). DT mNgon pa khu pa.

AKB   *Auto-Commentary on the Treasury of Abhidharma* (*Abhidharmakoṣaṃbhāṣyaṃ, chos mngon pa'i mdzod kyi bshad pa*). DT mNgon pa ku pa and khu pa.

DB   Devendrabuddhi. *A Textual Gloss on the Commentary of Validity.* (*Pramāṇavārttikapañjikā, Tshad ma rnam 'grel gyi 'grel pa*). DT Tshad ma che pa, 1a–326b.

DK   *Dergye Kangyur.* For convenience, the electronic version from ACIP was primarily used, but when necessary, it was checked against scans of the 1977 reprint by the Delhi Karmapae Choedhey, Gyalwae Sungrab Partun Khang. Works cited are also referenced by their number from the Complete Catalogue of the Tibetan Buddhist Catalogs by Hakuji Ui, et al.

DT   *Dergye Tengyur.* As with DK, the electronic text was the primary source, but it was checked against scans as well as against the actual folios and the critical *dPe zlur ma* edition.

Jewels   *Jewels from the Treasury: Vasubandhu's* Verses on the Treasury of Abhidharma *and Its Commentary,* Youthful Play: An Explanation of the Treasury of Abhidharma *by the Ninth Karmapa Wangchuk Dorje.* David Karma Choephel, trans. Woodstock: KTD Publications, 2012.

JK   *Jang (Litang) Kangyur.* Electronic version under preparation by The Dharma Treasure Association.

Orn   Prajñākaragupta. *The Ornament of the Commentary on Validity* (*Pramāṇavārttikālaṅkāra, Tshad ma rnam 'grel gyi rgyan*). sKal ldan rgyal po and Blo ldan shes rab, trans. Edited and corrected by Kumāra Śrī and 'Phags pa shes rab, ed. DT Tshad ma te pa and the pa.

PS   Dignāga. *Compendium of Validity (Pramāṇasamuccaya nāma prakaraṇa, Tshad ma kun las btus pa zhes bya ba'i rab tu byed pa)*. Vasudhararakṣita and dGe bsnyen seng rgyal, trans. DT Tshad ma ce pa, 1a–13a.

PSV   Dignāga. *Commentary on the Compendium of Validity (Pramāṇasamuc-chaya vṛddhi, Tshad ma kun las btus pa'i 'grel pa)*. Vasudhararakṣita and dGe bsnyen seng rgyal, trans. DT Tshad ma ce pa, 14a–85b.

PV   Dharmakīrti. *The Commentary on Validity (Pramāṇavārttikakārikā, Tshad ma rnam 'grel)*. Śākya Śrī Bhadra and dKun dga' rgyal mtshan bzang po, trans. DT Tshad ma ce pa, 94b–151a.

PV-s1   Dharmakīrti. *Pramāṇavārttikam*. Rāhula Sāṅkṛtyāyana, ed. In *Journal of the Bihar and Orissa Research Society*, Vol. XXIV (1938).

PV-s2   Dharmakīrti. *Pramāṇavārttikam*. R.C. Pandey, ed. Electronic version, http://www.dsbcproject.org/node/7975.

PVin   Dharmakīrti. *The Ascertainment of Validity (Pramāṇaviniṣcaya, Tshad ma rnam par nges pa)*. gZhan la phan pa bzang po, Blo ldan shes rab, et al, trans. DT Tshad ma ce pa, 152a–230a.

PVSV   Dharmakīrti. Autocommentary on the Commentary of Validity *(Pra-manavārtttikavṛtti, Tshad ma rnam 'grel gyi 'grel pa)*. DT Tshad ma ce pa, 261b–365b.

RZG   Chödrak Gyatso. *Tshad ma rigs gzhung rgya mtsho*. TBRC W1KG2778. Thimbu, Bhutan: Topga Tulku, 1973. http://tbrc.org/link?RID=O1PD 95368 | O1PD953681PD95374$W1KG2778

SB   Śākyabuddhi. *Pramāṇavārttikaṭīka (Tshad ma rnam 'grel gyi 'grel bshad)*. Subhutiśri and dGe ba'i blo gros, trans. DT Tshad ma je pa and nye pa.

SVI   Steinkellner, Ernst. *Verse-Index of Dharmakīrti's Works (Tibetan Versions)*. Vienna: Arbeitskreis für Tibetische und Buddhistische Studien, Universität Wien, 1977.

OTHER SOURCES

Beauregard, Mario. *Brain Wars: The Scientific Battle Over the Existence of the Mind and the Proof That Will Change the Way We Live Our Lives*. New York: Harper-Collins, 2012. Kindle Edition.

Dreyfus, George B. *Recognizing Reality: Dharmakīrti's Philosophy and Its Tibetan Interpretations*. Delhi: Sri Satguru Publications, 1997.

Dunne, John D. *Foundations of Dharmakīrti's Philosophy*. Boston: Wisdom Publications, 2004.

Franco, Eli. *Dharmakīrti on Compassion and Rebirth.* Wiener Studien zur Tibetologie und Buddhismuskunde 38. Vienna: Arbeitskreis für Tibetische und Buddhistische Studien, 1997.

Hopkins, Jeffrey. *Maps of the Profound: Jam-yang-shay-ba's Great Exposition of Buddhist and Non-Buddhist Views on the Nature of Reality.* Ithaca: Snow Lion Publications, 2003.

Karma Trinleypa. *Chos rje karma phrin las pa'i mgur dang/ thun mong ba'i dris lan bzhugs so//* Varanasi: Vajra Vidya Library, 2011.

Parnia, Dr. Sam and Josh Young. *Erasing Death: The Science That Is Rewriting the Boundaries Between Life and Death.* New York: HarperCollins, 2013. Kindle Edition.

Pawo Tsuglak Trengwa, *mKhas pa'i dga' ston,* Beijing: mi rigs dpe skrun khang, 1986. Scans downloaded from http://www.tbrc.org/#!rid=W7499.

Radhakrishnan, S. *Indian Philosophy, Vol. 2.* 2nd ed. Delhi: Oxford University Press, 2008.

Sakya Paṇḍita. *Tshad ma rigs pa'i gter gyi rtsa ba dang 'grel pa (The Treasury of Valid Logic Root Text and Commentary).* Qinghai: Bod ljongs mi dmangs dpe skrun khang, 1989.

Situ Chökyi Jungne et al. *bKa' brgyud gser phreng rnam thar zla ba chu shel gyi phreng ba.* Varanasi: Vajra Vidya Library, 2004. Vol. II.

Steinkellner, Ernst. *Dignāga's Pramāṇasamuccaya, Chapter 1: A hypothetical reconstruction of the Sanskrit text with the help of the two Tibetan translations on the basis of the hitherto known Sanskrit fragments and the linguistic materials gained from Jinendrabuddhi's Ṭīkā.* (April, 2005) www.oeaw.ac.at/ias/Mat/dignaga _PS_1.pdf.

Tāranātha. *History of Buddhism in India.* Lama Chimpa and Alaka Chattopadhyaya, trans. Delhi, Motilal Banarsidass, 1990.

Notes

Notes to the Translator's Introduction

1. In discussing Dignāga and Dharmakīrti's works, Chödrak Gyatso's student Karma Trinleypa said, "That Middle Way is the Great Middle Way, / It is no different than mahamudra." (*dbu ma de ni dbu ma chen po ste/ /phyag rgya che dang de la khyad par med*). From "Dris lan snang gsal sgron me zhe bya ba ra ti dgon pa'i gzims khang ba'i dris lan bzhugs so/ /" in *Chos rje karma phrin las pa'i mgur dang/ thun mong ba'i dris lan bzhugs so//* (Varanasi: Vajra Vidya Library, 2011), p. 164.

2. This section is largely based on George Dreyfus' overview of the development of epistemological traditions in India and Tibet found in "Introduction II: Dharmakīrti's Tradition in India and Tibet," *Recognizing Reality* (Delhi: Sri Satguru Publications, 1997), pp. 15–41.

3. Throughout this book, the Sanskrit *pramāṇa* and Tibetan *tshad ma* are translated alternately as valid, validly, valid cognition, or validity, depending upon the context and syntax. This term has been translated in a great variety of ways by different translators, but the most frequently encountered translation (at least in translations of works from the Tibetan tradition) is *valid cognition*. While this accurately reflects Dignāga, Dharmakīrti, and their followers' most frequent usage of the term on a narrow epistemological level, it does not encompass all of the different usages of the term in Dharmakīrti's work, let alone the range of senses in the broader Buddhist and non-Buddhist literature. Since the terms *valid* and *validity* do not limit the meaning in the same way, they are preferred here except in contexts where the term *valid cognition* seems clearer and less awkward.

4. Tāranātha, *History of Buddhism in India*, Lama Chimpa and Alaka Chattopadhyaya, trans. (Delhi, Motilal Banarsidass, 1990), p. 182.

5. For a list of all of Dignāga's works preserved in Tibetan, see Appendix 2. It should also be noted that in Tibetan, numbers such as 100 or 108 sometimes do not mean that number specifically but instead indicate a large number of several dozens.

6. Dharmakīrti's dates are difficult to ascertain, but most sources agree that

he was active in the seventh century. Tāranātha mentions that he was a contemporary of the Tibetan king Songtsen Gampo (617 to 697 CE) and also mentions that he was a disciple of Dignāga's student Īśvarasena (Tāranatha, p. 229).

7. Even Dignāga and Dharmakīrti's more original contributions may be viewed as ways to justify Buddhist positions in new language and terms. For example, Dignāga's presentation of the exclusion or *apoha* as the object of thought and Dharmakīrti's subsequent elaboration of it are quite original in many respects, but one also can see them as a way to explain one aspect of the selflessness of phenomena—how coarse relative phenomena such as water jugs can appear consistently to thought even though they are ultimately empty of any nature.

8. Dreyfus' *Recognizing Reality* treats this issue of Tibetan reinterpretations of Dignāga and Dharmakīrti clearly and in great depth, so readers who would like a more in-depth discussion of this are encouraged to look there. The terms "anti-realist" and "moderate realism" are taken from Dreyfus' presentation.

9. According to his biographies, in a previous lifetime, the First Karmapa Dusum Khyenpa was a bhikshu named Dharmakīrti, but it is not likely that this was the same Dharmakīrti as the one who wrote the seven treatises. Galo's biography of Dusum Khyenpa and Tāranātha's biography of Dharmakīrti in his *History of Buddhism in India* give different birthplaces and abbots for the bhikshu who was a previous incarnation of Dusum Khyenpa and for the author of the seven treatises. See Galo, "The Golden Isle: The Precious Lives of the Lord of Dharma in Eighteen Chapters" in *The First Karmapa: The Life and Teachings of Dusum Khyenpa*, Michele Martin and David Karma Choephel, trans. (Woodstock: KTD Publications, 2012), p. 7. See also Tāranātha, pp. 228–29.

10. Karma Trinleypa, *Dri lan rnam par thar pa'i don bsdus in Chos rje karma phrin las pa'i mgur dang/ thun mong ba'i dris lan bzhugs so//* (Varanasi: Vajra Vidya Library, 2011), p. 183.

11. At the end of the *Ocean*, it is written that "It is renowned that this was written by the Karmapa Ranjung Kunkhyen, the Dharma King Chödrak Gyatso at glorious Tsaritra." (*'di ni dpal tsa' ri trar karma pa rang byung kun mkhyen chos kyi rgyal po chos grags rgya mtshos sbyar bar mdzad do zhes grags pa las,* RZG ii.343a.) Though no date is given for its composition, it is known from the biographies of Chödrak Gyatso and from the autobiography of Shamar Chökyi Drakpa that the winter of 1494–95 was the only period Chödrak Gyatso went to Tsaritra as an adult. (Thanks to Karma Lekthong of the Duekhyen Library in Sidhbari, Dharamsala for supplying this information.)

12. An epithet for Chödrak Gyatso.

13. It is not clear what this refers, as there is no mention of calculations of the globe (*go la'i rtsis*) in the modern editions of the text. It may refer to a pas-

sage in one of the sections of the text that has been lost, or it may have been a question in regard to a different text.

14. Pawo Tsuglak Trengwa, *mKhas pa'i dga' ston* (Beijing: mi rigs dpe skrun khang, 1986), Vol. II, p. 1107–8. The scribe Dakrampa Khedrup Chögyal Tenpa was one of Pawo Tsuklag Trengwa's masters and told him this story directly. (*'jig rten gsum sgron 'di la zhu ba po nga rang 'dra ba zhig yod na myur du 'grub pa yod ste de med pas lan/ rigs gzhung rgya mtsho 'di la rtsom par yang ngas gsol ba btab/ rtsom yig pa yang rang gis byas/ rje thams cad mkhyen pa de gzhan dang rang mi 'dra/ tshad ma'i gzhung tsam yang sku 'khris na mi bzhugs/ phyag dpe ni mi gzigs/ dus rtag tu phyag mnyam gzhag spyan lta stangs thugs ting nge 'dzin las mi 'da' ba de'i ngang nas/ bka' chos gdams ngag chos kyi char pas mdzad skyong zad mi shes pa dgos [dgongs] pa'i gsol lcog gi 'khris su bdag gis snyug gu nag tung nge bzung nas bsdad/ gseng nam byung du thugs rtsom zhus pa na gang na yod gsungs pa tsam las thogs pa med par spyan lta stangs kyi ngang nas sha ra ra ljags dpod mdzad/ go la'i rtsis kyi skabs su cung zad go tshod zhus pa na/ de lta min pa'i rgyu mtshan mtha' dag nges pa dang bcas te bka' stsal nas phyag g.yas pa nam mkha' la cung zad brkyangs nas nged bgro gleng de ltar byed pa yin gsungs nas zhal 'dzum tsam mdzad byung/ drung gi phyag brkyang ba rdzogs par mthong ba sku 'khor ba la yang nga las med pa yin*)

15. The pledge to compose at the opening of *The Ocean* indicates that Chödrak Gyatso may have initially intended to include commentaries on all seven of Dharmakīrti's works on validity, but the finished work does not include commentaries on the four minor treatises.

16. There are eleven general discussions listed in the outline of the chapter, but one—the discussion of the truth of cessation—merely refers back to a previous topic and is thus not counted separately here.

17. *bKa' brgyud gser phreng rnam thar zla ba chu shel gyi phreng ba* (Varanasi: Vajra Vidya Library, 2004), Vol. II, p. 182 & p. 250.

18. *bKa' brgyud gser phreng*, p. 250. See also Dreyfus, p. 29.

19. From the colophon by Mikyö Dorje, RZG, Vol. II 343b. *gdul bya le lo che zhing shes rab chung ba dag gis bstan bcos de dag la rnam par dpyod pa'i blo gros kyis bzung bar ma nus nas glegs bam gyi phyi mo'ang legs par bsdu ba'i gzhi nyams par gyur pa na/*

20. I studied this chapter at the Vajra Vidya Institute, Sarnath, Varanasi, India, in 2003 and later received the reading transmission of the entire *Ocean* from Khenpo Sherap Phuntsok of the Vajra Vidya Institute. Khenpo Sherap received it from Khenpo Lobsang Tenzin, who received it from Khenpo Sönam Yönten, who received it from Satsa Drupkhen. Satsa Drupkhen received the transmission from Situ Pema Wangchuk Gyalpo, one of the main lineage masters of the Karma Kamtsang.

21. RZG, Vol 2, 348a.

22. There are differing opinions on the order of the chapters of the *Commentary:* this chapter is placed first in some editions, but many commentators and

editions place the chapter on inference for oneself first instead. Near the opening of *The Ocean*, Chödrak Gyatso explains in detail the rationales for each of the different orderings of the chapters and says that both are valid. However, he himself places "Establishing Validity" first, and this translation follows his lead. Thus the order of the chapters assumed throughout this translation is 1. Establishing Validity, 2. Perception, 3. Inference for Oneself, and 4. Inference for Others.

23. *Vinaya-kṣudraka-vastu* (*'Dul ba phran tshegs kyi gzhi*), D6, DK 'Dul ba tha, 162a–b. *dga' bo de ji snyam du sems/ de bzhin gshegs pa gzhan du 'gyur ba'i tshig gang yin pa de gsung ngam/ btsun pa ma lags so/ /dga' bo legs so legs so/ /de bzhin gshegs pa gzhan du 'gyur ba'i tshig gang yin pa de gsung ba ni gnas ma yin zhing go skabs med de/ dga' bo de bzhin gshegs pa ni yang dag pa gsung ba/ bden pa gsung ba/ chos gsung ba/ de kho na nyid gsung ba/ phyin ci ma log par gsung ba'o/ /de bzhin gshegs pa ni yun ring po nas 'jig rten la phan pa bzhed pa/ bde ba bzhed pa/ grub pa dang bde ba bzhed pa/ lam mkhyen pa/ lam grub pa/ lam ston pa/ lam brjod pa/ lam yongs su 'dren pa'o/ /de bzhin gshegs pa ni dgra bcom pa yang dag par rdzogs pa'i sangs rgyas rig pa dang zhabs su ldan pa/ bde bar gshegs pa/ 'jig rten mkhyen pa/ skyes bu 'dul ba'i kha lo sgyur ba/ bla na med pa/ lha dang mi rnams kyi ston pa/ sangs rgyas bcom ldan 'das so//*

24. DB 61b: *de de ltar na lugs las 'byung ba 'gro ba la phan par mdzad par bzhed pa nyid la sogs pa rgyu snga ma snga mas phyi ma phyi ma tham cad la srid pa'i rjes su dpag pas/ tshad ma shin tu mi srid pa med pa rab tu bsgrubs nas/*

25. Thorough descriptions of the non-Buddhist positions would require more verbiage than is appropriate for this sort of a translation. Those readers who want more thorough treatments of the non-Buddhist positions are encouraged to look at the excellent recent literature on Indian philosophy in general and Dharmakīrti in particular. Radhakrishnan's *Indian Philosophy* and Hopkins' *Maps of the Profound* both give good overviews of the various non-Buddhist schools, and Dreyfus' *Recognizing Reality* and Dunne's *Foundations of Dharmakīrti's Philosophy* also both give excellent descriptions of the positions of Dharmakīrti's opponents.

26. Verse 178ab.

27. John D. Dunne has some insightful comments on this issue in his *Foundations of Dharmakīrti's Philosophy* (Boston: Wisdom Publications, 2004), p. 59 n13.

28. As Dreyfus and Dunne both note, even this level of external realism is not monolithic; one can distinguish two main levels of analysis within it, which Dreyfus calls the "alternate interpretation" and "standard interpretation" and Dunne calls "Abhidharma Typology" and "External Realism." The distinctions between these two levels are rather technical and not critical for our purposes here. See Dreyfus, pp. 83–105, and Dunne, pp. 55–79.

29. One clear example of this is in the beginning of the second chapter of *The*

Commentary, where he states: "In this, the ultimately functional / Ultimately exists," (ii.3ab, *arthakriyāsamartha yat tadatra paramārthasat, don dam don byed nus pa gang/ /de 'dir don dam yod pa yin//*) In this passage, Dharmakīrti describes ultimate truth as meaning being able to function, which he and his commentators explain to mean causal efficacy—ultimately existent things are able to produce results. Yet just twenty-two verses later, Dharmakīrti shifts to a more profound level and states that the relationship between cause and result is not ultimate. "The relationship is made by thought," he says (ii.25c, *sambadhyate kalpanayā, rtogs pa yis ni 'brel par byed//*), meaning that it is purely relative. And if the relationship between cause and result is conventional, then causal efficacy itself can only be conventional and the earlier statement that the ultimate is causally efficient must be seen as a provisional statement made in a particular context for the sake of a particular argument, not as Dharmakīrti's own ultimate view. Indeed, Dharmakīrti has signaled this shift in levels of analysis in his earlier statement itself by qualifying it, saying only that it is ultimate "In this" (*atra*)—here in this context. Thus the statements frequently encountered in the secondary literature that Dharmakīrti considers only the causally efficient to exist ultimately should be taken with a grain of salt, for a close examination shows that Dharmakīrti only makes such a statement on a lower, provisional level of analysis.

30. This is in contrast to other Buddhist treatises whose primary aim is to present a Buddhist view, such as Vasubandhu's *Verses on the Treasury of Abhidharma* or Maitreya's *Ornament of Clear Realization,* for example, where comparatively few verses are refutations.

31. "Treatises that teach the characteristics" is another term for texts on validity.

32. *dbang po 'di dag gal te tshad yin na/ /'phags pa'i lam gyis su la ci zhig bya//*

33. Verse 210ab.

34. Karma Trinleypa, p. 170. *gzhan yang tshad ma grub pa'i le'u las/ /gnus lugs mngon sum rtogs pa'i lam bden ni/ /'gog pa'i bden pa nyid dang gcig par gsungs/ /de phyir dbu ma'i gzhung lugs yin zhes bzhed*

35. *Vinaya Vastu, 'dul ba lung gzhi.* This is based on a search of the Jang Litang Kangyur.

36. *Vinaya Vastu, 'dul ba lung gzhi,* JK 'Dul ba ga pa, 294a. *de na de rnams drang srong gi tshig ni tshad ma yin no snyam nas.*

37. Dunne, p. 19.

38. As Dunne points out, knowledge for the Pramāṇa theorists has a different connotation than for contemporary European and American philosophers. Rather than indicating a justified true belief or attitude, knowledge is instead considered a cognitive event that is an act of knowing indubitably. See Dunne, p. 18.

39. Verse 3a.

40. Verse 3b.

41. Specific characteristics (*svalakṣaṇam, rang mtshan*) refers to the actual particulars that can perform causal functions or fulfill aims, such as the atoms that make up coarse physical objects or specific instances of cognition that comprise a mental continuum. They are contrasted with universal characteristics (*sāmānyalakṣaṇam, spyi mtshan*), which are the conceptual ideas of a universal nature that inhabits the instances of a specific class, such as being a jug or being a cow.

42. Verse 8b-d.

43. PVin 167a. *tha snyad la mi slu la ltos nas 'dir tshad ma yin no/ /'di ni kun tu tha snyad pa'i tshad ma'i rang bzhin brjod pa yin no/ /'di la yang pha rol rmongs pas 'jig rten slu bar byed pa'i phyir ro/ /bsams pa las byung ba nyid kyi shes rab goms par byas pas rnam par 'khrul pas dben zhing dri ma med la ldog pa med pa'i don dam pa'i tshad ma mngon sum du byed do//*

44. In typical Dharmakīrtian fashion, he does also explore other, tangential issues during these two passages, but only in order to prove subsidiary aspects of his main proof.

45. Verse 148c.

46. Jonathan Franzen, "Jonathan Franzen: what's wrong with the modern world," http://www.theguardian.com/books/2013/sep/13/jonathan-franzen-wrong-modern-world.

47. Various Buddhist schools differ about whether there is a between state (*bardo*) between the moment of death and the moment of conception in the next life. Dharmakīrti does not mention this issue here, and it is immaterial to his argument. Whether there is a between state or not, the first cognition in a given lifetime would have to be part of a continuum that can be traced back to a previous state of existence.

48. Unless the condition of craving is absent, as Dharmakīrti discusses in v. 83 and v. 185–91.

49. On deeper levels of analysis, Dharmakīrti asserts that the body is merely a projection of the mind, and ultimately even that mind is emptiness, so this logic of rebirth only applies on the conventional level and on the levels of external realism. On these more profound levels of analysis, rebirth is seen as an illusion, but one that appears consistently to deluded beings and is thus called relative truth.

50. Dr. Sam Parnia and Josh Young, *Erasing Death: The Science That Is Rewriting the Boundaries Between Life and Death* (New York: HarperCollins, 2013), Kindle edition, p. 189.

51. Parnia and Young, p. 71.

52. Mario Beauregard, *Brain Wars: The Scientific Battle Over the Existence of the Mind and the Proof That Will Change the Way We Live Our Lives,* (New York: HarperCollins, 2012), Kindle edition, location 2409.

53. Some scientists posit that these experiences could be because of a lack of oxygen in the brain or because of seizures in the brain, but such arguments are not without their difficulties. See Parnia and Young, p. 148ff.

54. Additionally, there has been much discussion of cases where young children have memories of past lives that are then corroborated by independent researchers such as Dr. Ian Petersen, even in countries such as the United States where rebirth is not universally accepted. However, Dharmakīrti does not consider memory to be valid and does not discuss this line of reasoning in the chapter.

Notes to the Brief Introduction to Indo-Tibetan Logic

1. This term is often translated as *subject property*. However, since *subject* is usually used as a translation of *dharmin* (*chos can*), if you translate that back into Tibetan, you would arrive at the term *chos can gyi chos*, which Dharmakīrti rejects in the fourth chapter of *The Commentary* because it could lead to confusion between the subject in question and other subjects such as the analogy. Therefore Dharmakīrti uses the term *phyogs chos*, or *propositional property*. Though the word *proposition* properly refers to the subject and predicate together, here it refers as a nickname to the subject only.

2. *lakṣaṇa, mtshan nyid*. This term is frequently translated as *definition*, but that is not quite right because the term definition refers to a word or phrase that describes the nature of something. This term in Tibetan, however, does not refer to a verbal expression but to the characteristic properties of a phenomenon as they appear to thought (the entity universal) as Chödrak Gyatso describes early on in *The Ocean*. This is confused as being the specific characteristics of the object. But no one would confuse a definition for the specific characteristics—anyone who did mistake the definition for the entity would be terrified to look up "tiger" in the dictionary. Thus *definition* is inadequate as a translation. Some propose saying "defining characteristic" instead of characteristic, but that seems unnecessarily verbose since it really does not convey any meaning that the word characteristic does not already carry on its own.

3. This is frequently translated as *concomitant*, especially in academic literature. In normal usage, concomitant merely means that something accompanies something else but does not imply that whatever accompanies is necessarily entailed by what it accompanies, as *anvaya* does. Though in mathematics and logic concomitance might have been assigned that meaning, it seems that ordinary readers might not understand it easily, and the word *concomitant* is also somewhat awkward. Thus *entail* is preferred in this translation.

4. Though there are some photographs of rabbit-like creatures with racks of antlers, cognoscenti know that these are not rabbits but fabulous jackelopes.

Notes to *The Ocean of Literature on Logic*

1. This stanza is a prostration to Manjughosha (whose name literally means "gentle melody") and Maitreya, who is also known as Ajita.

2. *dge slong dag gam mkhas rnams kyis/ /bsregs bcad bdar ba'i gser bzhin du/ /legs par brtags la nga yi bka'/ /blang bar bya yi gus phyir min//* Though Chödrak Gyatso and many other masters attribute it to a sutra, in the Dergye Kangyur this exact citation appears in a tantra, the Śrī Mahā*balatantra* *R*āja Nāma (*dPal stobs po che'i rgyud kyi rgyal po zhes bya ba*, DK D391, rGyud 'Bum ga, 216b).

3. This topic should occur at the very end of *The Ocean of Literature on Logic*, but it seems to have been lost.

4. In this and other Tibetan commentaries, Dignāga's *Compendium of Validity* is often called *The Compendium Sutra of Validity* or simply the *Sutra*. The word *sutra* refers to the short, aphoristic quality of its statements, and does not mean that it was spoken by the Buddha. In this translation, *Compendium* will be used as the abbreviated title for clarity even when Chödrak Gyatso refers to it as the *Sutra* (*mdo*).

5. This last topic was probably intended to be placed at the end of the fourth chapter "Inference for Others." However it is not found in RZG or other present day editions; it is likely one of the portions of the work that was lost between the time of its writing and the time that Mikyö Dorje reassembled it.

6. Ācarya Jñānagarbha, *Satyadvayavibhagakārikā* (*bden pa gnyis rnam par 'byed pa'i tshig le'ur byas pa*), Tengyur dBu ma sa pa, 3a. *sems dang sems byung khams gsum pa/ /sgro btags rnam pa can rtog yin/ /de dag 'ching ba'i rgyu nyid du//*

7. *Support* here refers to bodily support: his teachings bring students to births in higher realms where they can practice the path of Dharma.

8. The twofold purity refers to freedom from adventitious stains and the completely pure nature.

9. A compilation in verse of Sanskrit poetic synonyms and epithets by Amarasiṃha.

10. Āryadeva, *Catuḥśatakaśāstrākārikānāma* (*bstan bcos bzhi brgya pa zhes bya ba'i tshig le'ur byas pa*), Tengyur, dBu ma tsha pa, 13a. *gzur gnas blo ldan don gnyer ba/ /nyan po snod ces bya bar brjod//*

11. PVSV, 261b. *don dang don ma yin pa rnam par 'byed pa ni rjes su dpag pa la brten pa'i phyir yin la/ de la'ang log par rtog pas de rnam par bzhag pa/*

12. In other words, the *Commentary* and Dharmakīrti's other works explain all six chapters of Dignāga's *Compendium*. The chapters are: 1. Perception, 2.

Inference for Oneself, 3. Inference for Others, 4. An Examination of Analogies and False Analogies, 5. An Examination of Exclusions, and 6. An Examination of False Refutations.

13. As this is the end of the introductory material and beginning of the actual chapter, the numbering of the outline topics is restarted at this point with capital Roman numerals so that the main topics of the chapter will be Roman numeral level headings. This clarifies the structure of the chapter itself and prevents the numbering from delving into too many levels of hierarchy.

14. Though Dignāga's original verse has two *pādas* and thus should probably be translated as a couplet, the verse is more pleasing as a tercet and so I have taken the liberty of translating it in three lines.

15. PSV 14a. Chödrak Gyatso's citation abbreviates the actual text. What follows is a translation of the passage as it appears in PSV, with the parts omitted by Chödrak Gyatso italicized:

> In the first chapter, there is a statement of praise of the Bhagavan who is valid through the perfect causes and results in order to instill respect. The causes are the perfect intent and training. *The intent is the wish to benefit beings, the training is teaching the teachings to beings, and the results* are the perfect benefits for self and others. The perfect benefit for oneself is the sugata, which has three meanings: impressiveness, like a person's handsome face; irreversibility, like having cured a contagious disease; and completeness, like a vase that has been completely filled. These three meanings are for distinguishing the perfect benefit for self as superior to non-Buddhists who are free of attachment, to learners, and to non-learners. *The perfect benefit for others is that through the meaning of liberating, he is a protector.* I prostrate to the teacher *who has such qualities.* (*'dir yang rab tu byed pa'i dang por rgyu dang 'bras bu phun sum tshogs pas tshad mar gyur pa nyid kyis bcom ldan 'das la bstod pa brjod pa ni gus pa bskyed par bya ba'i don du'o/ /de la rgyu ni bsam pa dang sbyor ba phun sum tshogs pa'o/* /bsam pa ni 'gro ba la phan par bzhed pa'o/ / sbyor ba ni 'gro ba la bstan ba ston pa'o/ /*'bras bu ni rang dang gzhan gyi don phun sum tshogs pa'o/ /rang don phun sum tshogs pa ni bde bar gshegs pa nyid kyis te/ don gsum nye bar blang bar bya'o/ /rab tu mdzes pa'i don ni skyes bu gzugs legs pa bzhin no/ /phyir mi ldog pa'i don ni rims nad legs par byang pa bzhin no/ /ma lus pa'i don ni bum pa legs par gang ba bzhin no/ /don gsum po de yang phyi rol ba'i 'dod chags dang bral ba dang/ slob pa dang/ mi slob pa rnams las rang don phun sum tshogs pa khyad par du bya ba'i phyir ro/ /gzhan don phun sum tshogs pa ni sgrol ba'i don gyis na* skyob pa nyid do/ /de lta bu'i yon tan can gyi ston pa *la phyag 'tshal 'tshal nas/*)

16. An isolate is a conceptual idea of an entity. Proposing that the characteristics and characterized are not separate in substance but have separate isolates means that although not substantially different, they are conceived in different ways and thus appear to the mind as separate phenomena.

17. ii.319ab (SVI iii.319a), PV 130b. *bya ba byed pa'i tha snyad dag / /thams cad de ltar rnam par gnas//*

18. Hot and burning are given as characteristics of fire and wet and liquid as the characteristics of water in many Buddhist scriptures.

19. "That which functions to support a beam" is the characteristic of a pillar given in traditional texts.

20. Verse 208ab.

21. That is, when someone with jaundice sees a yellow conch, there is no such thing as a yellow conch, so that cannot be the object of the cognition, but that individual does not have an awareness of a white conch, either. Such a cognition is therefore not an awareness of anything that exists, and therefore it has no object, according to the opponent.

22. PS 2a. *rtog pa'ang rang rig nyid du 'dod//* Skt: *kalpanāpi svasaṃvittāv iṣṭā* (PSVS 3).

23. ii.287d (SVI iii.287d). *de phyir de la kun mngon sum//*

24. In this context, *aspect* refers to the mental image of yellow. As explained in the chapter on perception, Dharmakīrti posits that cognitions have two aspects: the apprehended aspect (*gzung rnam*), which is a mental image of the object, and the apprehending aspect (*'dzin rnam*), which is the subject. Thus in this passage the nonconceptual misapprehension of a white conch as yellow is not a perception of the object (the conch), but it is a self-aware perception of the apprehended aspect, which is the object of the self-awareness.

25. As described at length in the chapter on perception, thoughts are not clear awareness of their engaged object because they do not apprehend it through perception. Instead, they apprehend a conceptual universal of the entity, which they mistake for the entity itself. Such an awareness of a universal is said to be unclear, and thus thoughts are said not to apprehend their object clearly. Hence a cognition of the engaged object cannot both be a clear apprehension of that object and a thought, which is by nature unclear.

26. RZG here reads *yongs su dpyod pa'i*, which would mean analyze rather than determine. However, Chödrak Gyatso bases this characterization of validity on the line from the *Ascertainment* quoted at the end of the paragraph, where the word used is *paricchidya* or *yongs su bcad pa*, translated here as *determined*. Additionally, SB 72a also describes as meaning *don yongs su bcad nas,* or after determining the entity. Thus *yongs su dpyod pa* (*analyzes*) seems to be a typographical error and it is translated as *determines*.

27. PVin 152b.*'di dag gi don yongs su bcad nas 'jug pa na don bya ba la bslu ba med*

pa'i phyir ro// The pronoun "they" refers to perception and inference, the two types of validity.

28. That is, if the propositional property of the syllogism is not proven.

29. DB 5b.

30. Sakya Paṇḍita, *Tshad ma rigs pa'i gter gyi rtsa ba dang 'grel pa (The Treasury of Valid Logic Root Text and Commentary)*, Qinghai: Bod ljongs mi dmangs dpe skrun khang, 1989, p. 21. *mtshan nyid gnyis kyis 'jog na ni//mtshon bya de yang gnyis su 'gyur//*

31. The cited text as Chödrak Gyatso has it (*ngo bo kho na rang nyid dang//*) does not appear in PS. However, a similar passage appears in PSV, 40b.

32. Orn 26b.

33. That is, Dharmakīrti.

34. Chapa Chökyi Senge (1182–1251).

35. *yid dpyod snang la ma nges dang/ /bcad shes log shes the tshom lnga//*

36. *yid dpyod rtags la gtan mi ltos/ /dam bca' tsam yin the tshom 'gyur//*

37. *gal te snang la ma nges pa/ /tshad ma min na mngon sum kun/ /tshad ma min 'gyur mngon sum la/ /nges pa nyid ni bkag phyir ro//*

38. *mngon sum rtog bral da ltar ba/ /bcad shes 'das pa dran pa yin/ /yul dus 'dzin stangs 'gal ba la/ /gzhi mthun pa ni ga la srid//* A common basis (*gzhi mthun*) between two sets is an object that is a member of both sets. For example, a gold vase is a common basis between gold and vase because it is both gold and a vase.

39. *ma rtogs log rtog the tshom ste/ /tshad ma'i 'gal zla rnam pa gsum//* These five citations are from Sakya Paṇḍita, p. 5–6.

40. Dharmottara, *Pramāṇaviniścayaṭīkā (Tshad ma rnam par nges pa'i 'grel bshad)*, D4229, DT Tshad ma dze pa, 16b. (Chödrak Gyatso refers to this text as *'Thad ldan* or *The Reasoned* throughout, though in the Tengyur that name is given to Dharmottara's commentary from volume Tshe on the third chapter of the *Ascertainment*.) The passage in question reads: "Thoughts that do not depend on evidence are doubt, so one cannot achieve their object." (*rtags la mi bltos pa'i rnam par rtog pa ni the tshom nyid yin pas de'i yul yang thob par mi nus te*).

41. When a respondent says something patently contradictory or wrong in debate, the presenter will shout "three circles!" meaning that the respondent has boxed themselves into three logical circles from which they cannot extricate themselves without contradicting themselves. *See* Dreyfus, "Tibetan Monastic Education," (http://www.thlib.org/#!essay=/dreyfus/drepung/monasticed/s/b42), note 47.

42. Higher states refers to the higher samsaric states of gods and humans, and true excellence refers to liberation and nirvana.

43. Verbal validity refers to one of the types of inference posited by the Naiyāyika, Mimāmsāka, and other Hindu schools, who posit that the Vedic

scriptures are verbal validity and thus authoritative. By refuting verbal validity, Dharmakīrti implicitly denies the validity of the Vedas. Cf. Radhakrishnan, 95–96. Dharmakīrti refutes verbal validity at greater length the chapter "Inference for Oneself."

44. Verse 6d.

45. Kāpilas is another name for adherents of the Sāṃkhya school, so called after the founder of the school, the sage Kapila.

46. Tengyur Dze pa (D4229), 10a. *nus pa nges par yang rjes su dpag pa dang don byed par snang ba'i mgnon sum ni rang kho na las 'gyur ro//*

47. Tengyur Dze pa (D4229), 10a. *'jug par byed pa'i mngon sum yang la la ni rang kho na las gyur te/ 'khrul bar dwogs pa mtha dag bsal nas rang bzhin gyi khyad par khong du chud pa gang yin pa'o//*

48. The bright red flowers of the *Butea monosperma* tree, native to South Asia, which are the same color as fire and curl upward in a flame-like shape.

49. Verse 7a.

50. A species of bovine, *Bos gaurus*, found on the Indian sub-continent and in Southeast Asia.

51. Sakya Paṇḍita, p. 23. *don rig gnyis dang rang rig dang //rjes su dpag rnams rang las nges//dang po ba dang yid ma gtad//'khrul rgyu can rnams gzhan las nges//*

52. In the Tibetan *de ldan bcom ldan tshad ma nyid*, the last syllable could be interpreted as saying that the Bhagavan is solely valid or that he is validity. However, the Sanskrit for this line (*tadvat pramāṇam bhagavān*) lacks any ending such as -*tva* that could justify such an interpretation, so it seems that the *nyid* in Tibetan is merely expletive and is thus omitted in the translation of the verse.

53. By teaching the virtues, he protects beings from the lower realms. By teaching the foundation vehicles of the listeners, he protects them from the suffering of existence. By teaching the great vehicles, he protects them from the lesser nirvana of the listeners and self-buddhas.

54. Chödrak Gyatso refers to Prajñākaragupta's *Ornament of the Commentary on Validity* by its abbreviated title. However, though Chödrak Gyatso attributes the citation to *The Ornament*, it actually appears in Jamāri's commentary on it, *Pramāṇavārttikālaṃkāraṭīkā supariśuddha-nāma* (*Tshad ma rnam 'grel rgyan gyi 'grel bshad shin tu yongs su dag pa shes bya ba*), D4226 DT Tshad ma me pa, 284a. *mtshan nyid gnyis po 'di ni bcom ldan 'das la yang ma god par snang ste/ ji ltar nye bar bstan pas mtho ris dang byang grol gyi lam mthong bar mdzad pa'i phyir dang / khyab 'jug dang dbang phyug la sogs pas ma mthong ba de kho na ston par mdzad pa'i phyir ro//*

55. RZG lists a third topic here (Rebutting that it is comparable for us) that does not appear later in the text and has thus been omitted.

56. Qualities refers to the three qualities of *sattva, rajas,* and *tamas.* Hopkins, Jef-

frey. *Maps of the Profound: Jam-yang-shay-ba's Great Exposition of Buddhist and Non-Buddhist Views on the Nature of Reality* (Ithaca: Snow Lion Publications, 2003), p. 153.

57. *gang zhig phra zhing gcig pu skye gnas 'dug/ de yis 'di kun skye zhing 'jig par byed//de ni dbang bdag mchog sbyin lha mchod bya//yon tan byed pa shin tu zhi ba thob//byed pa po la shes pa yod min te//bdag gi bde sdug bdag la rang dbang med/ /dbang phyug gis bskul yang na g.yang sa'am//yang na mtho ris dag tu 'byung bar 'gyur//* These two stanzas are quoted in several texts in the Tengyur and explained in detail in Avalokitavrata's *Prajñāpradīpaṭīkā* (*shes rab sgron ma rgya cher 'grel pa*, D3859, dBu ma wa pa pp. 122b–123b). To summarize that explanation briefly, the opening line of the first stanza (He who is subtle and single arises, dwells, and exists) teaches the quality of subtlety or creating and destroying sentient beings. The second line (He creates and destroys all of this) teaches that he is the creator of the external world. The epithet "powerful lord" indicates that creates and destroys both the external world and the worlds of sentient beings. "Confers boons" indicates that he has the power to benefit or harm all spirits. "God" means that his wishes are spontaneously accomplished. "Is worshipped" indicates that he is worshipped by all spirits. "He creates the qualities" means that he creates the qualities of sattva, tamas, and rajas and all he wishes. This teaches that he himself has achieved liberation or peace or alternately that he makes others achieve liberation. In the second stanza, the first line (There is no knowledge of this creator) means that living creatures have no mastery over him. The second line (And the self has no power over its pleasures and pains) indicates that because they do not see him, they have no power over whether they will experience pain or pleasure. The last two lines indicate that it is Īśvara who sends sentient beings to either the high realms or lower realms.

58. *dbang phyug bsgoms pas thar pa thob pa dang / /phra zhing rab srab kun rig byed pa thams cad byed/ /bsam gtan goms pas rnal 'byor pa yi bsam gtan yul/ /zhi ba'i bde ba 'dod pa rnams kyis dbang phyug rtag tu bsgom//*

59. RZG reads *de'ang dang po bzhi ni/ rags pa mi rtag bya ba dang bcas pa kun la khyab par 'dod cing/*, lacking a negative particle before the word for all-pervasive. Based on the context and other sources (Hopkins p. 163 and Khyenrab Wangchuk p. 112), I assume this is a typographical error and have translated it in the negative.

60. *dus kyis skye rgu sdud par byed/ /dus kyis 'byung ba smin par byed/ /dus kyis gnyid log sad par byed/ /dus 'da' bar ni dka' ba yin//*

61. *'obs ni rgya mtsho bsrung ba sum brtegs dang// /dmag mi srin po nor ni gnod sbyin byed/ /de yi bstan bcos pa sangs tshad med nyams/ /sgra sgrog bu de'ang dus kyi dbang gis nyams//* This somewhat cryptic verse is cited three times (with some slight variation) in the Dergye Tengyur including in Avalokitavrata's

Prajñāpradīpaṭīkā, but there is no word by word commentary, so this translation should be considered provisional until better source materials are found.

62. There are different enumerations of the qualities within the Vaiśeṣika school and different lists of the qualities in various Tibetan sources as well. Here Chödrak Gyatso's list differs from the twenty-four given by the Vaiśeṣika masters Kaṇada and Praśastapāda in that it sub-divides awareness (*buddhi*) into the five sensory awarenesses and leaves out the qualities of heaviness, fluidity, and viscidity (cf. Radhakrishnan 2006:184). Additionally, the Tibetan uses a different translation of the word for conjunction (*saṃyoga*) than is used later in the text (*phra rags* as opposed to *ldan pa*). This is perhaps due to Karma Pakshi basing his list upon different translations of the Sanskrit sources. Additionally, RZG omits sound, but that has been inserted into this translation because it is present in other sources and because without it there would not be twenty-five qualities.

63. Radhakrishnan gives four types of validity asserted by the Vaiśeṣikas: perception (*pratyakṣa*), inference (*laiṅgika*), remembrance (*smṛti*), and intuition (*ārṣajñāna*). He describes intuition as "the insight of seers." Here it is assumed that Chödrak Gyatso has omitted remembrance, and that what was translated into Tibetan as '*phrad pa'i tshad ma* most likely refers to intuition. Radhakrishnan, S. *Indian Philosophy, Vol. 2. 2nd ed.* (Delhi: Oxford University Press, 2008), p. 162 & 163.

64. As explained in AK, universes arise out of the force of karma, and karma arises from volition—"From karma various worlds are born. / Volition and what that creates." Thus volition is the cause of the universe. AK iv.1ab.

65. In other words, in the syllogism "Sound, the subject, is impermanent, because of being produced, like a jug," being produced in general proves the syllogism. However, the particular quality of a jug being produced (as in, "Sound, the subject, is impermanent, because of a jug's being produced.") would not be correct evidence because the evidence (a jug's being produced) would not be present in the subject—the proposition property would not be present. Thus the false refutation of a similar effect is to say that the general being produced is not correct evidence because the particular being produced (a jug's being produced) is not correct evidence.

Here Devendrabuddhi also states that the particular evidence of a sound being produced would also not be correct evidence because it would lack an analogy that could prove it (*dpe sgrub par byed pas stong pa nyid yin pa* DB 10a).

66. That is to say, the presenter and responder have different understandings of what the words mean.

67. The "Owlists," another name for the Vaiśeṣika school, so called because they wore owl feathers. Second Karma Trinleypa, *dus gsum gyi rgyal ba sras*

dang bcas pa'i bstan pa mtha' dag dang khyad par rdo rje 'chang karma pa'i dgongs pa gsal bar byed pa'i bstan bcos thar pa'i shing rta (Baijnath: Palpung Sungrap Partrun Khang, 2014), p. 23.

68. Here RZG 27b reads "in relation to the predicate" (*chos kyi lteng du*), but that seems to be an error as the predicate is not proven in relation to itself but in relation to the subject (*chos can gyi lteng du*).

69. This stanza does not appear in PV-s1 or s2 and is not commented on by Prajñākaragupta, but it does appear in the Tibetan in the Derge Tengyur and is explained by Devendrabuddhi. The phrases in question refer to Sanskrit idioms.

70. In other words, because a permanent creator would always exist, there is no way to prove that it is a cause because one cannot evaluate the reverse entailment of a case when the cause is not present. As Śākyabuddhi explains, "The reverse entailment is that if the cause does not exist, the result does not exist. Because he is permanent, Īśvara does not have that, and thus there is no reverse entailment." (*rgyu med na 'bras bu med pa ni ldog pa yin te/ de yang rtag pa nyid kyi phyir dbang phyug la yod pa ma yin pa de ltar na ldog pa med pa nyid yin no//* SB 85b)

71. Verse 9cd. Jaiminīya is another name for the Mīmāṃsaka school.

72. ii.532 (SVI iii.532, PV 138b). *gzugs sogs dang ni sems de ltar//gzung ba'i mtshan nyid dpyod pa 'di/ /ma dag blo can la yin gyi/ /rnal 'byor rtogs pa bsam mi khyab//*

73. Dharmakīrti, DT Tshad ma che pa, 359a. *bcom ldan 'das kyis don thugs su chud pa ni bsam gyis mi khyab ste/ rnam pa thams cad shes pa dang brjod pa'i yul las 'das pa'i phyir ro//*

74. iv.51cd. *gnas gsum par ni 'pho ba na/ /bstan bcos len pa rigs ldan yin//* In his commentary on the fourth chapter, Chödrak Gyatso explains this verse to mean that if one moves on to the analysis the third area of evaluable objects (the extremely hidden), it is logical to assert the treatises are authoritative (RZG II 224b–225a).

75. JK nyi khri nga pa, 17a. *rab 'byor rnam pa gang dag dang/ rtags gang dag dang/ mtshan ma gang dag gis chos rnams rab tu brjod pa'i rnam pa de dag dang/ rtags de dag dang/ mtshan ma de dag de bzhin gshegs pas thugs su chud do//* Here Cha de dag dang/ rtags de dag dang/ mtshan"*rnam pa gang dag dang / rtags gang dag dang / mtshan ma gang dag dang*" (those aspects, signs, or attributes), a formula that appears several times in the Kangyur, especially in Vinaya texts. However, the actual sutra reads "*rnam pa gang dag dang / tshul gang dag dang / mtshan ma gang dag dang,*" (those aspects, reasonings, or attributes).

76. JK, 'bum pha pa, 217ff. *chos gcig gi mdo dang rgyas pa shes na/ chos thams cad kyi mdo dang rgyas pa shes par 'gyur ro//*

77. *dngos gcig dngos po kun gyi ngo bo nyid/ /dngos kun dngos po gcig gi ngo bo nyid/ /gang gis dngos gcig de bzhin nyid mthong ba/ /de yis dngos kun de bzhin nyid du mthong//* Though attributed here to Āryadeva , this passage could not be

located in any of his works, though it does appear in four other works in the Tengyur: one on madhyamaka by Jang chub bzang po (D3852), two on prajñāparamita by Haribhadra (D3971 and D3973), and a work by Chos kyi bshes gnyen (D3796).

78. *mkhyen pa'i skad cig gcig gis ni/ /shes bya'i dkyil 'khor kun khyab can//* This citation appears in three works in the Tengyur: commentaries on the *Distinguishing the Two Truths* by Jñānagarbha and Śantarakṣita (D3882 and D3883), and in a commentary on *Reciting the Names of Manjushri* by Mi'i dbang po grags pa.

79. This should also be understood to mean previous and future lives.

80. *Madhyāmaka Āvatara (dBu ma la 'jug pa)*, D3861, DT dBu ma 'a pa, 201b. *nyan thos sangs rgyas 'bring rnams thub dbang skyes/ /sangs rgyas byang chub sems dpa' las 'khrungs shing/ /snying rje'i sems dang gnyis su med blo dang/ /byang chub sems ni rgyal sras rnams kyi rgyu//*

81. *De bzhin gshegs pa'i gsang ba'i mdo.* Cited in Śantideva's *Compendium of the Trainings* (D3940), Tengyur dBu ma khi pa , 6b. *bcom ldan 'das byang chub tu sems bskyed pa su'i lags/ rgyal po chen po gang gis lhag pa'i bsam pa ma 'khrugs pa'o/ /gsol pa/ bcom ldan 'das su'i bsam pa ma 'khrugs/ bka' stsal pa/ rgyal po chen po gang gis snying rje chen po skye ba'i'o/ /gsol pa/ bcom ldan 'das su'i snying rje chen po skye/ bcom ldan 'das kyis bka' stsal pa/ rgyal po chen po gang gis sems can thams cad la yongs su mi gtong ba'i sems skye ba'i'o//*

82. *Chos bcu pa'i mdo.* Cited in Prajñākaramati's *Byang chup sems dpa'i spyod pa la 'jug pa'i dka' 'grel*, DT 3872 dBu ma la pa 74b–75a. *rigs kyi bu 'di la byang chub sems dpa'i rigs la gnas pa byang chub tu sems bskyed na/ de bzhin gshegs pa'am de bzhin gshegs pa'i nyan thos kyis bskul zhing skyob par byas/ yang dag par 'dzin du bcug ste/ bla na med pa yang dag par rdzogs pa'i byang chub tu sems bskyed pa 'di ni byang chub kyi sems la mos pa'i rgyu dang po'o/ /rdzogs pa'i byang chub bam byang chub kyi sems kyi bsngags pa brjod pa thos nas bla na med pa yang dag par rdzogs pa'i byang chub tu sems bskyed pa 'di ni rgyu gnyis pa'o/ /sems can mgon med pa dang skyabs med pa dang dpung gnyen med pa rnams mthong nas snying rje'i sems nye bar bzhag ste/ bla na med pa yang dag par rdzogs pa'i byang chub tu sems bskyed pa 'di ni rgyu gsum pa'o/ /des de bzhin gshegs pa'i rnam pa thams cad kyi mchog yongs su rdzogs pa mthong nas dga' ba bskyed de/ bla na med pa yang dag par rdzogs pa'i byang chub tu sems bskyed pa 'di ni rgyu bzhi pa'o//*

83. Dignāga and Dharmakīrti.

84. *'jug stobs can.* I have not seen a Sanskrit name attested for this individual and therefore use the Tibetan.

85. These are contradictory because proving something due to evidence is by definition inference.

86. Verse 32.

87. iv.108, PV 143b. *mthong dang ma mthong ba dag la/ /rigs pas grub dang rang*

tshig gis/ /gnod med bstan bcos gang yin te/ /gzung bar bya phyir dpyod 'jug 'gyur//

88. The three analyses are examining whether or not scriptures are disproven by perception, inference, or internal contradictions.

89. iii.216cd (SVI i.216ab), PV 102b *yid ches tshig ni mi bslu ba'i/ /spyi las rjes su dpag pa nyid//*

90. PVin 167a. RZG misquotes it slightly. The actual text reads, "By becoming familiarized with the intelligence produced by contemplation, one is separated from confusion of misunderstanding and manifests ultimate validity, which cannot be turned back from the stainless." *bsams pa las byung ba nyid kyi shes rab goms par byas pas rnam par 'khrul pas dben zhing dri ma med la ldog pa med pa'i don dam pa'i tshad ma mngon sum du byed do//*

91. "And so forth" includes birth from an egg. These are posited as the four modes of birth for all sentient beings—the four manners in which sentient beings can take birth. See AK iii.8–9 and *Jewels*, p. 222–23.

92. That is the sixth, mental consciousness, which does not have a physical sense faculty as its dominant condition.

93. Volitional karmas are the volitions which impel us to act with body and speech. As Vasubandhu says, "Volition is mental karma, which / Creates the karma of body and speech" (AK iv.1cd). As Devendrabuddhi (DB 21a–b) and Prajñākaragupta (Orn 52a) make clear, since rebirth and the body of the next existence are caused by karma, the volitional karmas in the mental consciousness are the causes of the faculties, respiration, and so forth in the next lifetime.

94. Both Devendrabuddhi and Prajñākaragupta explain that this passage is a response to the hypothetical question of whether the mind is dependent upon a body that arises in a succession of instants or from a body that does not arise in succession. The latter is analyzed first. (DB 22b, Orn 52b.)

95. That is, if Cārvākas accepted the citation as valid, they would have to accept that there are arhats, and accepting arhats as validly proven would require accepting that there is a cycle of previous and future lives from which they can be liberated.

96. Though in most instances this translation of the root matches the Sanskrit rather than the Tibetan when there is a discrepancy, here it matches the Tibetan (*rgyu gcig phyir na lhan cig gnas*) as the translation reads smoother than would than a translation of the Sanskrit *hetvabhedāt sahasthitiḥ* (Since their causes are not separate, they coexist) would.

97. *'Phags pa sālu'i ljang pa'i mdo (Ārya Śālistambha Nāma Mahāyana Sūtra)*, DK mdo sde tsha pa (D210), 116a. *'di yod pas 'di 'byung/*

98. DB 26a. The actual passage reads: "There is no such determination of entailment between the body and mind in the womb and so forth, because

here there is no earlier observation of the body and later observation of the mind. The reverse entailment is also not determined." *(rjes su 'gro ba'i nges pa de 'dra ba dag ni mngal la sogs pa dag tu lus dang sems la yod pa ma yin te/ 'di la sngar lus dmigs pa yod na phyis sems dmigs pa med pa'i phyir ro/ /ldog pa nges pa yod pa yang ma yin no//)*

99. Chödrak Gyatso here briefly summarizes a long passage that appears in Orn 59b–60a.

100. DB 26b. *dper na 'dod pa sngon du song ba can gyis lag pa'i brkyang ba dang bskum pa lta bu ste/ dbugs 'byung rngub dag kyang sems kyi 'dod pa'i dbang gis 'jug pa dang ldog pa yin no zhes bya ba ni rang bzhin gyi gtan tshigs so//*

101. DB 28a. That is to say, just as a tree is not the cause of the ocean and therefore a change in its size does not affect the ocean, likewise the inhalation and exhalation are not related to the mind as its cause, and changes in them do not necessarily affect the mind.

102. DB 28a. *des na 'phen par byed pa'i dbang gis gnas pa'i dus nges pa yin pas/ de ltar na de phan chad rab tu 'jug pa ma yin pa'i phyir mtshungs pa ma yin no//*

103. The translation of the root in 57c follows Prajñākaragupta's explanation while the commentary follows the Karmapa. The Karmapa glosses the Tibetan *mnyam* (Skt. *śamīkṛte*) as meaning "together" (*mnyam du*) with death, while Prajñākaragupta describes it as bringing the humors (*nyes pa, doṣa*) into equality or balance (Orn 65b). Devendrabuddhi glosses it as meaning a weakening (*nyams pa*) of the humors and other causes of death (DB 28b), though this could be a typographical error.

104. The word *vikāra* in the Sanskrit original translated as "deterioration" means change and in particular change for the worse. This is the sense that Devendrabuddhi explains. ("For us, though the cause of deterioration (*vikāra*) is comparable, and its antidote is comparable. . ." (*kho bo'i ni 'gyur ba'i rgyu mtshungs pa dang de'i gnyen po mtshungs kyang... DB 30a*). The Tibetan translation reads *'gyur ba*, which means to be, to become, or to change but can also function similarly to a relative pronoun. Chödrak Gyatso interprets it as a relative program, but the translation of the root follows the sense expressed by Devendrabuddhi.

105. In the *Sutra of Entering the Womb* (which appears in the *Minor Topics of the Vinaya* (D6), JK *'Dul ba tha pa*, 139a ff), the Buddha describes how when a fetus forms in the womb, it first passes through a stage of being mushy (the consistency of yogurt) before forming into an oblong shape and then gradually developing into a recognizable child. This is also described in AKB *ad* iii.19. See also *Jewels*, pp. 233–34.

106. DB 31b. *gang gis gang la cung zad kyang mi byed pa de ni de'i rten ma yin te/ 'bigs byed kyis gangs can lta bu'o//* Vindhya and Himavān are two mountains in India separated by a great distance. They have no more relation to each other than do Everest and Kilimanjaro.

107. In the original for this line (*nāśasya saty abādho 'sāv iti / yod pa 'di gnod med pa'i phyir*), the word *saty* (*yod pa*) is glossed by Devendrabuddhi and Chödrak Gyatso as belonging to the preceding clause and functioning as the verb to be, but Prajñākaragupta glosses it as "*yod pa'i don*" or the entity that is present or exists (Orn 72B). Here the translation follows Devendrabuddhi's gloss ('*jig pa chos nyid gyur na*, DB 32B).

108. The word *abādho* (*gnod med*) in the original is ambiguous: it can mean both to harm or prevent and to logically disprove. Devendrabuddhi and Prajñā-karagupta are ambiguous, but Śākyabuddhi glosses it as meaning to prevent (SB 103a) as do some other Tibetan commentators, including Mipham. As that seems the more general interpretation, it is translated as *prevent* in the root and *disprove* in the commentary.

109. Here the Sanskrit reads *gamana* (moving or going) while the Tibetan reads '*bo ba* (spilling). Here the root verse follows the Sanskrit in order to keep the logical connection between the two couplets clear. The commentary, however, follows the Tibetan and reads "spilling."

110. Inherence (*samavāya*, *phrod pa 'du ba*) refers to a type of relation posited by the Vaiśeṣika and Nyāya schools whereby an existent universal is inherent in all its instances, a blanket is inherent in its threads, a whole inherent in its parts, or that predicated features are inherent in phenomena.

111. DB 34a, SB 104a, and Orn 75b.

112. Orn 80a. Chödrak Gyatso condenses the passage slightly. The full passage (with the phrases omitted by Chödrak Gyatso marked in italics) reads: "Just as formations of listening preceded by one's own experience are not evident during periods of deep sleep but are evident *at times* during waking periods, they would also be evident in the body *and would be perceived just as in the mind, because it is not separate.* Just as qualities of the body such as darkness are observed by others, why would not the mental qualities of the crafts and so forth also be observed?" *(rang gis myong ba sngon du song ba can gyi thos pa la sogs pa'i 'du byed gnyid log pa la sogs pa'i gnas skabs su mi gsal ba sad pa ni gnas skabs kyi dus kyis gsal ba de bzhin du lus la yang mngon par gsal bar 'gyur zhing sems ci lta ba bzhin du rtogs par 'gyur te/ tha dad pa med pa'i phyir ro/ /ji ltar lus kyi yon tan nag po la sogs pa gzhan gyis dmigs pa de bzhin du sems kyi yon tan bzo ba la sogs pa yang dmigs par ci ste mi 'gyur/)*

113. Orn 81a. *The Ornament* states that beings in the between state are perceptible only through yoga (*rnal 'byor tsam gyis*). The source for saying that they are only seen by beings of their own class is the AK iii.14, which states, "They're seen by their class, divine eye." See *Jewels* 228.

114. Instead they are called by the convention *body*. Devendrabuddhi explains: "At that time, the atoms are not the object of the convention. Well then, what is? you ask. They are the object of the conventions 'body' and so forth, just as the yarn during the period of a blanket is not called yarn but instead

is called a 'blanket.' In the same way, the atoms during the phase of the body and so forth are also not conventionally called atoms." (*de'i tshe rdul phran de dag tha snyad kyi yul ma yin no/ /'o na ci yin zhe na/ lus la sogs pa'i tha snyad du bya ba de dag yin te ji ltar snam bu'i gnas skabs can gyi snal ma rnams la snal ma zhes mi brjod kyi/ 'on kyang snam bu zhes bya ba yin pa de ltar na/ lus la sogs pa'i gnas skabs can gyi rdul phran rnams la yang rdul phran gyi tha snyad du mi byed pa yin no//* DB 40a.)

115. That is, someone might say that if there were no whole, a person's body would be see-through and objects would be able to pass through it because the individual atoms are not visible and not obstructive.

116. According to the Vaiśeṣikas, conjunction (*saṃyoga, ldan pa*) is the combination of other phenomena. It is asserted to be a single, substantially existent phenomenon that is separate from the constituents combined.

117. According to Dharmakīrti's presentation, the object of thoughts and words is an exclusion (*apoha, gzhan sel*).That is, the thought or word excludes everything that does not fit into that category and clings to what remains as the object. Thus it imagines the quality of singleness based on the jug being the opposite of not single, the quality of largeness based on it being the opposite of not large, and so forth. This is discussed in greater detail in the other chapters of Dharmakīrti's work.

118. That is, past and future objects do not exist—they either have ceased or not yet come into being—but we can still conceive of them in terms of number and so forth.

119. Sanskrit and Tibetan logicians contrast two different types of names: actual names (*dngos ming*) and nicknames (*btags ming*). One word can apply to one phenomenon as an actual name and others as a nickname, as with the word "lion," which is an actual name when referring to the king of beasts and a nickname when referring to a Brahmin boy who happens to look like a lion, as is described in the chapter on perception (ii.36). In this context, the opponent is arguing that when number such as singular or plural, possession, and so forth apply to a subject such as a jug, they would refer to a truly existing universal as an actual name, but when they refer to that subject's predicated qualities (the jug's form and so forth) as being singular and so forth, they are nicknames.

120. Orn 88b. *thog ma med pa'i rtog pas sgro btags pa nyid rgyu mtshan yin gyi/ dngos por btags pa'i skabs yod pa ma yin no//*

121. Here Chödrak Gyatso glosses the phrase *kun la* (literally, "to all") in the Tibetan as *yul kun la*—to all objects. The Sanskrit *sarvatra* has more of a sense of in all cases. In the translation, the root text reflects the Sanskrit while the commentary follows Chödrak Gyatso's gloss. The difference, however, is more linguistic than substantial.

122. As explained in the abhidharma, forms are said to be a conglomeration of a

minimum of eight kinds of substances: the four sources or elements (earth, water, fire, and air) and the four source-derived (form, scent, flavor, and touch). See AK ii.22, and *Jewels*, p. 162.

123. That is, the jug's ability to produce an eye consciousness is due to the jug's substance of form and not its substances of scent, flavor, and so forth, whereas the ability of the jug to hold water is due to all eight of its substances.

124. That is to say, some other schools say that the word jug does not signify the collection of atoms that makes up an individual jug but a kind or universal of jugness that is inherent in the jug but separate from the matter of which it consists.

125. That is, there are many instances of jugs, wood, and so forth, each of which is a collection, and the words that refer to them individually are expressions that signify collections. There is only Mount Vindhya, however, so the expression signifying a collection that refers to it only refers to only one collection, the mountain itself.

126. Devendrabuddhi clarifies that the opponents say that a single exhalation or inhalation makes a single mental consciousness know. DB 46a.

127. RZG reads "If that were not so" (*de ltar min na*), which seems to be a typographical error as it does not make sense here, and thus it is translated in the positive.

128. Devendrabuddhi explains the analogy further: "Exhalation would have a nature of multiple parts, like a herd and so forth." (*dbugs 'byung ba ni yan lag du ma'i bdag nyid can yin te/ khyu la sogs pa dang 'dra'o* DB 48a.)

129. DB 50a. *gang gi tshe lus tha ma lus phyi ma dang nying mtshams sbyor ba'i phyir blo lhan cig byed pa'i rgyu nyid du yang 'gyur ba de'i tshe lhan cig byed pa yin pa'i phyir lhan cig gnas pa de ltar na 'gal ba med do//*

130. Here and in the following verses, by "faculty" Dharmakīrti does not mean the retina, inner ear, and so forth described as the sense organs by Western science. Instead, he means what is described in the abhidharma as pure, clear forms that are present in the physical organs, such as the subtle, lucid form shaped like a flax flower that is said to be the eye faculty. These forms are described in AK i.9cd, "Supports of consciousnesses are / The eye, et cetera—lucid forms." (*Jewels* 110)

131. Verse 85d.

132. Verse 106d.

133. Verse 36a.

134. An earshot is a distance of 500 armspans or fathoms (ca. 3000 ft or 914 m), and a league is eight earshots (ca. 4.5 miles or 7.3 km). AK iii.87–88.

135. In PV-s2 and Orn, there appears before this verse the couplet "One will achieve perfection of compassion / And spurred by others' unbearable suffering," (*niṣpannaḥ karuṇotkarṣaḥ paraduḥkhākṣmeritaḥ, thugs rje phul byung*

grub ,gyur te/ /gzhan sdug mi bzod pas bskul ba'i//) In PV-s2, the couplet is in brackets, indicating that it appears in some sources but not in others. As it does not appear in PV, Devendrabuddhi, or most Tibetan commentaries including this one, it has been omitted from the main text of this translation.

136. Though Chödrak Gyatso explains the third person pronoun *de* (them) as referring to meditators, Devendrabuddhi and Prajñākaragupta explain it as referring to the qualities of cultivation and the faults of the impediments (DB 56b, Orn 102b).

137. The rhinoceros-like self-buddhas are so called because they keep to solitude, like a rhinoceros. Though some self-buddhas are congregating self-buddhas who gather in groups of five hundred, the name "rhinoceros-like" is often applied to all self-buddhas.

138. Buddhahood and other results of the spiritual way (arhatship, stream entry, and so forth) are considered results of removal because they are attained through the removal of defilements and obscurations.

139. Nonlearner arhats and self-buddhas.

140. Verse 141.

141. AK vi.3cd. *sdug bsngal nyid gsum ldan pa'i phyir/ /ci rigs ma lus sdug bsngal lo//* Chödrak Gyatso only cites the last two lines of the stanza, which in full reads: "The attractive and the unattractive, / And the defiled other than those / Are suffering without exception / Because they have three sufferings."

142. Verse 142cd.

143. Verse 142ab.

144. Though Chödrak Gyatso credits it to the *Praise of Superiority* (*Viśeṣa-stava, khyad par 'phags bstod*) by mTho btsun grub rje (D1109, bstod tshogs ka, 1a–4b), it actually appears in the *Praise of the Bhagavan Buddha Called In Praise of Him Who Is Worthy of Praise though Unable to Be Praised* (*Varṇārdhavarṇa Bhagavato Buddhā Stotra Aśaya Staba Nāma, Sangs rgyas bcom ldan 'das la bstod pa bsngags par 'os pa las bstod par mi nus par bstod pa zhes bya ba*) by Ācārya Maticitra, D1138, DT stod tshogs ka pa, 96a. *khyod kyi bstan las phyir phyogs pa'i/ /skye bo ma rig gis ldongs pa/ /srid rtse'i bar du song nas kyang/ /sdug bsngal yang 'byung srid pa sgrub//*

145. The instinctive view of the self (*bdag lta lhan skyes*) is the instinctive sense of me based on the five aggregates. All sentient beings possess this instinctive view. According to the Mahayana presentation, this is a discard of meditation; it is harder to discard because it is based on the five aggregates and habituated through innumerable lifetimes in beginningless samsara. This is discussed further at verse 201.

146. The imaginary view of self (*bdag lta kun btags*) is the belief in a self or soul based on the teachings of a mistaken teacher or philosophy. Because it lacks

any basis in anything concrete, the imaginary view of the self is easier to discard and once discarded does not recur.

147. Verse 138a–d.
148. Verse 144a.
149. AK vi.24d (Jewels 66).
150. AK iii.94cd (Jewels 33).
151. Verse 143b & d.
152. Analytic cessation is the removal of obscurations attained by the power of analyzing suffering and the other noble truths with one's own intelligence. (Jewels, p. 104).
153. The truth of origin has two parts: karma and the afflictions. Nirvana with remainder is the cessation of the latter; arhats who have attained this state are still subject to the ripening of karma until they pass into nirvana without remainder.
154. That is, listener arhats have realized the selflessness of the individual and eliminated all the afflictions of the three realms of samsara. In addition to that, self-buddhas have realized that the apprehended aspect of phenomena is selfless and empty, so they have a partial realization of the selflessness of phenomena. However, they do not have a full realization of selflessness, because they have not realized the emptiness of the apprehending mind.
155. The Sanskrit word *samudbhava* in the original verse can have two meanings: either origin or to rearise or revive. In the Tibetan, it was translated as *kun 'byung*, which is also used for the truth of the origin (*samudaya* in Sanskrit). Chödrak Gyatso thus comments on it as meaning the latter, but Devendrabuddhi, Śākyabuddhi, and Prajñākaragupta all gloss it as meaning to rearise, so it is translated as "rearising" in the verse and "origin" in the commentary.
156. The three fires of greed, hatred, and delusion. Mikyö Dorje, *Chos mngon pa mdzod kyi 'grel pa rgyas par spros pa grub bde'i dpyid 'jo zhes bya ba bzhugs so* (Varanasi: Kagyud Relief & Protection Committee, 2005), Vol. IV, p. 259.
157. *prakṛti*. The Sāṃkhya school posits that all phenomena that are known arise out of this universal nature of all that is known.
158. Skt. *śabdabrahma*, Tib. *sgra'i tshangs pa*.
159. Verse 272.
160. Though RZG reads "*zab mo*" (profound), it appears to be a misprint for *za ba po*.
161. This and the following several paragraphs draws heavily upon Asaṅga's *Compendium of Abhidharma*, D4049, DT sems tsam ri pa, 13ff.
162. That is, all phenomena, both defiled and undefiled.
163. Eye, ear, nose, tongue, body, and mind.
164. Eye consciousness, ear consciousness, nose consciousness, tongue consciousness, body consciousness, and mind consciousness.

165. Form, sound, scent, taste, touch, and dharmas.

166. Maitreya, *Madhyāntavibhaṅgakārikā (dBus dang mtha' rnam par 'byed pa'i tshig le'ur byas pa)*, D4021, DT sems tsam phi pa, 41a. *de bzhin nyid dang yang dag mtha'/ /mtshan ma med dang don dam ste/ /chos kyi dbyings rnams rnam grangs so/ /gzhan min phyin ci log ma yin/ /de 'gags 'phags pa'i spyod yul dang/ /'phags pa'i chos kyi rgyu yi phyir/ /rnam grangs don de go rim bzhin//*

167. *med dgag*

168. *ma yin dgag*

169. DT sems tsam, phi pa, 41a. *gang zag dang ni chos rnams kyi/ /dngos po med 'dir stong pa nyid/ /de dngos med pa'i dngos yod pa/ /de ni de las stong nyid gzhan//*

170. Asaṅga, *Mahāyāna saṃgraha (Theg pa chen po bsdus pa)*, D4048, DT sems tsam ri pa, 10b–11a. *de la thos pa'i bag chags kyi sa bon chung ngu dang 'bring dang chen po yang chos kyi sku'i sa bon du blta ste/ kun gzhi rnam par shes pa'i gnyen po yin pas kun gzhi rnam par shes pa'i ngo bo nyid ma yin pa dang/ 'jig rten pa yin yang 'jig rten las 'das pa'i chos kyi dbyings shin tu rnam par dag pa'i rgyu mthun pa yin pas 'jig rten las 'das pa'i sems kyi sa bon du 'gyur ro/*

171. DT sems tsam ri pa, 11a. *byang chub sems dpa' las dang po ba rnams kyi 'jig rten pa yin kyang chos kyi skur bsdus pa dang/ nyan thos dang rang sangs rgyas rnams kyi rnam par grol ba'i lus su bsdus par yang blta'o//*

172. Here there appears to be a misprint in RZG, which reads "causally compatible results of the realization of the thoroughly pure dharma expanse" (*chos kyi dbyings shin tu rnam par dag pa rtogs pa'i rgyu mthun gyi 'bras bu yin pa'i phyir*). However, the *Compendium of the Mahayana* reads "causally compatible with the thoroughly pure dharma expanse" (*chos kyi dbyings rnam par dag pa'i rgyu mthun pa yin pas*, DT sems tsam ri pa 19b).

173. Dharmin and dharmatā.

174. Vasubandhu, *Triṃśika kārikā (Sum cu pa'i tshig le'ur byas pa)*, D4055, DT sems tsam shi pa, 2b. *de phyir de nyid gzhan dbang las/ /gzhan min gzhan ma yin pa'ang min/ /mi rtag la sogs bzhin du brjod//*

175. DT sems tsam phi pa, 42b. *dam pa'i don ni gcig pus so//*

176. DT sems tsam bi pa, 10b. The commentary is by Vasubandhu. Vasubandhu's actual commentary does not include the word "conventionally" (*tha snyed*).

177. Verse 148c.

178. Personality view (*satkāyadṛṣṭih, 'jig tshogs la lta ba*) is to view the five aggregates as a self. It is synonymous with the view of the self (*bdag lta*).

179. Though this quote could not be located in the Kangyur, a similar passage is cited by Vasubandhu in AKB: "As it was said, 'Bhikshus, when any spiritual person or brahmin holds the view thinking 'I am', all such views are viewing nothing more than these five aggregates of grasping." (*ji skad du dge slong dag dge sbyong ngam/ bram ze gang la la bdag go snyam du yang dag par rjes su lta ba na yang dag par rjes su lta ba de dag tham cad ni nye bar len pa'i*

phung po lnga po 'di dag la lta ba kho nar zad do zhes gsungs pa lta bu'o//, AKB 239b).

180. Verse 258.

181. *Entering the Middle Way*, D3861, DT dbu ma 'a pa, 210a. *nyon mongs skyon rnams ma lus 'jig tshogs la/ /lta las byung bar blo yis mthong gyur cing/ /bdag ni 'di yi yul du rtogs byas nas/ /rnal 'byor pa yis bdag ni 'gog bar byed//*

182. Here the Sanskrit word *vikārād* translated in the root as *change* is translated in the Tibetan with the verb *'gyur*, which can either mean change or function as an auxiliary verb. Though the meaning of the root is clearly change, Chödrak Gyatso parses it as an auxiliary verb for the verb to *skye ba* (to arise), thus specifying the nature of the change.

183. The Tibetan translation of the root for v. 153d reads literally "Arise from pleasure and from pain," but the extant Sanskrit and both Devendrabuddhi and Prajñākaragupta say "Arise from pleasure and so forth" (*sukhādijaḥ*). Thus here the translation of the root reflects the Sanskrit text, but the commentary reflects the Tibetan root.

184. Throughout this passage, it is important to remember that because of the societies in which they lived, Dharmakīrti and Chödrak Gyatso wrote primarily for a heterosexual male audience and thus use a beautiful woman as an example. But one could use any being—male, female or otherwise—as an example. The underlying logic that the object of lust is not the direct cause of lust but is merely a contributing factor by way of being the objective condition applies equally regardless of whether the lustful person or the object of lust is male, female, hermaphrodite, eunuch, or transgender.

185. Orn. 115b–116a. Prajñākaragupta's full explanation of this line reads: "Or if that [phlegm] were both of their [desire and hatred's] nature, it would follow that they both would be at the same time. If you say that is how it is, it is not so, because they would be necessarily seen. Here they are not necessarily seen at the same time." (*yang na gal te de gnyi ga'i rang bzhin na/ de'i tshe gnyi ga yang dus mtshungs pa nyid du thal bar 'gyur ro/ /de bzhin nyid do zhe na/ de ni ma yin te/ nges pa mthong ba'i phyir ro/ /'di la dus mtshungs pa nyid du nges pa mthong ba ni med do//*)

186. DB 68b. *rlung la sogs pa'i nyes pa ni 'byung ba'i rang bzhin yin pa'i phyir*

187. Verse 65a.

188. Orn. 116b. The actual passage reads: "If they were supported by earth and so forth, one would have accepted that at that time form and so forth are separate from the elements, contradicting the assertion that they are just the elements. If they are asserted to just be the elements, they would not be entities that are supporter and supported." (*gal te sa la sogs pa la brten pa yin na ni de'i tshe gzugs la sogs pa 'byung ba dag las tha dad par khas blangs pas 'byung ba tsam du khas len pa la gnod par 'gyur ro/ /'byung ba tsam du khas len na ni/ rten dang brten pa'i dngos por 'gyur ba ma yin no//*)

189. PV-s1 gives two versions of the last *pāda*. The translation is of the version that matches the Tibetan (*avinirbhāgartitvādāśrayo'yuktamānyathā*), which is the version commented on by Prajñākaragupta. Devendrabuddhi explains the other version (*avinirbhāgartitvādrūpāderāśrayo'pi vā,* From their supports, they are supports / For form and so forth).

190. Forms that are made of the four elements, such as visible forms, scents, and so forth, are called elementally derived. (*Jewels,* 130–31.)

191. Though PV reads *ngo mtshar* (astonishing), that appears to be a misprint for *ngo tsha* (modest), corresponding to the Sanskrit *salajjaḥ.*

192. The Sāṃkhya school asserts that results exist in the causes in the form of potential. If that were so, cognition would exist in the elements supposed to cause it and elephants in the grass they eat.

193. Therefore, they would not all necessarily have desire and so forth. Devendrabuddhi's text reads: "Even were a person not to transcend the character of the elements, his color, shape, faculties, and other qualities of his body at some times do not exist, so it is uncertain." (*skyes bu 'byung ba'i bdag nyid las ma 'das pa de ltar na yang/ 'di'i kha dog dang dbyibs dang dbang po la sogs pa lus kyi chos 'ga' zhig gi tshe med pa can nyid yin pas ma nges pa yin no//* DB 73a.) That is, just as not all people have eyes, arms, and so forth, not everyone would have greed, hatred, and so forth.

194. PV does not include the word *not*: it reads *yin* (is) rather than *min* (is not). However, the Sanskrit clearly is in the negative, and both Devendrabuddhi and *The Ornament* explain it so. Hence the phrase "not so" in the root does not appear in the commentary.

195. Verse 169a.

196. Verse 148d–149a.

197. The Tibetan root verse is ambiguous as to whether the pronoun is singular or plural, and so Chödrak Gyatso glosses it as referring to the five aggregates of grasping. However, the pronoun in the original Sanskrit is singular, and Devendrabuddhi glosses it as referring to suffering (*sdug bsngal de mi rtag pa yin no//* DB77a). This is why the root uses the singular pronoun *it* and the commentary the plural *they.* One should note that this is not a significant divergence, as Dharmakīrti identifies the five aggregates as being the truth of suffering—"Suffering is the samsaric aggregates."

198. Orn 124a. The quotation is from a verse recorded in the vinaya that the Buddha spoke on several different occasions:

> Others' control is always suffering.
> One's own control is always happiness.
> The ones in common are harmful.
> The link is very hard to transcend.

(*gzhan dbang thams cad sdug bsngal te//bdag dbang thams cad bde ba yin//thun mong dag gis gnod byed do/ /'brel pa shin du 'da' bar bka'//* Vinaya Vastu, JK 'Dul ba nya pa, 47a and other locations).

199. Verse 187d.

200. As explained below in verses 186–88, this is the greed for future possessions and enjoyment or for a future place of birth.

201. Verse 137ab.

202. Verse 186b–d.

203. Verse 190d–191c.

204. The Sāṃkhya school posits the existence of an aware being called the *puruṣa* who is separate from the primal substance and consumes or experiences everything that manifests from it.

205. Orn 126a.

206. *bshad ma thag pa'i skye ba'i gnas su nye bar 'gro ba'i sred pa gang yin pa de ni srid pa'i sred pa zhes bya ba'i ming can no//* (DB 79b).

207. Orn 126a.

208. That is, ordinary individuals take birth under the power of craving, which is therefore one cooperating condition for rebirth, but noble bodhisattvas who are free of craving take rebirth out of compassion, which is thus another condition. Orn 126b.

209. The word in the Sanskrit translated here as *existence* (*bhave*) does not appear in the Tibetan root and is not commented on by Chödrak Gyatso, though it is clearly commented on by Devendrabuddhi. Additionally, there is a typographical error in RZG, which read "Since it increases the cause" (*rgyu ni 'phel bar byed phyir dang*) rather "Since that propels the continuum" (*rgyun ni 'phen par byed phyir dang*).

210. See the general discussion under the topic "i. The explanation of the perfect benefit for oneself, the sugata" on page XXX above.

211. Orn 127b–128a. *'ga' zhig bcings pa de ni thar pa yod pa ma yin te/ de'i rang bzhin yin pa'i phyir/ /thar pa la yang bcings pa yod pa ma yin te/ de ni rtag tu thar pa'i rang bzhin yin pa'i phyir ro/ /'on kyang sems kyi rgyun ma dag par 'gyur ba tshogs pa'i khyad par las dag pa'i cha gzhan bskyed pa 'ba' zhig go/ de la phyi ma dag pa'i cha ni 'khor ba nyid du ma grub bo/ /don dam par ni 'khor ba pa 'ga' yang yod pa ma yin te/ skad cig rnams 'khor ba ma yin pa'i phyir dang/ rgyun kyang don dam par med pa'i phyir ro/ /des na 'khor ba'i phyir zhes bya ba'i gtan tshigs ni ma grub bo/ /gang la thar pa yod pa'i thar pa po yang med do//*

212. That is, those free of desire or craving for any of the realms of existence.

213. In RZG, the last line reads *kho bo dus la stong pa bzhin*, which makes little sense and appears to be a misprint for the quote as it appears in DB: *kho bo dus la sdod pa yin* (DB 83b). Thus the translation follows the text in DB.

214. That is, they would view sentient beings as existent.

215. The three undefiled paths are the paths of seeing, meditation, and no learning.

216. The word *logical* (*yujyate*) in the root does not appear in the Tibetan translation and is thus omitted from Chödrak Gyatso's commentary.

217. The varying sources do not agree as to whether this should read permanent
or impermanent. PV-s2 gives it as *'nityaḥ, (impermanent)*, but PV-s1 places
brackets around the *avagraha* (*[']nityaḥ*), suggesting that the original lacked
the negation. PV, DB, and Orn all read permanent. RZG gives impermanent
in the root and in the first two appearances in the commentary but reads
permanent the third time. Thus in this translation, the translation of the
root reflects the Tibetan root and Devendrabuddhi, whereas the translation
of the commentary leaves the inconsistency of RZG.

218. DB 87a. *byis pa'i rtsed mo'i rtog pa dang 'dra bar lung du ma bstan pa'i tshig la
dmigs pas ci zhig bya/*

219. *ci ste gal te gzhan du mi 'gyur na/ gnyis ka'i rang bzhin du 'gyur ro zhe na/*

220. Orn reads "permanent" here but is misquoted in RZG.

221. Orn 132a. *gang gi rang bzhin 'jig med pa/ /de la mkhas rnams rtag ces brjod/ /des
na ngo tsha'i lta ba 'di/ /spongs la de mi rtag par smros/ /'jig pa yang yin rtag pa
yang yin no zhes bya ba 'di ni 'gal lo/ /gang gi phyir 'jig pa med pa de ni rtag pa yin
te/*

222. Verse 216b–d.

223. Orn 133a. *da ni lam gyi zhar la 'gog ba'i rnam pa nges par 'byung ba nyid bstan
pa'i phyir bshad pa/ bshad zin lam de goms pa las//*

224. Verse 207ab.

225. Verse 137.

226. AK vi.5.

227. Verse 225cd.

228. Verse 280.

229. Verse 276ab.

230. Verse 214a–c.

231. Verse 210ab.

232. Verse 212.

233. The original lists a fourth topic here, "(d) Refuting that exhausting karma
and the body is liberation." That topic, however, does not appear separately
in the headings in the actual text, although the meaning is covered under
the third topic.

234. Verse 138ab.

235. The Sanskrit *āśrayaḥ parivartate* translated in the root as "the basis is transformed" was rendered in Tibetan as *gnas gyur*, which literally means to
change (*gyur*) the basis (*gnas*) but idiomatically means transform. Hence
Chödrak Gyatso does not gloss the word for "basis" separately, though he
does provide *The Ornament*'s explanation, which identifies it as referring to
the all-ground.

236. Orn 133a. *sngar bshad zin pa'i lam gyi bden pa de nyid goms pa las/ gnas sems kyi
rgyun nam kun gzhi dag par 'gyur te/ bdag dang bdag gir 'dzin pa dang mi mthun*

pa bdag med pa de'i bdag nyid du gyur pa na nyes pa mtha' dag dang bral bar 'gyur ro//

237. The Tibetan of this clause in RZG (*nyes pa nyams te las bzlog pa'i phyir ro//*, "because the faults have weakened and karma been blocked") appears to be corrupt, so here the passage from *The Ornament* that seems to be its source (*nyes pa rnams ni de las bzlog pa yin pa'i phyir ro//*) has been translated instead.

238. Verse 207ab.

239. Skt. *vitarka*. Tib. *rtog pa*. The mental factor that considers the features of an object in general.

240. The opponents are the Exposition school and so forth (SB 135b). For example, in the AK (iii.28–29) Vasubandhu describes the Kashmiri Exposition's position that personality view is not ignorance and instead is an aspect of the mental factor intelligence. *See Jewels*, p. 241.

241. JK Phal po che ga pa, p. 113a. *de 'jig rten du 'byung ba dang/ 'jig pa las rnam par lta ba'i tshe/ 'di snyam du sems te/ 'jig rten du dogs pa byung ba gang ji snyed pa de dag thams cad ni bdag tu mngon par zhen pa las byung ste/ bdag tu mngon par zhen pa dang bral na 'byung ba'ang med par 'gyur ro snyam mo/ /de 'di snyam du sems te/ byis pa'i blo can bdag tu mngon par zhen pa mi shes pa'i rab rib kyis bsgribs pa yod pa dang med pa la mngon par 'dod pa can du tshul bzhin ma yin pa'i yid las byung ba/ lam log par zhugs pa/ log par rjes su 'brang ba de dag ni bsod nams dang/ bsod nams ma yin pa dang/ mi g.yo ba'i 'du byed rnams kyang bsog ste/ 'du byed de dag gis yongs su bsgoms pa'i sems kyi sa bon zag pa dang bcas pa/ nye bar len pa dang bcas pa ni phyi ma la skye ba dang rga shi'i rang bzhin yang srid pa mngon par grub pa 'byung ba nye war 'gro ba yin te/* This citation appears in SB as well, with with a few textual differences that seem mostly due to difference of translation from the Sanskrit. The text for this citation in RZG seems corrupt, particular the last line, so the translation follows the text from the sutra. Śākyabuddhi explains that this teaches that ignorance is personality view because it teaches the first of the twelve links of interdependence, ignorance, to be the fixation on a self, which is the view of the self. This is "because it says that all of that is 'out of fixation on a self.'" (*de dag thams cad ni bdag tu mngon par zhen pa las zhes bya ba gsungs pa'i phyir ro//* SB 136b.)

242. *Butea monosperma*, also called the *kiṃśuka*.

243. Orn 137a. *des ni 'gog bden gyi nges par 'byung ba'i rnam pa yang bshad pa yin no//*

244. People who follow non-Buddhist worldly paths of meditation to achieve freedom from attachment to the Desire realm, mistaking that for liberation from samsara.

245. Orn 139a. *bsdu ba'i tshigs su bcad pa'o//*

246. Orn 139a. *sdug bsngal gyi rten ni dang po nyid du bdag yin te/ bdag yod na zhen pas phyis sdug bsngal gyi rgyur 'gyur gyi/ bdag med na su zhig sdug bsngal/*

247. That is, the opponent says that the logic of the preceding verse is not proven.

248. The Tibetan word *'dod pa* (desire or wish) that translates the Sanskrit *vallabha* (dear or desired) can also mean to assert, which is the sense in which Chödrak Gyatso glosses it.

249. Verse 222cd.

250. The Sanskrit *paryāyeṇa* translated in the root as "in order" was translated into Tibetan here (as almost always) as *rnam grangs kyis*, which Chödrak Gyatso interpreted as "through a variety."

251. In this couplet, the Sanskrit *viṣayaḥ* (object) was translated into Tibetan as *yul can* (subject). Thus if the couplet were translated from the Tibetan, it would read:

> Attachment would then be a faultless subject,
> And the means to accomplish would be faultless.

Thus while the Sanskrit specifies that if the object of attachment (the self) were faultless, attachment to it and the means to attain its enjoyments would be be faultless as well, whereas the Tibetan merely implies that the object is faultless. Here the translation of the root follows the Sanskrit, but the commentary follows the Tibetan.

252. Tibetan grammarians say that drawing distinctions between members of a list is one of the functions of the word *dang* (and), and Chödrak Gyatso is merely specifying that this is the sense it is used in here.

253. PV-s1 gives two variants for this line: *bālāderapi sambhavāt* ("As it occurs in children and so forth,") and in a note, *bālāderapi darśanāt* ("As it is seen in children and so forth,"). Though Devendrabuddhi comments on the former, the Tibetan translates the latter, and so this translation follows the Tibetan.

254. As the pronoun "they" is only implied in Sanskrit and the Tibetan translation, Chödrak Gyatso does not elaborate on whom it refers to. (The Sanskrit uses a third person singular verb, which is rendered in the plural here to avoid gender specificity.) Devendrabuddhi clarifies that it refers to an individual: "They, the individual, once again return naturally to their own nature, which has the characteristic of arising from clinging to 'mine.'" (*skyes bu de rang nyid kyis bdag gi'i chags pa las byung ba'i mtshan nyid can gyi/ rang bzhin yang ni brten par 'gyur//* DB 107b).

255. DB 108a. *'on kyang gnyis ka la rjes su chags pa dang khong khro ba med pa'i mtshan nyid can gyi btang snyoms su gnas par 'gyur ro//*

256. Orn 147a. *kho bo cag gi phyogs la ni//chos nyid tsam mthong bas sems mnyam pa nyid thob ste/ rjes su chags pa dang/ khong khro dang bral bas na/ rnal 'byor pa rnams chags pa dang bral ba yin gyi/ gzhan du ni ma yin no//* The last sentence of the original, which Chödrak Gyatso abbreviated, reads, "Because they are free of attachment and aversion, yogis are detached."

257. *Abhiṅskramana sūtra* (*mNgon par 'byung ba'i mdo*), JK sa pa, 66b. This is

quoted in both Devendrabuddhi and *The Ornament*. *(dge slong dag gzugs rtag pa yin nam/ mi rtag pa yin/ btsun pa mi rtag pa lags so/ /gang mi rtag pa de sdug bsngal ba yin nam/ bde ba yin/ btsun pa sdug bsngal ba lags te/ gang mi rtag pa de ni sdug bsngal ba rnam par 'gyur ba'i chos can lags so/ /de la 'di ni nga'i'o/ /'di ni nga'i bdag go zhes lta rung ngam/ btsun pa de ni ma lags so//)*

258. Here the Sanskrit *santāna* (continuum) was rendered in Tibetan as *rgyu* (cause). This might be a misprint for the Tibetan word *rgyun* (continuum); if so it must have occurred early on as all the versions of the Tengyur say *rgyu* (cause). Thus Chödrak Gyatso comments using the word *rgyu* (causes) rather than *rgyud* (continuum), so the root reflects the Sanskrit and the commentary reflects the Tibetan. There is no conflict in meaning, however, as a continuum is no more than a conceptual projection based on a sequence of causes and results.

259. DB 110b. *thog ma med pa'i dus nas 'jug pa zhes bya ba'i don to//*

260. The scriptures here refers to the Vedas.

261. The text for this sentence in RZG ("All efforts at mantras established from empowerment rituals are pointless" *de'ang dbang bskur ba'i cho ga las grub pa'i rig snags kyi rtsom pa tham cad don med do*) seems to be corrupt, so the sentence from *The Ornament* on which this passage was based (*de yang dbang bskur ba la sogs pa'i cho ga las grub pa yin pa'i phyir sngar gyi rtsod pa thams cad med do//* Orn 148a–b) has been substituted for RZG's text.

262. The Mīmāṃsakas and other Hindu sects posit that the words of the Vedas are eternal sound that is not produced or authored by any human being. This gives them intrinsic authority. The verse and the opponents' claim appear verbatim in Orn 148b.

263. The original outline lists three points, but the third (C. Rebutting that the reason is unproven) does not appear in the text itself.

264. The ten virtues and ten nonvirtues (SB 145b).

265. DB 112a–113b. *'dzin 'phen 'khrug dang 'gog pa dag/ sems pas 'gyur gyis dbang gis min/ /ces smos te/ rang gi yul la 'jug pa la bzlog pa med par 'dzin pa'o/ /'phen pa ni rang gi yul la 'jug par byed pa'o/ /'khrug pa bsnun pa la sogs pas blo ni 'gyur ba bskyed pa'o/ /'gog pa ni blo'i rjes su mthun pa yod na yang 'khrug pa ldog pa yin no//*

266. Orn 150a. *des na dbang bskur ma thag tu grol bar 'gyur ro//*

267. Verse 24.

268. Though the pronoun that is the subject of this clause is singular in the Sanskrit, Chödrak Gyatso comments on it in the plural.

269. Orn 151b. The actual passage appears slightly differently in Orn: "Samsara is unreal projection, and ultimately samsara does not exist. The unreal is the sixteen aspects. Because of projecting them, those with craving imagine that they are in samsara due to karma, but samsara is not otherwise possible." *(yang dag pa ma yin pa sgro 'dogs pa nyid 'khor ba yin gyi/ don dam par ni*

'khor ba med do/ /yang dag pa ma yin pa ni rnam pa bcu drug po ste/ de sgro 'dogs pa'i phyir na/ yongs su sred pa can las kyis 'khor bar mngon par rlom pa yin gyi/ gzhan du ni 'khor ba sred pa ma yin no//)

270. Orn 151b. *ma rig pa mtha' dag log pa'i mtshan nyid mya ngan las 'das pa'i yul mngon du byed par 'gyur ro/ /de'i phyir de kho na mthong bas sred pa log pa ni thar pa yin no//*

271. For example, arhats such as Śariputra and Maudgalyana who attained nirvana with remainder had bodies and also experienced the ripening of karma before they passed into nirvana without remainder. The opponent is questioning how such arhats could be said to be liberated.

272. Orn 152a. *sred pa bzlog pa ma gtogs par las dang lus dag gi gnyen po gzhan ni yod ma yin no//*

273. Cited in DB 117b–118a, but the original source is unclear. *bde 'gro 'am ni ngan 'gro yang/ /skye mched lnga yi rkyen can gyi/ /sems ni mi 'dod skye gang gi/ sdig pa'i las kyi 'bras bur 'dod//*

274. Orn 152a. *rnam 'gas de bskyed 'bras bu ni/ /chung 'gyur rigs mi mthun rkyen gyi/ /'bras bu nyams su myong bas ni//* RZG misquotes *The Ornament* here as reading "In some ways, the results that are produced / Are lessened, not those of a different kind. / Experiencing the result. . ." (*rnam 'gas de bskyed 'bras bu ni/ /chung 'gyur rigs mi mthun can min/ /'bras bu nyams su myong bas ni//*) The translation is of the citation as it appears in Orn.

275. Orn 152a. *las gang gis de'i rigs can nyid kyi 'bras bu nye bar bskyed par bya'o/ /'bras bu de'i cha nyams su myong ba'i phyir las des bskyed pa'i 'bras bu nyid nyams par 'gyur gyi/ de dang mi mthun pa'i 'bras bu ni 'grib pa ma yin no//*

276. Jina, *Pramāṇavārttikālaṃkāraṭīkā (Tshad ma rnam 'grel gyi rgyan gyi 'grel bshad)*, D4222, DT tshad ma de pa 362b. *shin tu brgal dka'i las rnams byas pa ni/ /bdag nyid rnam par smad pas bsrab par 'gyur/ /bshags dang sdom par byed pa de dag gis/ /brtan du drungs nas bton pa ma yin no//* The text in DT gives paths (*lam*) instead of actions (*las*) in the first line, but given the context, it seems that might be a typo in the Tengyur. The citation here is as it appears in RZG.

277. DB 119a. *gal te 'das pa'i las la brten nas brjod pa de'i tshe ma grub pa yin la/ ma 'ongs pa'i las la brten nas ni grub pa la bsgrub pa yin no//*

278. Orn 153a. *gang zhig gdon mi za bar 'bras bu 'byin nus pa gang yin pa de ni gdon mi za ba kho nar 'bras bu 'byin pa yin te/ de'i don du'ang dka' thub can dag mngon par sbyor ba ma yin te/ de'i stobs kyis 'ong ba'i phyir ro//*

279. The original *viparyayāt* was translated as into Tibetan as *bzlog las*, which can mean "from the opposite" or alternately "from blocking" or "from turning away." Chödrak Gyatso comments on it in the latter meaning, but Devendrabuddhi explains it as "not from those who do not have faults" (*skyon dang ldan pa ma yin pa las ma yin no//* DB 119b). As that seems closer to the Sanskrit, the root follows that interpretation while the commentary reflects Chödrak Gyatso's explanation.

280. Chödrak Gyatso glosses *gzhan don ngor* (*aparārthatantratvam*) as meaning *gzhan gyi ngor*, or from the perspective of others. However, the Sanskrit commentaries of Devendrabuddhi, Sūryagupta, and Jina all explain *aparārthatantratvam* as meaning that he is dependent upon or primarily acts for others' sake. Hence the divergence between the root and the commentary. Here the translation as "compelled by others' needs" is a slightly freer translation of *aparārthatantratvam* in order to convey its meaning in idiomatic English.

281. That is, the existence of a result, the shoot, proves the prior existence of the cause, its seed. Likewise, the existence of the teacher proves the prior existence of its cause, compassion.

282. PSV 14a. *phyag 'tshal nas tshad ma bsgrub par bya ba'i phyir rang gi rab tu byed pa rigs pa'i sgo la sogs pa rnams las 'dir gcig tu btus te tshad ma kun las btus brtsam par bya'o//*

283. DB 122a. *bstan bcos kyi dang por phyag 'tshal ba'i tshigs su bcad pa phyed 'og ma rtogs sla ba nyid kyi phyir/ phyed gong ma nyid kyi bshad pa yongs su rdzogs par mdzad nas/*

Notes to Appendix 1

1. As in the main text of the chapter, the numbering hierarchy is restarted at the end of the introductory material and the beginning of the discussion of the chapter itself.

INDEX

green press
INITIATIVE

KTD Publications is committed to preserving ancient forests and natural resources. We elected to print this title on 100% post consumer recycled paper, processed chlorine free. As a result, for this printing, we have saved:

17 Trees (40' tall and 6-8" diameter)
7,853 Gallons of Wastewater
8 Million BTUs of Total Energy
525 Pounds of Solid Waste
1,448 Pounds of Greenhouse Gases

KTD Publications made this paper choice because our printer, Thomson-Shore, Inc., is a member of Green Press Initiative, a nonprofit program dedicated to supporting authors, publishers, and suppliers in their efforts to reduce their use of fiber obtained from endangered forests.

For more information, visit www.greenpressinitiative.org

Environmental impact estimates were made using the Environmental Defense Paper Calculator. For more information visit: www.papercalculator.org.